Pini Dunner

Mavericks, Mystics & False Messiahs

Episodes from the Margins of Jewish History

The Toby Press

Mavericks, Mystics & False Messiahs
Episodes from the Margins of Jewish History

The Toby Press, LLC
POB 8531, New Milford, CT 06776–8531, USA
& POB 2455, London W1A 5WY, England

www.tobypress.com

The publication of this book was made possible through the support of Torah Education in Israel and The Jewish Book Trust.

ISBN 978-1-59264-510-7, *hardcover*

A CIP catalogue record for this title is
available from the British Library

Printed and bound in the United States

In loving memory

of

my dear parents

Aba Dunner
(1937–2011)

&

Miriam Dunner
(1941–2006)

*You are my inspiration
each and every day*

In honor of our father

Hershel Golker

*who always teaches us
the importance of learning Torah
and the reverence of Jewish leaders.
May he continue to do so*
עד מאה ועשרים

*With everlasting gratitude,
his children and grandchildren*

*From London to LA,
Rabbi Pini and Sabine lead and inspire wherever they are.
Distances don't separate
our admiration, friendship, and respect.
Proud to be their friends for decades
and, God willing, decades to come.*

*Maurice and Gabriella
Jerusalem, Israel*

Supporting this book is but a small way
of showing appreciation
to our friend and Rav, Pini Dunner.
He made Yiddishkeit sing for us and our family.

Penny and Mike Sinclair
London, England

~~~~

Michael and Sheryl Rosenberg
and family
are proud to dedicate this book
in memory of their dear father

Stanley Diller *z"l*
שמואל זנוויל בן אהרן יעקב דילער ביגלאייזען ז״ל

a Holocaust survivor who became one of
the Los Angeles Jewish community's
greatest philanthropists and leaders.
נפטר לבית עולמו עשרה בטבת תשע״ב

~~~~

To Pini
Congratulations on the publication of your book,

Mavericks, Mystics & False Messiahs,

an apt subject for you.
I wish you every success with this wonderful publication.

Lee Samson
Beverly Hills, California

In loving memory of

ימין בן מסעוד ז״ל
חיים בן ימין ז״ל
גבריאל בן ימין ז״ל
יהודה בן מסעוד ז״ל
מרק בן הודה ז״ל

Jacques and Natalie Wizman
Beverly Hills, California

~~~~

In loving memory of

my dear wife	*my dear husband*
Andy Curry	**Laurence Beresford**
עלקא מאשא ע״ה	ר׳ אליעזר ז״ל
בת ר׳ חיים זלמן	בן ר׳ בערל

Dedicated by
Lionel Curry and Ruth Beresford-Curry
London, England

Contents

Foreword

Jewish history has produced a host of peculiar characters from biblical times onward but the gallimaufry of those depicted in this book is remarkable by any standard.

Some of the personalities described by Rabbi Dunner were revered religious leaders; others were confidence tricksters. In several cases (and these are the most perplexing) they were both at the same time.

What brings together all these stories is the clash between credulity and evidence-based reasoning – a conflict that lies at the heart of the Jewish experience since the Enlightenment.

In my book *The Secret Lives of Trebitsch Lincoln*, on which Rabbi Dunner bases his account of that adventurer, I compared him with the eighteenth-century "pseudo-Messiah" Jacob Frank, who led his followers out of Judaism into Christianity. Trebitsch moved from Judaism to Buddhism. The most famous such figure, Shabbetai Tzvi, turned from Judaism to Islam.

These are merely three of the large number of such characters who emerged throughout the Jewish world – and beyond. History has tended to consign such men (and in a few cases women) to the margins, labeling them pretenders and pathologizing them as mentally ill. They are often seen as products of pre-modern societies prone to mass enthusiasms and delusions.

In all these cases spiritual enthusiasm, whipped up to a frenzy, gave rise to a revolutionary religious movement. Sometimes, as in the case of Trebitsch, this was pitifully small and short-lived. The Sabbatian sect known as Dönme was much larger and persisted until the twentieth century as a distinctive element within Islam. In the case of Jesus, what began as a sect of Judaism changed the history of the world.

Rabbi Dunner notes that both Shabbetai Tzvi and Trebitsch-Lincoln insisted even after their conversions that they remained Jews. The same is, of course, true of many converts who regard their apostasy not as betrayal but as ultimate fulfillment; one need only think of St. Paul and "Jews for Jesus." Another significant recent example was the late Cardinal Lustiger, archbishop of Paris. At his funeral at Notre Dame Cathedral his great-nephew recited the Kaddish.

But how wide a gulf really separated them from a latter-day holy man such as the late Menachem Schneerson (the Lubavitcher Rebbe), many of whose followers worship him as the Messiah?

It might be said that one difference is that Schneerson, unlike Shabbetai Tzvi, never himself claimed such a status. But even if that is true, it does not dispose of the matter. The same might, after all, be said of the Jew Jesus. The Jewishness of the mainstream Lubavitch movement is largely unquestioned nowadays, but given the historical precedent, whether this will continue to be the case in future generations remains to be seen.

Judaism, particularly that minority part of it that calls itself "Orthodox," often prides itself on its singularity and freedom from the taint of external influences. Yet the evidence of historical reality tells a different story. The Talmud, for example, is riddled with the intellectual influences of Hellenistic, Babylonian, and other surrounding cultures.

A diasporic society such as that of the Jews could not be isolationist. Intellectual openness and syncretism formed an essential condition of Judaism's development and survival. It is impossible to understand Maimonides outside the context of the circumambient Islamic and

Mediterranean worlds. Similarly, Moses Mendelssohn was not only the founder of the *Haskala* (the Jewish Enlightenment) but part and parcel of the German and European age of reason.

What is new in the post-Enlightenment Jewish world is the phenomenon of Jewishness without Judaism, sometimes without any religion at all. One aspect of this is the "non-Jewish Jew" – to use the term that the secular socialist historian Isaac Deutscher used about himself. Another aspect is the secular Zionist such as Theodor Herzl, whose path to Jewish nationalism began with the vision of himself leading a procession of his coreligionists to the baptismal font. Both socialism and Zionism began among Jews as revolutions against religious authority. Yet both assumed quasi-messianic features as they grew into mass movements.

In the fusion since 1967 of hyper-religiosity with ultra-nationalism among some Jews in both Israel and the Diaspora, we encounter another form of Messianism. Its adherents see this as rooted in Jewish tradition; others condemn it as a perversion akin to that of the "pseudo-Messiahs" of yore.

The historian's task, it is often said, is not to judge. I am not so sure. There is certainly a requirement to do more than just record. If the historian is to transcend the level of the mere chronicler, there must be at least an effort at interpretation – or, to put it another way, at evidence-based analysis. That surely is what distinguishes the historian from the traditional *maggid* who told fantastic tales to receptive audiences. Yet in what follows Rabbi Dunner marries the two together in exemplary fashion by bringing the fruits of professional historical scholarship to a broad readership.

The battle between credulity and reasoned argument endures in our own time. This book affords ample testimony to the epic nature of this struggle within the soul of the Jew over the past several centuries.

Bernard Wasserstein
Professor Emeritus of Modern European Jewish History,
The University of Chicago
Amsterdam, December 2017/5778

Introduction

"There is nothing new in the world except the history you do not know."

HARRY S. TRUMAN

"We are not makers of history, we are made by history."

MARTIN LUTHER KING JR.

Winston Churchill is frequently quoted as having said that history belongs to the victor. It is not clear that he actually did say these words, but it is certainly the case that history belongs to those who survive long enough to tell the tale. The question is: What happens to those historical actors who have left no distinctive impression on the broader story? For the most part they are consigned to the margins and footnotes – if they are remembered at all – and the majority of them disappear completely from mainstream consciousness, deemed by posterity to be irrelevant.

Curiously, it is these marginal characters that have always fascinated me. I believe their influence on events as they unfolded, during the period in which they lived and on the future, was far stronger than may seem years later. Take the messianic pretender Shabbetai Tzvi, about whom you will find a chapter in this book. Shabbetai Tzvi was hugely important for a few years, but ultimately – at least if judged by his own ambitions – he and his supporters were an utter failure. His story was a flash in the pan, nothing more than a noisy distraction. Even if he was a dangerous fraud and a successful troublemaker in the years he was active, in the end he achieved nothing meaningful. His impact on Jewish life was certainly important at the time, but today, hundreds of years later, it appears that his life and actions have no bearing on any person or movement within the Jewish world.

In reality, however, he had a profound effect on Judaism then and now, even if it was entirely inadvertent. It is an effect that continues to reverberate to this day. His irregular activities and the furor they created crystallized some important theological issues for the rabbis and community leaders of his era, who through him and the impact of his messianic aspirations recognized the stark dangers posed by not defining in the clearest possible terms Jewish mystical ideas that could be easily misinterpreted and manipulated, so that someone like him could succeed. The fact that Shabbetai Tzvi existed and created such chaos in the Jewish world prompted responsible leadership in the Jewish world – people who had seen him in action and witnessed the chaos he had generated as it unfolded – to put up the guardrails and prevent such a disaster from happening again in the future.

As a case in point, another chapter of this book contains an account of the Emden-Eybeschutz controversy, which was a continuation, one hundred years later, of the Shabbetai Tzvi controversy. Rabbi Yaakov Emden's stand against Rabbi Yonatan Eybeschutz – whether he was justified in his accusations or not – was a final battle against covert Sabbatian mystics and their insidious publicists who were secretly insinuating themselves into the mainstream Jewish world. So although Shabbetai Tzvi's story was inconsequential in terms of his attempt to lead the Jews out of exile and back to the Promised Land, it would be foolish to dismiss it as a historical sideshow.

We tend to look at the history of Jewish life in a linear way, ignoring or dismissing the influences and the stimulators from beyond the comfort zone of traditional Judaism. But we must ask ourselves: What were the outside factors that influenced what happened on the inside? How did the Shabbetai Tzvi and Emden-Eybeschutz controversies affect how we live our lives as Jews in the twenty-first century? How did the *Get* of Cleves controversy – another episode included in this book – influence Jewish law going forward, so that rulings arrived at today are determined by this seemingly marginal episode?

Rather than looking at the broad narrative of history, the uniting theme of this book is the very individual personalities of these marginal characters and the impact they had during the time in which they lived. But all the mavericks whose lives are explored in this book somehow represent – in their individuality and their unique stories – aspects of the broader narrative of their eras.

So, in the first instance, I am fascinated by how aspects of Jewish history which occur outside of the spotlight have a residual effect on what is happening onstage.

But truthfully, I am also fascinated by historical aberrations and am drawn to bygone eccentrics. I would like to think this is because oddities tend to shed light on what is wrong with the system that produced them. If one asks any sociologist or therapist, they will say that the irregularities they deal with on a daily basis are often consequences of problems within contemporary society at large.

A good example of this phenomenon is Ignatz Trebitsch-Lincoln, the protagonist of another chapter in this book. Trebitsch-Lincoln was brought up in a fully observant Orthodox Jewish home in Hungary, but evolved into something comparable to the "Zelig" character from the eponymous Woody Allen movie, jumping from one personality to another, working hard to blend in. He is constantly on the margins of important events, but in the end is just a noisy shadow whose enduring impact was negligible, but whose peculiar life tells you much about the era in which he lived, both in terms of his own journey, and in relation to the different groups he attempted to join and influence.

In my view, Trebitsch-Lincoln, and other flamboyant Jewish characters of the nineteenth and early twentieth centuries, are extreme examples of numerous others of their era who had also drifted away from the Orthodoxy and values of their upbringing and adopted bewildering new personas while attaching themselves to causes or creeds that were entirely unconnected or only loosely connected with their past.

Most of them remained embedded in their new communities for the rest of their lives, having abandoned their past to a greater or lesser extent for some kind of alternative. This description encapsulates most of the Jews who emigrated out of Eastern and Central Europe, and made new lives for themselves in Western Europe, the United States, or Ottoman Palestine. Many of them completely abandoned their past and adopted new behaviors and new life ideals.

As preposterous as it may sound, perhaps this phenomenon can be highlighted by comparing the debonair Hungarian-born trickster Trebitsch-Lincoln to Israel's first president, Chaim Weizmann, who doesn't belong in this book. His success as an international statesman is never questioned, but perhaps it is no coincidence that his origins were not dissimilar to those of Trebitsch-Lincoln.

Weizmann is almost exclusively remembered as an urbane Russian-born British-based scientist, and as the smooth-talking cultured diplomat who was comfortable mixing with the ruling classes of the world's major powers. But his origins in Russia do not chime with this image. He was the third of fifteen children; his father was a wood wholesaler and devoutly Orthodox. In order to become the man he would later be, Weizmann utterly abandoned his past and adopted an entirely new persona, quite foreign to the *shtetl* milieu of his youth.

As it turned out, Weizmann leveraged this guise for the benefit of his coreligionists and devoted his life to furthering the cause of Zionism – unlike Trebitsch, who was a narcissist and a scoundrel and did nothing for anyone but himself. Nonetheless, the pathology is remarkably similar. Both Weizmann and Trebitsch were brought up in an insular Orthodox setting and were part of a deeply traditional Jewish community, and both of them, when they abandoned their origins, shaped their public personas around a sophisticated and cultivated modern society that was very far removed from the way of life they had seen in the homes of their parents.

For some reason, we only ever examine Weizmann's life through the lens of his Zionism and his political activism, ignoring or only superficially giving any attention to the total shift from his origins that enabled him to become such a successful Zionist advocate and activist, and for that reason alone it might be important to read Trebitsch-Lincoln's story so that we can truly encounter this elusive and intriguing side of that period in Jewish history.

After all, if we properly appreciate the extent of the upheavals such personal transformations required, we might better understand the huge sacrifices made not just by Weizmann but also by the Zionist pioneers who moved from Lithuania, or Russia, or Rumania, or Poland, to join a new agricultural settlement in Ottoman Palestine in the late 1800s. Or we might understand the tribulations experienced by Jewish immigrants to the United States – both those who succeeded and those who struggled to prosper.

In order to obtain an accurate reading of the social dynamics that produced these kinds of Jews, and to appreciate the extent of the transformations they all went through to do what they did, one needs to focus on an extreme – and Ignatz Trebitsch-Lincoln is the perfect foil. By traveling along the roller coaster that was Trebitsch-Lincoln's life we gain an insight into the lifestyle transformations required of a person like Chaim Weizmann, which he undertook so that he would succeed in his quest for a Jewish national home.

Finally, it goes without saying that the stories of an intriguing eccentric such as Trebitsch-Lincoln, or of the very peculiar Shabbetai Tzvi, or about the very disturbing Emden-Eybeschutz controversy, are diverting and compelling in their own way, and it is certainly the case that this is an important factor when it comes to studying history. Of course, in pure historical terms, it is primarily important for us to be familiar with the broad details of history – the factors that led up to the French Revolution, for example, or the military history of the First World War – but that kind of broad-brush narrative is never going to be as interesting as the story of a crazy fraudster, or how it was that a messianic pretender could have convinced devout rabbis he was the Messiah.

I think that when people get excited about some marginal aspect of history they are inevitably going to become more interested in the conventional historical narratives that are rather less engaging. As a student of history, who is fascinated by history and who loves the rich tapestry that is history, I strongly believe this book will excite its readers through the very entertaining anecdotes and vignettes that recall marginal characters within the Jewish historical narrative, and will consequently stimulate a wider audience to look further into Jewish history.

Perhaps, after reading about the characters and episodes in this book, the reader will want to find out more about the rather more mundane aspects of the origins of Jewish life, including details of Jewish community history, and the rabbis and significant figures who led those communities that made the Jewish world what it is today. Knowing how Judaism evolved throughout its history can only enrich Judaism and the engagement with Jewish identity. If the stories in this book succeed in acting as the conduit to a strengthened Jewish identity, for that reason alone this book will have been worth every effort.

ACKNOWLEDGMENTS

No book of any subject or length can be produced without the help of others. The byline may have the author's name, but in the background are numerous others whose assistance and encouragement created the platform for the author to produce his written work.

First and foremost I would like to thank all those people who have fed my insatiable appetite for obscure information on random subjects of Jewish and general interest. I am a self-confessed information addict, and over the years I have been generously enabled by numerous information providers on every topic that has ever grabbed my attention.

Although this is not an exhaustive list, hopefully it includes everyone who has had a hand in providing me with nuggets of information that have found their way into this book, in one form or another: the indefatigable Menachem Butler of Harvard Law School, Allan Engel (the first person to introduce me to the insane world of Ignatz Trebitsch-Lincoln), Rabbi Eliezer Katzman, Professor David Latchman, and my dear friend Moshe Leib Weiser of London. My profound appreciation to all of you for sharing your knowledge with me and for helping me put this collection of historical episodes together.

I would also like to thank Professor Bernard Wasserstein for his invaluable research into Ignatz Trebitsch-Lincoln and the comprehensive book he wrote on this enigmatic figure. I wish to thank him for agreeing to write the foreword, and for his generous words about my humble attempt to summarize his valuable tome for a wide readership.

My thanks, too, to Professor Shnayer Leiman, who kindly agreed to read through the extended chapter on the Emden-Eybeschutz controversy, the chapter on the Shabbetai Tzvi affair, and the chapter on the notorious literary forger, Rabbi Yehuda Yudel Rosenberg, and to offer his insights and observations, based on his decades of research into these particular aspects of modern Jewish history. His comments, delivered in typically humble style, were extremely helpful and insightful, and I am grateful for his scholarship, but most of all for his friendship.

My appreciation also goes to Daniel Kestenbaum, of Kestenbaum Judaica Auctions in New York, and to his able assistant, Jackie Insel, for kindly assisting me in obtaining the image of the Baal Shem of London.

I also thank Deborah Thompson, the diligent author's assistant who stepped in toward the end of the preparation period to ensure that all the details of the book's manuscript were in order so that it could be submitted for publication. Deborah expertly pulled all the strands together and made it happen.

Which brings me to Toby Press, who enthusiastically embraced this project and did everything to turn the dream of this book into a reality. In particular, I would like to thank Toby Press's editor-in-chief, Gila Fine, and her esteemed colleague, Matthew Miller, publisher of Toby. Thanks are also due to editors Nechama Unterman, Ilana Sobel, and Shira Finson.

This book would never have happened without the eager enthusiasm for Jewish history articles of Shalom Rubashkin, editor of our local Jewish newspaper in Los Angeles, *Jewish Home LA*. Without his delivery deadlines, and gentle reminders to submit the articles on time for press day, all of the incredible historical episodes in this book might have remained unwritten. I am forever indebted to Shalom for showcasing my Jewish history knowledge on these quite obscure events and people in the pages of his newspaper. Other newspaper editors might have pushed me to take a more mainstream approach to my chosen topics, but Shalom vigorously encouraged me to share unusual narratives, which ultimately allowed for the preparation of this book, using the original articles as the draft manuscript.

Last, and by no means least, let me thank my dear wife, Sabine, whose incredible patience and enduring forbearance for my literary obsession, as I clatter away on my laptop keyboard late at night and randomly scatter books around the house, is deeply appreciated. She has an equal share in all of my output. Her constant encouragement for me to write, to speak, to teach, and to involve myself in communal affairs is the engine that makes everything I do possible, and better. No "thank you" will ever truly suffice, but I must thank her nonetheless, for this book, and for every other one of my successes.

Chapter 1

Shabbetai Tzvi: Notorious Messianic Deceiver

Constantinople, 1666

> "From his first maturity [Shabbetai Tzvi] was peculiar, different from other youths his age – a fact which some interpret in his favor, calling him an angel rather than a human being, while others condemn him for it as a lunatic."
>
> – Rabbi Avraham ben Levi Conque (1648–c. 1730) of Hebron, a faithful follower of Shabbetai Tzvi

SABETHA SEBI
Vermeynden Meſſias Der Ioden

Portrait of Shabbetai Tzvi, drawn in Izmir (Smyrna), 1666

To truly fathom the incomprehensible Shabbetai Tzvi episode, first one must have an understanding of its origins in Kabbala and Jewish mystical tradition. The study of Kabbala had historically not focused on Messianism or on the process of Jewish redemption from the *galut*, the exile from Jerusalem that began after the Second Temple was destroyed in 70 CE, which was followed by the wide dispersion of Jews across the known world. For hundreds of years the study of Kabbala was mainly concerned with the mystical and symbolic view of the universe and its creation, and on understanding God and how to connect with God through the performance of commandments found in the Hebrew Scriptures and the Oral Law.

The early kabbalists – small, secretive groups of Jewish mystics – saw the concept of messianic redemption in much the same way as did non-kabbalists: a firm belief in an ultimate moment in time, when a Messiah chosen by God would lead the Jews back to the Holy Land, at which point the Temple would be rebuilt. It was an essential part of the Jewish belief system, but it was not considered particularly mystical.

After the dramatic expulsion of Jews from Spain in 1492, this paradigm shifted. The upheaval caused by the Spanish Expulsion, and by the Inquisition that followed in its wake, shook the Jewish world to its foundations, probably more than any other event since the destruction of the Jerusalem Temple 1,400 years earlier. During the sixteenth century, Safed (Tzfat), a small community in the northeast of *Eretz Yisrael* – then under Ottoman rule – emerged as the headquarters of Kabbala in the Jewish world. Its emergence proved to be pivotal, particularly as the Kabbala espoused by Safed kabbalists was mainly eschatological in theme and content. Eschatology is the branch of theology concerned with the "end of days."

Some of Judaism's greatest minds and most spiritual of souls found their home in sixteenth-century Safed, and to this day the principal mystical and legal texts of Judaism can be traced to these Safed kabbalists. The greatest of these kabbalists, and the one with the broadest influence, was Rabbi Yitzhak Luria Ashkenazi (1534–1572), who later became known as the Arizal or the Ari. The Arizal had a close and devoted circle of disciples who recorded all his teachings. He never wrote anything down himself, and everything we know of him and his teachings emanates from these disciples, mainly via a mystic called Rabbi Hayim Vital (1542–1620).

The Arizal's kabbalistic system – today referred to as Lurianic Kabbala – revolved almost exclusively around this previously overlooked topic of exile and redemption. In the most basic of terms, it posited that the whole of creation was directly tied into the exile and eventual redemption of the Jewish nation. In summary, God can only allow for the existence of a physical world through an act of withdrawal. The calibration of "withdrawal" and "God" within creation is the balance between spiritual and unspiritual, or physical, in the universe.

The sin of Adam and Eve created a state of imbalance, in need of *tikkun*, or correction. The exile of the Jewish people in the physical world is a reflection of this imbalance. If the Jewish nation achieves ultimate perfection, as reflected through messianic redemption, then all of creation can at last be in balance, and God will have realized His original purpose for creation.

Interestingly, the Arizal did not devote much attention to the Messiah himself. Who he would be, what he might do or say, and how he might reveal himself, seemed of little relevance to the Arizal. But among the few scattered references within Lurianic mysticism that discuss the Messiah figure one in particular is worth noting. The Arizal predicted that the messianic redeemer would possess an "evil side," and in the course of his activities the Messiah would perform actions or be involved in events that might seem antithetical to his messianic mission.

One fascinating example of this idea can be found in a text from the 1550s, authored by an anonymous rabbi who was part of the Safed kabbalist group. He discusses how frequently some biblical heroes were somehow connected with "inappropriate" women: Judah and Tamar, Joseph and the wife of Potiphar, Moses and Zipporah, Joshua and Rahab, Samson and Delilah, Boaz and Ruth. The text offers a number of explanations and interpretations – for example, the necessity for God's chosen hero to have a relationship with those whom God needs to vanquish; or another one: the need for a male, representing good, to effect *tikkun* on a female, representing evil; or another one: through a union of two disparate elements from opposite ends of the spectrum

God can realize the purpose of creation. Shabbetai Tzvi's apologists would later use these ideas to justify his peculiar behavior and public desecration of Jewish law.

Lurianic Kabbala's focus on the redemption had the effect of generating a new enthusiasm for the Messianic Era and heightened expectation for its imminence in the Jewish world, in a way that had not been seen since Bar Kokhba's tantalizing rise and devastating defeat by the Romans at Betar in 135 CE. There was a sudden proliferation of Jewish groups devoted to bringing about the redemption, and between 1630 and 1660 the sense of an impending redemption was promoted and discussed in many different communities.

THE EARLY LIFE OF SHABBETAI TZVI

Let us turn now to the protagonist of our story: the messianic pretender, Shabbetai Tzvi. His biography is unsurprisingly full of contradictions. Glorified by acolytes, and vilified by detractors, the truth about him is hard to pin down. But some of the facts are incontrovertible. He was born on August 1, 1626, which that year was also the Ninth of Av, Tisha B'Av, when Jews fast and spend the day mourning the destruction of the two Jerusalem Temples. But there was no fast or mourning on the day Shabbetai Tzvi was born, as it was a Saturday and fasting is prohibited on the Jewish Sabbath. Mystical literature is insistent that the Messiah will be born on Tisha B'Av, to signal that final redemption will emerge out of the ashes of destruction. In any event, it was in honor of the day of his birth – in Hebrew, *Shabbat* – that the parents of the newborn boy named their son Shabbetai.

Shabbetai Tzvi was born in the town of Izmir, in Turkey, known in those days as Smyrna. His family was originally from Greece, but his father, Mordechai, had moved the family to the coastal city to more easily and profitably conduct his international trading business. It is possible that the family was of Ashkenazic origin, as Tzvi is not a typical Sephardic family name. Mordechai Tzvi was a trading agent, acting on behalf of English traders who lived in Izmir. This type of arrangement was very common – Western European traders would hire local Jews to act for them, as they generally spoke multiple languages and were extremely well connected.

Shabbetai was the second of three sons, and his family was wealthy, prosperous, and prominent. Both his parents died before the Messiah saga – his father in 1663, his mother many years earlier. Shabbetai's main teacher was a man called Rabbi Yosef Escapa (1572–1662), author of a halakhic work titled *Rosh Yosef*. The young Shabbetai was an earnest and competent student who mastered Talmud and Jewish law at an early age, and he was just eighteen when he received his rabbinic ordination.

No one knows exactly when Shabbetai Tzvi first started studying Kabbala but it was certainly at a young age. Evidently, he studied it on his own, which was highly unusual. Aspiring kabbalists are expected to master their subject with guidance from a mentor – hence the term Kabbala, or "received" teachings.

At twenty, Shabbetai Tzvi married for the first time, but the marriage was never consummated and shortly after the wedding, following a complaint to local rabbis by his new wife's father, the young couple divorced. Almost immediately Shabbetai Tzvi married again, but once again the marriage was not consummated and ended in divorce. At around the same time people began to notice that Shabbetai Tzvi's behavior was erratic and unpredictable. Sometimes he was enthusiastically joyful, exuberant, and ecstatic, while at other times he was depressed, anxious, paranoid, and passive. Today we recognize these wild mood swings as symptoms of acute manic depression, or bipolar syndrome, but in the seventeenth century such symptoms were interpreted somewhat differently. To Shabbetai Tzvi's detractors his behavior was evidence that he was an evil madman. To his supporters and devotees, however, his strange behavior attested to the fact that he was a divine and holy man. Shabbetai Tzvi told people that he regularly experienced visions and he would often stay awake for days at a time without food. Occasionally he would disappear for weeks at a time, and no one knew where he had gone. Despite these strange disappearances, his supporters refused to acknowledge that there was anything wrong with him and instead claimed that he needed time on his own to atone for the world's sins.

One of the most unusual aspects of his manic episodes was his transformation from a meticulously observant Jew into a flagrant violator of Jewish law. His supporters would later refer to his public violations of halakha as *"maasim zarim"* – strange or paradoxical acts.

Notwithstanding the support for Shabbetai Tzvi in Izmir, his odd behavior eventually began to seriously concern the senior Jewish leadership in the town, and after an emergency meeting they decided to expel him from the community, before his malign influence began to seriously disrupt the equilibrium of the insular and conservative-minded Jewish population. The year was 1651, and Shabbetai Tzvi was twenty-five years old.

FROM OUTCAST TO REDEEMER

Before we follow Shabbetai Tzvi on his journey from Izmir, let us get to know him a little bit better. Numerous people who were acquainted with him during these wilderness years – whether they were his detractors, his supporters, or just neutral observers – would later offer their opinions and reflections on the Shabbetai Tzvi they remembered from that time, describing all the facets of his fascinating, if troubled, personality. The composite picture that emerges is mesmerizing, and remarkably consistent, despite the many different motives behind the diverse accounts.

Shabbetai Tzvi was exceptionally charming and charismatic. He was also musically talented, handsome, extremely kind and generous spirited, very diplomatic, gregarious, and a brilliant conversationalist. He was fluent in several languages, and had wide knowledge in numerous subjects. All these attributes, combined with his family's relative wealth, ensured him easy access wherever he went, enabling him to befriend anyone with whom he came into contact. Those who met him were immediately impressed, and he would easily win people over with his endearing personality and acute intelligence. Sadly, this also meant that people were blinded, at least initially, to his severe mental illness.

In any event, following his expulsion from Izmir, Shabbetai Tzvi proceeded to Salonica (Thessaloniki), in Greece, where he was received respectfully, and he soon befriended all the local rabbis. But the honeymoon in Salonica was very short-lived. Within weeks his behavior had deteriorated and he had begun to act strangely. One fateful day, Shabbetai Tzvi invited all the local rabbis to his home. They arrived to discover that he had set up a wedding canopy in his yard. As they looked on, he proceeded to perform a marriage ceremony between himself and a Torah scroll, as if he was marrying a woman. Shocked by this bizarre behavior, they immediately arranged to have him evicted from Salonica, and he was gone within a matter of days.

From Salonica he drifted to Athens, then Peloponnese, then Patras, and finally – in 1658 – he was back in Turkey, in Constantinople (Istanbul), where he remained for several months. His strange behavior had by this time escalated exponentially. In one particularly notorious incident, he purchased an oversized dead fish, dressed it up in baby clothes, put it into a crib, and announced to startled onlookers on the street that fish represent liberation and redemption, and this particular fish was the childlike Jewish nation in need of redemption. Shortly after this bewildering episode, Shabbetai Tzvi announced that he was implementing a "festival-week ceremony." Over the course of seven days he celebrated every major Jewish festival – High Holy Days, Pesaḥ, Shavuot, and Sukkot – with all the associated laws, customs, and prayers, each day a different festival. He explained that by doing this he was atoning for all the sins committed by Jews throughout history who had done something wrong during any of these festivals, or had not observed them properly.

It was at the conclusion of this strange week that Shabbetai Tzvi announced an innovation – a blessing over sin. The blessing ended with the words "*mattir issurim*" – a corruption of the blessing recited every morning that ends "*mattir assurim,*" which describes God as "He who liberates the imprisoned." This new blessing, to be used every time someone sinned to please God, changed the meaning of the phrase to "He who permits the forbidden." By this stage Shabbetai Tzvi was in full manic mode and announced to the group of bewildered spectators that a new era had begun, with new laws and commandments, and by doing what he was about to do he would effect the final mystical perfection of God's physical creation. He then took a piece of pork, uttered the altered blessing, and proceeded to eat it.

When the local community heard what he had done there was an uproar. Local rabbis were compelled to react harshly, and they arranged for Shabbetai Tzvi to be publicly flogged. He was then excommunicated and no one was permitted to speak to him, feed him, or house him. Shunned by every Jew in the city, and unable to support himself, Shabbetai Tzvi left town and returned to his birthplace, Izmir, where he disappeared from sight. He would not be seen for the next three years. Then, in 1662, he reemerged with his confidence recovered, and departed Izmir for *Eretz Yisrael*. The trip required a stopover in Egypt, and while he was there he became very friendly with the local rabbis and community leaders, and in particular a man called Raphael Joseph, the government-appointed *chelebi* (community president) of Egyptian Jewry.

After a few months in Egypt, Shabbetai Tzvi traveled to Jerusalem, where he seems to have impressed the small community. He spent a year in Jerusalem, and the community's leaders then sent him back to Egypt as their official representative to raise funds. It was there, on March 31, 1664, that Shabbetai Tzvi got married for the third time. Sarah, his bride, was a girl with her own remarkable life story. Orphaned during the infamous Chmielnicki Massacres of 1648–49 in Poland and Ukraine, she was brought up by gentiles as a Christian. She only discovered her Jewish origins on reaching adulthood, and thereafter began drifting from community to community, possibly in search of her family – a rootless woman, very beautiful, and by all accounts very seductive.

Although Sarah had a reputation for immoral behavior, she would often made the strange claim that she was destined to marry the "Messiah," a prediction that was the object of great amusement to everyone who knew her. Somehow she came across Shabbetai Tzvi in Egypt, and decided to marry him. The wedding took place at the home of Raphael Joseph.

THE PROPHET FROM GAZA

It was at this point that Shabbetai Tzvi stumbled across someone whose involvement in his messianic pretensions was to prove absolutely crucial – Avraham Natan ben Elisha Hayim Ashkenazi, later known to Sabbatians as Natan HaNavi (Nathan the Prophet) and to everyone else as Natan Azzati (Nathan of Gaza).

Nathan was born in approximately 1643 in Jerusalem. Despite his family being Ashkenazic – hence his last name – it was part of the Sephardic community in Jerusalem. In reality, though, Nathan's father was rarely there as he spent the vast majority of his time collecting money for the Jerusalem community in towns and cities outside *Eretz Yisrael*. Even as a young boy, Nathan was known to be highly intelligent, extremely diligent in his studies, and he was particularly admired as a gifted writer. At the age of twenty he married the daughter of a wealthy Sephardi from Gaza and, with the promise of full financial support by his wife's father, he moved to Gaza and took up the study of Kabbala.

The change from Talmud and Jewish law to Kabbala seems to have had a profound and unsettling effect on Nathan. He withdrew from society, began to fast regularly, and engaged in intense prayer and regular ritual bathing, as well as other forms of self-mortification. Before long he informed his family and friends that he was having mystical visions and that angels appeared to him to tell him about the past, present, and future.

Like Shabbetai Tzvi, Nathan was a very talented and engaging individual, but he had many qualities that Shabbetai Tzvi did not. He was a relentless campaigner for ideals he held important; he was highly motivated and focused; and he was consistent in his Judaism – unimpeachably mitzva observant, with none of the highs and lows or aberrant behaviors of Shabbetai Tzvi; he was an original and systematic thinker, very fast on his feet; and last but not least, he was an exceptionally talented writer, which would prove critical in the messianic propaganda campaign.

Nathan would end up as the catalyst that allowed a messianic movement to flourish around the flawed character of Shabbetai Tzvi. Before he entered the picture Shabbetai Tzvi had not succeeded at anything, except for attracting attention to himself in an assortment of Jewish communities, usually for the wrong reasons. Without Nathan, Shabbetai Tzvi would probably have disappeared without a trace, confined to the trashcan of forgotten historical eccentrics who have proliferated throughout Jewish history. But that was not to be. A fateful meeting between the two of them would launch a toxic partnership that wreaked havoc across the Jewish world.

In 1665 Raphael Joseph heard about this young man in Gaza who was claiming to have spectacular visions. By this time Nathan was being visited by countless pilgrims and he had acquired a reputation as a healer. Intrigued by what he was hearing, Joseph told Shabbetai Tzvi about Nathan. Shabbetai Tzvi immediately resolved to visit this "healer" to seek help for his tormented soul. Within a few days Shabbetai Tzvi set off on a journey from Egypt to Gaza, and as soon as he arrived he arranged to meet Nathan.

The moment Shabbetai Tzvi entered his room Nathan fell to the ground in a trance. When he awoke he informed Shabbetai Tzvi that he possessed a precious and unique soul and was none other than the Messiah. Shocked by this startling revelation, Shabbetai Tzvi burst into laughter and dismissed Nathan's pronouncement as nonsense. When the meeting was over Shabbetai Tzvi began organizing to leave Gaza, but Nathan simply refused to give up. For three weeks he relentlessly cajoled Shabbetai Tzvi to accept what he was telling him and to concede that he was the King Messiah, destined to lead the Jews out of exile back to the Promised Land.

Nathan encouraged Shabbetai Tzvi to visit Jerusalem and Hebron to pray at Jewish holy sites, and accompanied him to both places, all the while badgering him to accept his mission. But when they returned to Gaza, Shabbetai Tzvi slipped into one of his periodic depressions. It was shortly before the festival of Shavuot, and on the first night of Shavuot Nathan fell into a trance in the presence of local community members and while in the trance said some amazing things about Shabbetai Tzvi. When he eventually awoke he informed everyone that he was in no doubt that Shabbetai Tzvi was the Messiah.

With the pressure now mounting, it took just one more week for Shabbetai Tzvi himself to concede, and on 17 Sivan, coinciding with May 31, 1665, for the first time Shabbetai Tzvi publicly declared himself as the Messiah, King of the Jews and Redeemer of Israel. His first act as "Messiah" was to abolish the fast of *Shiva Asar BeTammuz* (the Seventeenth of Tammuz). The decree was greeted enthusiastically in Gaza, and not only did the community feast on the fast day, they also recited Hallel and rejoiced with live music, singing, and dancing. The community in Hebron was next to join the believers. In Jerusalem, however, the story was different. The community there knew Shabbetai Tzvi, and the local rabbis were incredulous, refusing to accept that the Shabbetai Tzvi they knew so well was actually the Messiah.

Shabbetai Tzvi arrived in Jerusalem together with Nathan shortly afterward, but they were both ridiculed – every time Shabbetai Tzvi walked past a group of children they would mockingly chant at him, "He left as a *shaliaḥ* (charity collector) and he returned as the *Mashiaḥ* (Messiah)!" Shabbetai Tzvi tried to gain entry to the Temple Mount to bring a sacrifice but was prevented from doing so by the Ottoman authorities. A fight then erupted between him and the local Jewish leadership, who accused him of having misappropriated some of the monies he had collected in Egypt on behalf of the community. The case was brought to the local Ottoman leader for adjudication, and Shabbetai Tzvi was exonerated. His supporters immediately claimed that the legal victory was a miracle and proved he was the Messiah.

But very quickly afterward, Shabbetai Tzvi was in trouble again. At a party celebrating his victory he personally cooked and served non-kosher meat and recited the "*mattir issurim*" benediction. Nathan's teacher and former mentor, the highly regarded Rabbi Yaakov Hagiz, called together the local rabbis. They unanimously decided to excommunicate both Shabbetai Tzvi and Nathan, and the defiant duo were unceremoniously expelled from the Holy City. They left without putting up a fight and were never to return.

The rabbis of Jerusalem were not satisfied with a mere expulsion. Extremely concerned by the actions of the two intoxicated fraudsters, as well as by the behavior of their awestruck supporters and the possible repercussions of the messianic campaign, they wrote dozens of letters to rabbis in Jewish communities across the world to warn them of the dangers posed by this lethal duo, and to inform them about what had transpired during their time in Jerusalem. But despite the ease with which they had managed to dispatch Shabbetai Tzvi and Nathan from their own jurisdiction, putting a stop to the growing messianic movement would prove to be completely beyond their grasp.

ON A MESSIANIC MISSION

After their eviction from Jerusalem, Shabbetai Tzvi and Nathan decided that they would split up. While Shabbetai Tzvi embarked on a tour of Jewish communities, to introduce himself to as many people as possible so that he could create a wide base of support among the general Jewish public, Nathan launched a propaganda campaign, using correspondence with leading players across the Jewish world as a door opener for Shabbetai Tzvi wherever he went.

Nathan returned to Gaza – which he declared the new holy city of Judaism – while Shabbetai Tzvi headed toward Izmir. On his way he stopped at any town or city that had a Jewish community. The news of his messianic declaration traveled ahead of him and he was enthusiastically welcomed wherever he went. And although his behavior remained erratic and unusual, the enthusiasm generated by the belief that he was the Messiah seemed to render any aberration irrelevant – whether he behaved normally or strangely, his personal conduct was completely overshadowed by the euphoric feelings of the thousands of Jews who believed he had come to liberate them from exile.

Meanwhile, as Shabbetai Tzvi zigzagged triumphantly from community to community, Nathan launched a feverish propaganda campaign. In numerous letters dispatched to every major Jewish center he called for mass repentance in anticipation of the imminent redemption. He began to refer to Shabbetai Tzvi as *"AMIRAH"*: *"Adoneinu Malkeinu Yarum Hodo"* – "Our lord, our king, may his majesty be exalted." His flowery predictions for the great redemption and how it would unfold became more fanciful with each letter. His "prophecies" were apocalyptic and supernatural. A blazing fire would surround Jerusalem and Hebron, he wrote, to prevent any uncircumcised gentiles from entering these holy places. Mosques and churches would spontaneously disappear without a trace. These bizarre predictions were lapped up by the masses, as fact and fiction became indistinguishable. With hindsight, it is evident that the entire movement had set itself up for crushing failure from very early on.

Shabbetai Tzvi arrived in Izmir in September 1665 and stayed there for four months. He secluded himself upon arrival and rarely emerged. Throughout his time there, letters from supporters and detractors piled up at the homes of local rabbis and leaders. Two distinct groups emerged – those who enthusiastically believed in him and those who emphatically did not. At the head of the unbelievers was the chief rabbi of the city, Rabbi Hayim Benveniste, acclaimed author of the authoritative halakhic work *Knesset HaGedola*.

Tension in the city mounted but remained under control until, on Saturday, December 12, 1665, Shabbetai Tzvi led a mob of supporters to the Portuguese synagogue, where he disrupted the service and read the Torah portion from a printed book instead of the Torah scroll. He announced that he was appointing one of his brothers the new sultan of Turkey, and his other brother the emperor of Rome. While everyone looked on disbelievingly, he began to hurl insults at the local community rabbis, including Rabbi Benveniste.

Suddenly he changed the subject. "Why has Jesus been so abused by Jewish tradition?" he asked disparagingly, and then declared that under his leadership Jesus would henceforth be considered one of the Jewish prophets. He performed a number of strange rituals and then announced to the astonished worshipers that the date of the redemption was 15 Sivan, 1666. At this point Rabbi Benveniste stood up and demanded that Shabbetai Tzvi prove to everyone that he was the Messiah, as he claimed. Shabbetai Tzvi sneered and began hurling vile insults at the rabbi, threatening him with excommunication. The synagogue erupted in complete pandemonium as Shabbetai Tzvi screamed abuse and the rabbi's supporters screamed back at him.

Inexplicably, within a matter of days Rabbi Benveniste reconciled with Shabbetai Tzvi, and he suddenly became one of the impostor's most ardent supporters. Rabbi Benveniste was a man with a stellar reputation, both as a pious Jew and as a wise and learned rabbi, and his declaration of support was a turning point in the messianic campaign, as numerous doubters changed sides and began to support Shabbetai Tzvi. In response to Rabbi Benveniste's decision to back him, Shabbetai Tzvi arranged for a rival local rabbi to be fired and began to treat Rabbi Benveniste with great respect. Now led by their chief rabbi, Izmir's Jewish community erupted with messianic fervor, and those unbelievers who remained skeptical were utterly marginalized. Sadly, the respected rabbi's support for the charlatan Messiah continued throughout the remainder of the nine-month episode, a tragic miscalculation that stained his reputation until his passing and which continued to haunt his legacy even after his death.

In Gaza, Nathan continued his energetic campaign to promote the redemption. Believers began to proliferate throughout the Jewish world. The legend soon began to feed on itself – the more people there were who believed that Shabbetai Tzvi was the Messiah, the more ambassadors there were for the cause. With the excitement growing, and the anticipation increasing, Shabbetai Tzvi and his acolytes decided it was time to inform the Ottoman authorities, and in particular the Sultan, about his messianic mission and to request their full cooperation.

In early 1666, Shabbetai Tzvi set sail for Constantinople. Rough seas disrupted the ten-day journey, and the ship floundered at sea for more than a month. Meanwhile, the news of his imminent appearance in the Ottoman capital created a massive stir, and the Jewish-community leadership struggled to formulate a cogent strategy. While some of them believed it was possible that Shabbetai Tzvi was indeed who he claimed to be, acknowledging him as Messiah, King of the Jews, was a treasonable offense, punishable by imprisonment or possibly even execution. But what if he was the Messiah? Not welcoming him would be a blatant denial of his elevated status and would amount to a terrible dishonor and a desecration of God's name. Meanwhile, there were those in the community who utterly refused to believe the messianic claims, and there were some who even urged the community's leaders to arrange for Shabbetai Tzvi to be assassinated.

While all this was being deliberated in Constantinople, such was the power of the propaganda emanating from Gaza and Izmir that Jews as far away as Germany, Holland, Poland, and North Africa were selling their businesses and wrapping up their affairs as they prepared for the imminent redemption and their return to Zion. The scene was set for a dramatic climax.

MESSIANIC MISSION ABORTED

By this time, the Turkish authorities had caught wind of the affair and an emergency meeting was called between government officials and the Jewish leadership to decide what to do. After examining the evidence, and based on first-hand accounts of the pretender's personal history, the authorities and Jewish leaders concluded that Shabbetai Tzvi was an impostor and determined that he had to be stopped in his tracks. As a result of this decision, when Shabbetai Tzvi's ship drew close to Constantinople on February 5, 1666, a group of Turkish soldiers sailed up to his vessel before it docked, unceremoniously arrested him, and escorted him to shore.

The arrest marked the end of the messianic adventure in practical terms, and Shabbetai Tzvi was taken into custody. Unsure what to do with this unlikely revolutionary leader, the authorities decided that the grand vizier, Köprülüzade Fazil Ahmed Pasha, would take personal charge of the case. Shabbetai Tzvi did not present a military threat to the Ottomans, and it seems no one was too concerned by his political ambitions either. As far as the Ottoman authorities were concerned, the main problem posed by the eccentric rabbi and his following was economic. With Jews in control of so many trade routes, the potential disruption to Turkey's trade and industry as a result of the religious awakening provoked by this furor was of grave concern, and the grand vizier understood that this matter needed careful and delicate handling.

In the meantime Shabbetai Tzvi was treated benignly, a fact misconstrued by his supporters as further proof that he was the Messiah. He was kept in a comfortable suite at the local prison, and friends and supporters were permitted to visit him in a constant stream. Shortly before Passover, Shabbetai Tzvi was transported just under two hundred miles to a fortress across the water from Gallipoli. Thousands of believers traveled from all over the world to catch a glimpse of their Messiah. So great was the influx of pilgrims that local food prices began to rise, and boat owners were able to charge exorbitant rates to ferry believers to the prison fortress and back. The surreal pantomime persisted for several months and, although the declared date of redemption came and went, the hysteria continued unabated.

On the fast of *Shiva Asar BeTammuz*, Shabbetai Tzvi ate heartily, and so did his supporters. During the traditional three weeks of mourning that followed the fast, Shabbetai Tzvi announced he was canceling the fast of Tisha B'Av, a decision hailed by his followers as a new high point of the redemptive era. But by now people were beginning to realize that things were not going as planned, and nothing seemed to match Nathan's ever-escalating predictions and "prophecies." One did not need to be particularly perceptive to see that Shabbetai Tzvi had failed to lead the Jews to redemption. In fact, he wasn't even getting out of jail. In addition, there were worrying reports emerging from the jail of his involvement with various young women who were being supplied to him by the prison staff on a regular basis.

The sultan of Turkey, who had been receiving reports from his grand vizier about the strange prisoner and his following, decided that the matter needed to be addressed once and for all, before it got completely out of hand. In September, without any warning, Shabbetai Tzvi was suddenly spirited away to Adrianople, where the sultan resided during the summer months. As soon as he arrived he was brought to the palace for an audience with the sultan, who was joined by a group of senior advisers, as well as the royal physician, a Jewish convert to Islam.

Questioned about his messianic pretensions, Shabbetai Tzvi denied that he was the Messiah, claiming it was all an elaborate fabrication. When it was pointed out to him that an enthusiastic messianic movement had developed around him, and that the movement was in danger of escalating into a rebellion against Ottoman rule, he shrugged his shoulders dismissively and did not offer any comment. One of the sultan's advisers mentioned that he had heard Shabbetai Tzvi was a miracle worker, and requested that he perform a miracle for them, but the bashful Messiah tactfully declined.

The apostate royal physician then told him in no uncertain terms that there was only one solution to the crisis – Shabbetai Tzvi's immediate conversion to Islam. If he refused, the sultan would have no choice but to have him executed on the spot on the grounds that he was a dangerous revolutionary. Shabbetai Tzvi did not hesitate for a moment. He tore off his Jewish cap and spat on it, and to everyone's surprise began speaking viciously against the Jewish faith. A Muslim cleric was quickly summoned to convert him, and the conversion was performed there and then, witnessed by the sultan and all his advisers.

After the conversion was over, the sultan presented Shabbetai Tzvi with a special turban and formally changed his name to Aziz Mehemed Effendi. He was appointed keeper of the palace gates and awarded a generous government-funded salary. Those who were present at the meeting later reported that both Shabbetai Tzvi and the sultan appeared delighted by their meeting, and they parted in very good spirits.

The news of Shabbetai Tzvi's conversion was greeted with astonishment. At first it was dismissed as lies. For believers it was inconceivable that their Messiah would choose apostasy over martyrdom, while critics could not believe that the sultan had allowed such a dangerous revolutionary to remain alive. Confusion reigned. As time went by, and Jews in Adrianople witnessed the newly turbaned Shabbetai Tzvi manning the palace gates, the news of his apostasy began to spread across the Jewish world, and so began a long and tortured journey back to normality for the masses of Jews who had been animated by this eccentric pretender, a man who had proven to be nothing more than a disappointing fraud.

FALSE MESSIAH DIES – HIS MISSION DOES NOT

Shabbetai Tzvi lived on for another ten years. At times he assumed the role of a pious Muslim and criticized Judaism; at other times he associated with Jews and acted as a Jew. In March 1668 he let it be known that God had appeared to him in a prophetic vision and revealed that he was still the true Messiah, in spite of his conversion, and that his conversion had been a holy act meant to attract Muslims to Judaism as part of the redemption process.

This statement and other peculiar acts were too much for the authorities to tolerate. Shabbetai Tzvi was fired from his palace job, his salary was terminated, and he was banished to a Muslim district of Constantinople, with strict instructions not to interact with the Jewish community. But it seems he was unable to stay out of trouble. Within a short period he was discovered leading Jewish prayer groups, resulting in his immediate exile to a small coastal village in Montenegro. There he died in total isolation, supposedly on September 17, 1676, which coincided with Yom Kippur. He was hastily buried by the local authorities in an unmarked grave, and his burial site remains unknown.

The vast majority of those who had believed that he was the Messiah rejected him as soon as they found out about his conversion to Islam. There was, however, a significant group which tenaciously clung to his messianic promises, finding convoluted kabbalistic explanations to prove that the conversion was part of the grand messianic scheme. Most prominent among those believers was Nathan of Gaza, who spent the remainder of his life traveling around the world, shoring up belief in the Muslim Messiah, even after he had died.

In 1680, Nathan suddenly died at the age of thirty-seven in Skopje, Macedonia. Despite the death of the movement's main life force, belief in Shabbetai Tzvi and the mystical teachings he had espoused persisted for well over a century, and it wasn't until the end of the 1700s, and only after numerous notorious and bitter battles, that the remnants of Shabbetai Tzvi's messianic movement finally disappeared from mainstream Jewish life, bringing to an end one of the strangest episodes of modern Jewish history.

Chapter 2

"Dr." Samuel Falk:
Kabbalist or Charlatan?

London, 1742

> *"I am sorry that I cannot furnish you with anything more tangible on the subject [of the Baal Shem], but I think that the majority of his reputed miracles are like the epitaph on his [gravestone] – neither legible nor plausible."*
>
> *– J. Myers, in a letter about the Baal Shem of London to British Chief Rabbi Dr. Hermann Adler, dated November 8, 1895*

Portrait of "Dr." Samuel Falk, Baal Shem of London, artist unknown

THE SALE OF AN ICONIC IMAGE

The auction room in midtown Manhattan suddenly went quiet. It was late afternoon, Thursday, January 31, 2013. With a dramatic flourish the auctioneer began the bidding for Lot #287. The room was filled with an eclectic mix of seasoned collectors, hasidic Judaica dealers, and inquisitive aficionados of Jewish art. There was an atmosphere of eager anticipation as the bidding commenced. The lot on sale was a well-executed oil painting portrait of a man known as the "Baal Shem of London." It is without any doubt one of the most recognized eighteenth-century Jewish-themed paintings in the world. Strangely enough, however, no one in the auction room was particularly interested in the Baal Shem of London or knew too much about him. That is because interest in this painting has nothing to do with its subject. Quite the contrary; the interest in this painting is based solely on the fact that the benign, avuncular-looking individual it depicts has for well over a century been consistently misidentified.

The auction catalog got straight to the point in its description: "For more than a century this eighteenth-century portrait of the kabbalist Rabbi Dr. Chaim Samuel Jacob Falk has been broadly misidentified and popularly thought of as being a depiction of the founder of the hasidic movement, the Baal Shem Tov himself." As remarkable as that sounds, it is absolutely true. In the strictly observant Orthodox Jewish community every child growing up hears numerous stories about the mythic founder of Hasidism, Rabbi Yisrael Baal Shem Tov, as well as stories about all the other great hasidic luminaries of that era – the Maggid of Mezeritch, Rabbi Levi Yitzhak of Berdichev, Rabbi Nahman of Breslov, and many more. But the colorful stories about these extraordinary individuals are never accompanied by illustrations or depictions of the rabbis they describe. After all, there were no cameras in eighteenth-century Russia and Poland, and none of these rabbis had ever sat to have their portrait painted by a well-known rococo or neoclassical artist except, apparently, for the Baal Shem Tov.

Every child growing up in strictly Orthodox communities around the world is familiar with the picture of the Baal Shem Tov. It is ubiquitous, and no one ever questions its authenticity, which is very strange. How can anyone imagine that an exotic-looking man wearing a large black beret, with a compass in his hand, is the revered founder of the hasidic movement? Why would he be wearing a beret? Surely he should be wearing a fur *streimel*? And why is he holding a mathematical instrument, of all things? If anything, he should be holding a volume of Talmud, or some other sacred book – or holding nothing at all!

Of course, the answer to all these questions is very simple: the man in the portrait isn't the Baal Shem Tov who founded the hasidic movement. The portrait is of Chaim Samuel Jacob Falk, a mysterious character who lived in London during the latter part of the eighteenth century. The confusion about this portrait stems from a simple misunderstanding. Falk purported to be a kabbalist, and was known during his lifetime as the "Baal Shem of London." The title "Baal Shem," or "Master of the Name," was frequently used at that time to describe people who knew how to write kabbalistic amulets using God's name. So who was the Baal Shem of London and how did the confusion about this portrait first arise?

ORIGINS OF A LONDON KABBALIST

Chaim Samuel Jacob Falk, also known as Dr. Falk or Dr. Falcon, was a bizarre character. His origins are obscure and shrouded in mystery. He was probably born in Poland around 1710 although, like so many other aspects of his life, this "fact" is based on guesswork and speculation. Almost nothing is known about his early years, other than the time he spent in Fuerth, Germany, where his mother died and was buried. The only thing we know for certain is that he lived in London for the last forty years of his life.

Throughout his time in England, Falk presented himself as a kabbalist who could perform remarkable magical feats. It seems his claim to have magical abilities had begun long before he moved to London. One contemporary writer claimed to have read an account of Falk publicly performing magic in Germany in the presence of various prominent non-Jews, and apparently his sudden and hasty arrival in London in 1742 was the direct result of his fondness for such performances. After a public demonstration of his "powers" in Westphalia, he was summarily arrested and thrown into jail for sorcery – in those days punishable by death. Falk's lucky escape to London undoubtedly saved his life.

England in the eighteenth century was known for its tolerance of eccentrics, whether locally bred or foreign born. Falk found that the Jewish community had readily adopted this broad-minded attitude, and both the Sephardim and Ashkenazim in London warmly welcomed him. Although he was fairly reclusive, his interest in Kabbala, and apparent practical skills using Kabbala, quickly became known. Legends and myths describing his incredible powers were whispered around the community, and these incredible stories continued to circulate long after his death. The stories were fantastic, to say the least. The candles in his home stayed alight for weeks at a time. When he ran out of coal for his fireplace, he would utter a kabbalistic prayer and his cellar would mysteriously fill up with new coal. It was told that on one occasion, after a fire threatened to destroy the Ashkenazic community's "Great Synagogue" on Duke's Place, Falk prevented any damage by writing four Hebrew letters on the doorposts, which halted the fire at the entrance of the synagogue. And these are just a fraction of the fables that swirled around Falk. So, who was he?

Through scattered pieces of recorded information we are able to piece together a more accurate picture of Falk than anything gleaned from these fantastic fairytales. Falk seems to have arrived in London completely penniless. For a few years he struggled, and his faithful assistant records that his personal life was fraught with difficulties as he and his wife constantly argued about finances. Eventually things began to change for the better. People were surprised at his sudden change of fortune. How was it possible that someone who had been so insolvent that he was forced to pawn all his belongings had suddenly achieved such great material success? Rumors began to spread that he possessed mystical powers that he had used to attain his new-found wealth.

The truth, however, was far more mundane. Falk was an exceptionally charismatic individual and particularly attractive to the type of people who are drawn to enigmatic personalities. Two of those people were the affluent Jewish banker Aaron Goldsmid and his son George. At some point they became enraptured with Falk and consulted with him on all personal matters, as well as on matters of business. He, in turn, took their advice on investments, which resulted in him becoming extremely prosperous. He began to live in fine accommodations, surrounded by servants and an array of wealthy acquaintances. He launched a pawn-broking business and bought a large home in an upscale residential enclave called Wellclose Square, in the East End of London, where he built his own private synagogue. He rode everywhere in an extravagant coach drawn by four horses and became an avid collector of books and art. Remarkably, although he was not considered a scholar, this in no way detracted from his reputation as a kabbalist, nor did the fact that he regularly performed extremely peculiar rituals prevent senior com-munity leaders – including Chief Rabbi David Tevele Schiff – from considering him their friend.

On one occasion he withdrew into his home for six weeks, and allowed it to be known that he was not eating or sleeping for the entire period. After six weeks had passed he sent for a group of ten men to join him – but only after they had immersed themselves in a *mikve*. The men arrived at midnight and were asked to clothe themselves in white robes and to remove their shoes. They were then invited into a large room lit only by flickering candlelight. One of the ten men later described in a letter to his son the scene as they entered the room:

> The saintly man was seated on his throne arrayed like an angel of heaven, diademed with a golden miter, a golden chain round his neck reaching to his waist, from which hung a great star, and holy names were engraved on the star. His face was covered with a star-shaped veil, and his headgear was marvelously fashioned out of parchment, with holy names written on it. A star of pure gold was fastened on each corner of his turban, and names were engraved on them. Who could possibly describe the beauty of the painting on the tapestries that were hung on the walls, with sacred figures, as on the heavenly throne in Ezekiel's vision?

The letter describes the strange "throne room" as having been divided into an inner section and an outer section delineated by silver chains. Falk instructed five men to sit within the chains, and the other five to sit outside of them, following which he took out an engraved shofar and an engraved trumpet and blew on them. The letter writer and his nine companions were overwhelmed by this melodramatic scene and became Falk's avid devotees.

RELATIONSHIP WITH THE JEWISH COMMUNITY

Strangely enough none of these activities – which reflected occult rituals rather than anything related to Judaism – elicited any criticism from the leaders of the London community, nor did they lead to any public warnings that he was a fraud. In Europe, however, things were different, and it wasn't long before Falk's odd behavior began to ring alarm bells. During the eighteenth century controversies were constantly erupting in the Jewish communities of Germany and Poland as the rabbinate tried to root out crypto-Sabbatians, a subculture of individuals who secretly continued to believe in the messianic mission of Shabbetai Tzvi. Although Shabbetai Tzvi had died in 1676, a cult of believers still maintained that he was the Messiah, and secretly perpetuated this and other subversive ideas, employing twisted interpretations of Lurianic Kabbala.

The Sabbatian phenomenon resulted in a deep antipathy toward unsupervised study of Jewish mystical texts, and anyone discovered studying Kabbala, or purportedly using practical Kabbala, became an object of suspicion, often resulting in vilification and even banishment. One famous victim of this attitude was Rabbi Moshe Hayim Luzzatto, known as Ramhal, who was subjected to a relentless campaign of condemnation and then threatened with excommunication after it became known that he claimed to be studying Kabbala with an otherworldly *maggid* who regularly appeared to him while he was in a trance-like state.

Another famous target of the fierce anti-Sabbatian crusade was the revered rabbi of Hamburg, Rabbi Yonatan Eybeschutz, whose amulets for pregnant women were examined by the equally revered Rabbi Yaakov Emden, who controversially alleged that the amulets contained references to Shabbetai Tzvi. In his latter years Rabbi Emden made it his life's mission to unmask crypto-Sabbatians, and he went to great lengths to seek them out so that he could ensure none of these alleged heretics would be able to influence any normative and unsuspecting Jewish community.

It was in this context that the Baal Shem of London came to the attention of Rabbi Yaakov Emden. Almost as soon as he heard about him the crusading rabbi swung into action – and he did not hold back. In a letter written to a colleague, Rabbi Emden wrote:

> Although I do not know him personally, I have heard that he pretends to be an expert in practical Kabbala, and that he claims to have the ability to discover hidden treasures. He is married to an immoral woman with whom he moved to London. There he found supporters – especially among the lower classes – who tried to use him to enrich themselves. Some rich non-Jews also believed in him, thinking that he could discover treasure for them. Using trickery he succeeded in entrapping one wealthy non-Jewish captain, who spent his entire fortune on him and has now been reduced to poverty and is only able to survive as a result of Falk's charity. Incredibly this captain continues to praise him among wealthy Christians, so that they give him a lot of money. In this way the Baal Shem is enabled to live as a man of wealth, and he uses his money to bribe his close followers so that they continue to spread his fame.

Rabbi Yaakov Emden's assertion that Falk was a Sabbatian was an assumption he based on Falk's close friendship with a known Sabbatian by the name of Moshe David of Podhajce, who had been expelled from a number of communities. But the assumption is problematic. Falk kept a private diary, as did his trusted assistant Tzvi Hirsch. Neither of them ever mentioned Shabbetai Tzvi, nor recorded kabbalistic ideas associated with Sabbatianism. Although Falk was certainly friendly with Moshe David, it is far more likely that Moshe David sought him out and befriended him when he discovered that they shared a fondness for strange occult-style rituals. Perhaps they even colluded together to create pseudo-kabbalistic rituals that would impress gullible people who then paid them money for advice.

Whether or not he was a Sabbatian sympathizer, one aspect of Falk's character is undeniable – he was extremely charitable, and this benevolence is probably what enabled him to carry on with his activities without censure for so long. There was a constant stream of poor people at his door, and none of them ever left empty handed. Shortly after Pesah in 1782, Falk wrote his last will and testament. His wife had already died and there were no children. Aaron Goldsmid and his son were appointed executors, along with Goldsmid's son-in-law, Lyon de Symons. Everything was bequeathed to charity via an endowment fund that would grant annual payments. Three days after writing his will Falk died and was buried in the Jewish cemetery in Mile End, East London, where his grave can be seen to this day.

Miracle worker, charlatan, psychic, Sabbatian, physician, alchemist, heretic, philanthropist – every one of these terms has been used to describe the Baal Shem of London. As is the case with most dubious characters who purport to be something they are not, Falk was probably not a complete fraud and possessed certain skills and intuitions that he used as a foundation to create an aura of mystique around himself in order to profit financially.

This was the time just before the era of scientific sophistication, and anyone with knowledge of basic chemistry could dazzle an uninformed audience. Add kabbalistic symbolism and dramatic rituals into the mix, and the credulous were easily convinced that Falk possessed supernatural powers. We have no reliable records of his successes and failures, or to what extent his clientele were disappointed by his unfulfilled promises. He was never sued in court, nor charged with any crime. His devotees seem to have been pleased with what he did for them, and, notwithstanding Rabbi Yaakov Emden's accusations, he was remembered fondly in London's Jewish community long after he died.

PORTRAIT OF A BAAL SHEM

It can certainly be said that had it not been for the portrait of him, Falk, like so many other minor historical characters, would have eventually been forgotten, except perhaps for the odd mention in historical footnotes. But a fateful lecture was to change all that. At the turn of the twentieth century, British Chief Rabbi Dr. Hermann Adler delivered a lecture at the Jewish Historical Society of Great Britain titled "The Baal Shem of London." In the lecture he attempted to look beyond the myths surrounding Falk and offer an accurate biographical sketch that took all the known details of his life into account. The public lecture included a viewing of the portrait, which had been in a private art collection belonging to the Goldsmid family since Falk's death. In 1908, the lecture was published together with a picture of the portrait. This is what Rabbi Adler had to say about it:

> The annexed portrait is from an original painting in the possession of Mr. W. H. Goldsmid by [John Singleton] Copley, and is fully worthy of the artist. The likeness bears out the description of the Baal Shem given by a contemporary, who writes that "when he walks abroad he is garbed in a flowing robe, which strikingly harmonizes with his long white beard and venerable features."

Rabbi Adler's assertion that Copley was the artist who painted the portrait was guesswork, as the portrait is unsigned. In fact, it is highly unlikely that Copley was the artist, and there is speculation that the portrait was painted by Philip James de Loutherbourg, a close friend of the Italian adventurer and occultist Giuseppe Balsamo – also known as Count Alessandro di Cagliostro – who spent time with Falk in London after his dramatic expulsion from France. Perhaps Cagliostro introduced Loutherbourg to Falk, as all three of them shared a fascination with alchemy and the supernatural. In truth, we will never know.

What is clear is that the publication of the picture resulted in a mix-up that created the wide misconception about the portrait's subject. Within a matter of months the picture of the portrait was appearing elsewhere in Jewish publications identified as a likeness of Rabbi Yisrael Baal Shem Tov. The confusion was based on a simple misunderstanding. In the eighteenth century any rabbi who was skilled at amulet writing could be referred to as a "Baal Shem," but by 1908 there was really only one Baal Shem who was widely known by that title – the founder of the hasidic movement. And so, even though the rabbi depicted in the portrait did not appear to be a saintly Ukrainian rabbinic leader, the title "Baal Shem" attached to this portrait was enough for people to draw the wrong conclusion, and it was used to illustrate articles and books about the Baal Shem Tov.

That is how an obscure portrait of a smiling, weirdly attired charlatan mystic became one of the best-known images of any eighteenth-century Jew. The auction house estimated the painting would sell for

$30,000–50,000. They were wrong. In a heated bidding war it eventually sold to a private buyer for $75,000. Once again the self-styled Baal Shem of London had been the center of attention. One may well ponder over the fact that people are still talking about Chaim Samuel Jacob Falk more than two hundred years after his death. Does the fact that he remains an object of discussion prove that he did have the mystical powers he claimed for himself and that they are still at work? It is an intriguing thought, although the answer will forever remain as elusive as the man himself.

Chapter 3

The Emden-Eybeschutz *Maḥloket*: Amulets, Accusations, and Controversy

Hamburg, 1751

> *"A rabbinic scholar cannot be ignorant of history and changing times… and must never be considered a fool or a simpleton in worldly affairs. One is obliged to know history to understand our talmudic sages and Jewish law."*
>
> – *Rabbi Yaakov Emden (1697–1776)*

"Rabbis in Hamburg argue over Kabbala amulets," woodcut, 1765

The atmosphere in the room was somber and tense. The elderly rabbi lay on a rickety bed, surrounded by family and a handful of close friends, his breathing labored, his wrinkled face sunken and pale. This wasn't any ordinary elderly rabbi; this was one of Europe's most influential rabbinic figures, Rabbi Yaakov Emden, and these were his final moments.

At seventy-nine years he had reached a ripe old age. He had outlived two of his three wives and most of his twenty children. Once a wealthy and successful businessman, his fortunes had reversed, and just a year earlier his family had been compelled to seek assistance from the community fund. His health had been in decline for some time, and his waning eyesight had ultimately resulted in total blindness, denying him his one remaining pleasure – reading and studying the numerous books in his private library.

It was April 19, and the year was 1776. For over a quarter of a century most of Rabbi Yaakov Emden's energy had been devoted to one thing – ensuring that every God-fearing Jew was made fully aware that the chief rabbi of Hamburg and revered rabbinic leader, Rabbi Yonatan Eybeschutz, was not the devout Jew he purported to be, but was in fact a secret believer in the false Messiah, Shabbetai Tzvi, and that he had cunningly insinuated Sabbatian heresy into mainstream Jewish life.

Rabbi Yonatan Eybeschutz had died in 1764, but his demise had not halted Rabbi Yaakov's campaign. In fact, the death of his nemesis seemed only to have increased the campaign's ferocity. Rabbi Yaakov was absolutely determined that the man he considered the epitome of evil would never be adulated. Even as Rabbi Yonatan was being buried twelve years earlier Rabbi Yaakov delivered a "eulogy" in which he accused him of religious deviancy and worse, astounding his audience with the vehemence of his denouncements.

But now, as the small group of relatives and friends stood silently watching the aged rabbi as his life ebbed away, the last thing on their minds was Rabbi Yonatan Eybeschutz. All they were concerned with was the imminent final breath of this titan of Jewish leadership, a man who had been at the center of European Jewish life for well over fifty years. The bitter dispute between him and his archrival was utterly remote at that moment, and if anyone in the room gave the saga any thought at all, it would only have been to reflect on the fact that the controversy was finally coming to an end.

Suddenly, unexpectedly, Rabbi Yaakov opened his unseeing eyes. He grabbed the hand of the person closest to him, a member of the *ḥevra kaddisha* at his bedside, and began to speak in a whisper. It sounded as if he was greeting someone: a long-lost relative or friend. His voice was barely audible, and the man whose hand he had clutched leaned toward him, trying to make out what he was saying. He put his ear next to Rabbi Yaakov's mouth and listened intently, then gasped and went pale.

"What is he saying? What is he saying?"

The young man seemed unable to respond. He leaned back toward Rabbi Yaakov's head and listened again, and then shook his head in bewilderment.

"The rabbi is saying over and over again, '*Barukh haba,* my revered father; *barukh haba,* Rabbi Yonatan,' that is what he is saying!"

There was a sharp intake of breath from everyone in the crowded room. What could it mean? How was it possible that in his final moments Rabbi Yaakov was mentioning his beloved father in the same breath as the name of his hated adversary? What did he mean by "*Barukh haba,*" a phrase usually said when welcoming someone? The family members muttered to each other quietly, trying to figure out some explanation for what was going on. One of them suggested that someone should ask Rabbi Yaakov what he had meant, but Rabbi Yaakov had gone quiet again and his eyes were closed. His breathing began to slow, and within a matter of minutes he was gone. The *ḥevra kaddisha* cleared the room and – in keeping with tradition – they lifted the rabbi's fragile body off the bed and onto the floor.

Outside, the family began discussing the funeral and burial arrangements with community officials. Obviously, Rabbi Yaakov would be buried in the most distinguished portion of the cemetery, where only community leaders and important rabbis were buried. After all, aside from being one of Europe's preeminent rabbis, he had lived in Hamburg for most of his life, and his father, Hakham Tzvi Ashkenazi, had served as chief rabbi. No one would dare to deny him his rightful place in the cemetery.

The community representatives began shifting from foot to foot, looking down at the floor. There was a problem, a big problem. Who was going to break the news to the family? The only available gravesite in the cemetery was a few feet away from where Rabbi Yonatan was buried, and on the same row. There was no way the family would agree that Rabbi Yaakov be buried there, and nor would the Hamburg community leadership, whose loyalty to Rabbi Yonatan had been absolute over the years, be willing to see the man who had caused so much strife buried near the object of his relentless crusade.

One of the community's representatives blurted out the news to the family. There was dead silence. The head of the *ḥevra kaddisha* spoke up. He wanted to suggest a solution.

> I hear that Rabbi Yehezkel Landau, chief rabbi of Prague, is in town, presiding over a court case. Perhaps let us ask him to rule whether Rabbi Yaakov can be buried near Rabbi Yonatan. He knows the history between them very well. For my part, I can speak on behalf of the community. We will follow the Rabbi of Prague's direction – as long as the family also agrees to do so.

The family members looked at each other and nodded their agreement. What choice did they have? Every minute they delayed the funeral was disrespectful to their father. A meeting was hastily set up with Rabbi Landau. His relationship with both Rabbi Yaakov and Rabbi Yonatan had been fraught and difficult over the years, which at the very least meant that both sides would treat his ruling as objective. A senior member of the Emden family and a representative of the *ḥevra kaddisha* were shown into Rabbi Landau's room, and he listened intently as they explained the problem at hand. He pondered for a moment, and asked how Rabbi Yaakov had spoken of Rabbi Yonatan over the last few months of his life. Had there been any change of attitude? Had he softened his stance?

Not really, the family member responded – his harsh criticism had been unceasing. Except, he added, in the moments just before he died; and he related the strange episode that had taken place just minutes before Rabbi Yaakov had drawn his last breath.

Rabbi Landau smiled. "I think we can announce the funeral," he said, "and it is absolutely fine for Rabbi Yaakov's final resting place to be so close to Rabbi Yonatan. Clearly, as his soul was departing from this world,

Rabbi Yaakov finally reconciled with Rabbi Yonatan, and none other than the great Hakham Tzvi was there to witness it. *Barukh Dayan Ha'emet!*"

And with that one of the worst rabbinic battles in modern Jewish history appeared to have reached its natural conclusion. A controversy that had embroiled multiple communities, ruined careers, split families, involved the gentile authorities of more than one country, and devastated lives, seemed – finally – to be at an end. With the death of the second of the two protagonists whose names were synonymous with this epic fight, on what possible grounds would it continue?

But had anyone breathed a sigh of relief as they buried Rabbi Yaakov Emden on that spring day in Hamburg, they would have been completely mistaken. The root causes of the controversy, the two principal combatants, and the impact of the controversy on Jewish life and on the development of Judaism would fascinate and polarize scholars and rabbis of every subsequent generation, as well as captivate aficionados of Jewish history – and they continue to do so to this day.

ORIGINS OF THE CONTROVERSY

In 1666, the false Messiah, Shabbetai Tzvi, converted to Islam. His conversion was all it took for most of the Jewish world to draw the obvious conclusion that he was a fraud. The vast majority of those who had publicly declared their allegiance to him shamefacedly admitted their folly and went back to normative Judaism, wounded and wiser. But there was a significant group who simply refused to accept that his apostasy negated his messianic identity. They were too emotionally and religiously invested in Shabbetai Tzvi, and they remained fiercely loyal to him. Nathan "the prophet" of Gaza, Shabbetai Tzvi's lead publicist, outlived his messianic foil, and came up with convoluted kabbalistic propositions to explain away his hero's conversion and to rationalize his failure to materialize the messianic mission.

In 1676 Shabbetai Tzvi died in obscurity, having never recanted. Astoundingly, devotees considered his death a temporary setback, and within every community there were those who clandestinely continued to believe that Shabbetai Tzvi was the true Messiah. What was more, it was their fervent view that they had to insinuate their warped kabbalistic ideas into mainstream Judaism so that the abortive messianic mission of their hero could be fulfilled.

Surprisingly, although Sabbatians – as they came to be known – were very much a minority group, their number included many rabbis and distinguished leaders. They were also almost impossible to detect, behaving in every way like fully observant Jews, indistinguishable from any other Jew. Time after time during the decades after Shabbetai Tzvi's death, crypto-Sabbatian activists were exposed and banished from their communities. Although they seemed to be ordinary and faithful Jews, at some point they had fallen under the spell of a Sabbatian propagandist, and their theology and faith beliefs had deviated from accepted norms, while outwardly they continued to behave like faithful, observant Jews.

THE NEHEMIAH HAYYUN AFFAIR

One particularly notorious propagandist was a Bosnian-born scoundrel called Nehemiah Hiya Hayyun, who wandered from community to community during the early years of the eighteenth century. A scholar who was a gifted teacher and writer, he authored a number of books that interspersed Sabbatian heresies with regular Torah interpretations. In 1711 he arrived in Prague, where he maneuvered himself into the circle of the local kabbalistic rabbi, Rabbi Naftali Katz, esteemed author of *Semikhut Ḥakhamim*, a widely admired book on *Mishnayot*.

Rabbi Katz was very taken by Hayyun, who was a smooth talker and well versed in rabbinic scholarship, and agreed to write an approbation letter for his new book. So did Prague's respected chief rabbi, Rabbi David Oppenheim. In Berlin, Hayyun gained the approval of the local chief rabbi, Rabbi Aharon Binyamin Wolf. With these endorsements in hand he arrived in Amsterdam in 1713, where he requested permission from the leaders of the prestigious Sephardic community to sell his books. The Sephardic chief rabbi, Rabbi Shlomo Ayllon, was not sufficiently qualified to spot dangerous material in Hayyun's work, so the community leaders submitted Hayyun's book to the rabbi of the local German congregation, Hakham Tzvi Ashkenazi, and asked for his opinion. Hakham Tzvi, unlike Rabbi Ayllon, was renowned across Europe for his erudition and scholarship, and a positive review from him would have carried weight throughout the Jewish world.

But when Hakham Tzvi, together with his friend and colleague, a local Sephardic rabbi from Jerusalem, Rabbi Moshe Hagiz, looked through the book, they both quickly came to the conclusion that Hayyun was a closet Sabbatian masquerading as a normative Jew. Hakham Tzvi reported his findings back to the Sephardic lay leadership and warned them that Hayyun posed a grave danger to the Amsterdam community.

For a variety of reasons, mostly unrelated to Hayyun himself, the issue quickly degenerated into an ugly communal battle, with Hakham Tzvi and Rabbi Hagiz on one side and powerful members of the Sephardic community on the other. Rabbi Ayllon, who was rumored to be a closet Sabbatian himself, launched a campaign to discredit Hakham Tzvi and Rabbi Hagiz, claiming that they had no right to interfere in a matter that concerned the Sephardic community. Fistfights broke out between the supporters of both camps, and Hakham Tzvi was eventually put under house arrest by the gentile authorities, probably for his own protection. Hayyun, emboldened by the support he was receiving from Rabbi Ayllon and his admirers, published a number of vicious attacks against Hakham Tzvi and Rabbi Hagiz, actively fomenting the animosity toward his detractors.

The saga spiraled out of control as the months went by, and eventually, in early 1714, Hakham Tzvi fled Holland for England, never to return. He was offered the post of chief rabbi in London, but declined, and ultimately returned to mainland Europe, where he took up the position of chief rabbi of Lemberg (Lvov) in 1717. He died there in 1718, at the age of fifty-eight.

THE AFTERMATH OF THE HAYYUN AFFAIR

Throughout the period of the Hayyun affair, Hakham Tzvi's family, and especially his teenage son Yaakov, were caught in the eye of a ferocious storm. Yaakov was just fifteen years old – an impressionable teenager – and the experience stayed with him for the rest of his life. He watched as his innocent and distinguished father was dragged into the foul politics generated by the controversy, and how he was pilloried for his honestly held views and his unshakeable integrity. Additionally, he was exposed to the tenacity of Sabbatian activism and the vicious tactics Sabbatians were willing to use to gain a foothold in Jewish affairs. In Hakham Tzvi's case it resulted in the loss of his rabbinic position and being subjected to appalling abuse at the hands of Hayyun's supporters. It was a lesson the young Yaakov learned and never forgot.

Shortly after Hakham Tzvi's escape from Amsterdam, community leaders asked Hayyun to leave the city so that the controversy could die down. As he traveled through Europe, Hayyun discovered that his widely publicized alleged association with Sabbatianism had resulted in a general revulsion toward him. Wherever he went he found that doors were closed. He left Europe and moved to Safed in northern *Eretz Yisrael*, then under Ottoman rule, and opened up a Sabbatian "yeshiva." The enterprise failed, and he moved to Constantinople, where he tried desperately to rehabilitate himself.

In 1725 Hayyun resurfaced in Western Europe claiming that the rabbis in Turkey had readmitted him into the fold, but everywhere he went he was refused entry. Even his former defender in Amsterdam, Rabbi Ayllon, refused to meet him. In Vienna he was forced to stay in an enclosure reserved for Turkish Muslims. In Glogau and Berlin he found no refuge whatsoever. When he arrived in Hanover he tried to hide his identity, but was soon recognized and quickly expelled. He made his way to Prague but there, too, was prevented from entering the city. Soon afterward he disappeared from sight, and was reported to have died in 1730.

Hayyun's final abortive attempt to gain prominence was very significant in terms of the Emden-Eybeschutz battle twenty-five years later, as not only did it coincide with a new and even fiercer battle against the Sabbatians than the one of 1713–14, but it also generated evidence of a link between him and a brilliant talmudic scholar and rising rabbinic superstar – a young man living in Prague called Yonatan Eybeschutz. According to Rabbi Moshe Hagiz, who had been Hakham Tzvi's co-campaigner against Hayyun in Amsterdam, just before Hayyun was ejected from Hanover in 1726 community officials searched his possessions and found correspondence that was "Sabbatian in nature, including letters from Yonatan Eybeschutz." When Hayyun arrived in Prague shortly afterward, on the last leg of what was his pathetic final journey, no Jew was willing to house or feed him, except for the wife and daughter of Rabbi Yonatan, who brought him food and took care of him until he left.

In order to truly appreciate the significance of this unlikely association, not only is it important to know that Nehemiah Hayyun was a devious rogue, it is also imperative to realize just how illustrious and mainstream Rabbi Yonatan was. The son of the rabbi of Eybeschutz (Ivančice, Moravia), he became the star student of Rabbi Meir Eisenstadt of Prosnitz, author of *Panim Me'irot*, who was undoubtedly the most influential talmudic teacher of his generation. Rabbi Yonatan outshone all his peers and in 1715, at the age of twenty-five, he moved to Prague and quickly gained prominence as a remarkable speaker and an energetic communal activist. He engaged amicably with local Christian leaders, and during the many absences of Prague's chief rabbi, Rabbi David Oppenheim – who was often called away to take care of his vast business interests – Rabbi Yonatan would fill in for him. Although there was considerable friction between the two rabbis, Rabbi Yonatan had a captivating personality that won him numerous allies, enabling him to withstand the senior rabbi's hostility.

SUPERSTAR RABBI FALLS UNDER A CLOUD

It is not possible to overstate Rabbi Yonatan's qualities. His intellect was unparalleled, he was charismatic, exceptionally warm, a gifted communicator, versed in every aspect of Torah knowledge, remarkably good looking, and possessed of an inexhaustible energy. Apart from Rabbi Yaakov Emden, no one would ever question his superior rabbinic qualities, nor cast any doubt on his abilities as a teacher and scholar. If anything, it was these sterling credentials that precipitated the widespread astonishment when rumors began to emerge in 1725 – long before the *maḥloket* with Rabbi Yaakov Emden – that Rabbi Yonatan was a leading crypto-Sabbatian, engaged in the most sordid attempts to inject Sabbatian beliefs into the Jewish mainstream.

The controversy began quite unexpectedly in Frankfurt. In the early summer of 1725 an itinerant preacher called Moshe Meir of Zolkiew arrived in Frankfurt, where his conduct led to his being suspected as a crypto-Sabbatian. Concerned by his presence and the potential danger of his influence, a group of young local rabbis raided his room while he was out preaching, and discovered a manuscript work in his luggage that began with a verse from Genesis (24:42): "*Vaavo hayom el haayin*," "When I came today to the spring." The manuscript contained a detailed heretical kabbalistic description of God that both denied His oneness and posited that His power was in the process of diminishing.

The investigators took the manuscript to the senior rabbis in Frankfurt, who were horrorstruck. Such ideas were heresy and utterly reprehensible to Judaism. They located the hapless Moshe Meir and forcefully interrogated him to find out who the author of this deviant material was. Under huge pressure he finally revealed that he had received the manuscript from none other than Rabbi Yonatan Eybeschutz of Prague, who, he claimed, was also its author.

The rabbis were aghast. Everyone had heard of Rabbi Yonatan. He was a celebrity, acclaimed by anyone who had ever met him. How was it possible that this bright rabbinic scholar, the rising star of the European rabbinic fraternity, could have written, or was even associated with, such a disgusting literary composition? It was utterly incomprehensible. The rabbis of Frankfurt felt that this was far bigger than anything they could deal with, and decided to involve senior rabbinic authorities in Europe who would be able to address this grave matter and would be taken seriously if tough decisions needed to be made.

THE ANTI-SABBATIAN CAMPAIGN OF 1725

The challenge in 1725 was exponentially greater than it had been in the battle against Hayyun more than a decade earlier. During that conflict the Sabbatian adversary had been an itinerant preacher, who for all his talent and charm was essentially an easy prey. None of Hayyun's allies had been his friends – in the main they were recently acquired acquaintances. If there were those among them whose support for him was rooted in their own Sabbatian beliefs, ultimately Hayyun was just a means to an end, and as soon as the fight was lost, they abandoned him to his sorry fate without a second thought.

Rabbi Yonatan Eybeschutz could not have been more different. He was the ultimate insider, with pedigree, a devoted non-Sabbatian following, and status as a noted rabbinic scholar and preacher. Even the people who were totally dedicated to the task of rooting out insidious Sabbatian influences shied away from open warfare with someone like him. The stakes were simply too high. If Rabbi Yonatan

Eybeschutz was branded a flagrant deviant, what would that mean for every other rabbi of his stature? How would it be possible for Jewish community life to remain stable if every distinguished rabbi with an enemy could have his career and reputation wrecked in a frenzy of anti-Sabbatian zealotry?

And yet, while the evidence against Rabbi Yonatan was never more than anecdotal and circumstantial, it was still hard to ignore the fact that his name kept on cropping up in the hunt for crypto-Sabbatians. What was even harder to ignore was that both Sabbatian-hunters and the Sabbatians themselves concurred over Rabbi Yonatan, all of them claiming he was a longstanding and committed Sabbatian. Both sides maintained that Rabbi Yonatan was inducted into Sabbatianism by a man called Leibel Prosnitz, a former peddler turned Sabbatian "prophet," with whom he had come into contact while studying in the town of Prosnitz under Rabbi Meir Eisenstadt.

Leibel Prosnitz may have or may not have believed in Shabbetai Tzvi's messianic identity, but he was certainly a gifted hoaxer who used "magic" and "miracles" to convince credulous people that he was a holy man with unique powers. Over the years Prosnitz had been involved in several attempts to infiltrate Sabbatianism into mainstream Jewish life, and in 1706 had even announced the imminent return of Shabbetai Tzvi. When this prediction failed to materialize he began to wander from community to community, joining up with crypto-Sabbatians wherever he went.

During the 1725 campaign, Prosnitz became the subject of an intensive and aggressive investigation by the rabbinate of Mannheim. The inquiry was triggered after his son-in-law was discovered staying at the home of a known Sabbatian, Yeshaya Hasid, who lived in Mannheim. In the course of the investigation Hasid shockingly divulged that Sabbatians now believed that Leibel Prosnitz was "*Mashiah ben Yosef*," while Rabbi Yonatan Eybeschutz was "*Mashiah ben David*" – in other words, some kind of reincarnation of Shabbetai Tzvi.

This disturbing revelation was rendered even more alarming when it emerged that Prosnitz had lobbied Hasid to use his influence to ensure Rabbi Yonatan would be offered the position as rabbi of Mannheim. What emerged out of the investigation was that Sabbatians thought of

Rabbi Yonatan as their supreme leader and as an integral part of their secret mission to inject Sabbatianism into the highest levels of Jewish life.

This view of Rabbi Yonatan was not exclusive to Hasid and Prosnitz. Rabbi Moshe Hagiz, who relentlessly and quite ruthlessly led the 1725 anti-Sabbatian crusade, was also totally convinced that Rabbi Yonatan was a Sabbatian and the author of *"Vaavo hayom el haayin."* In correspondence with numerous rabbinic colleagues Rabbi Hagiz repeated this view countless times, and sought support for a confrontation with the young rabbi.

But the confrontation never occurred. On September 16, 1725, Rabbi Yonatan publicly took an oath denying any connection to Sabbatianism and then affixed his signature to a strongly worded ban issued by all the rabbis in Prague against Sabbatians and Sabbatianism. His supporters cited these actions as incontrovertible proof that he was not a Sabbatian. Even many of those who believed he was a Sabbatian were ready to take Rabbi Yonatan's readiness to publicly condemn Sabbatians as a sign that he had either repented, or that he would never again be so reckless as to involve himself with Sabbatianism, even covertly. After all, why would a man of his quality and ability wish to descend into the sordid world of disreputable crypto-Sabbatians such as Prosnitz, Hasid, and their ilk?

Sabbatian manuscripts and incriminating letters ascribed to Rabbi Yonatan continued to circulate, but were generally dismissed as forgeries or fantasy. The best Rabbi Hagiz could do was try to convince his colleagues to avoid sending students to Prague to study under Rabbi Yonatan, but even in that endeavor he failed. Rabbi Yonatan was unassailable. The murmurings continued, but his signature on the ban along with his consistent denials of any involvement with Sabbatianism made it impossible for his adversaries to gain traction against him. Meanwhile the anti-Sabbatian fight focused on those whose connection with Sabbatianism was certain, and whose neutralization was uncontroversial. By the end of 1726 the crisis was over and Rabbi Yonatan's popularity and reputation continued to grow.

In 1736, the chief rabbi of Prague, Rabbi David Oppenheim, died. Rabbi Yonatan seemed the natural choice to succeed him, but it was not to be. Bitter acrimony between Rabbi Yonatan and Rabbi Oppenheim dating back many years meant that the community leadership would not allow him to replace the late chief rabbi. A compromise between those who wanted him as chief rabbi and those who did not resulted in his appointment as chief *dayan* for the Prague *beit din*. But a man of Rabbi Yonatan's caliber was not realistically going to occupy a secondary spot for very long.

In 1741, Rabbi Yonatan was offered the chief rabbinate of Metz, France, when the incumbent chief rabbi, Rabbi Yaakov Yehoshua Falk, elder statesman of the European rabbinate and author of the celebrated *Pnei Yehoshua* on Talmud, left to take up the chief rabbinate of Frankfurt. Rabbi Yonatan left Prague for Metz and led the community there until 1750, the year he was offered the coveted chief rabbinate of Altona-Hamburg-Wandsbeck, known as the Triple Community, one of the most prestigious and influential Jewish communities in Europe.

THE TRIPLE COMMUNITY AND RABBI YAAKOV EMDEN

The Triple Community had boasted some of the greatest European rabbinic luminaries of the previous century, including Hakham Tzvi Ashkenazi, who presided over the community in various roles from 1690 until 1710. It was also the birthplace of Hakham Tzvi's son, Rabbi Yaakov Emden, and it was here that Rabbi Yaakov now lived, a prominent local rabbinic scholar, although he had no formal position in the community. Rabbi Yaakov's attitude to Rabbi Yonatan's appointment, irrespective of the accusations of Sabbatian heresy, would prove a contentious issue in the years that followed, but even before delving into the origins of the devastating dispute that engulfed the two rabbis, let us catch up with Rabbi Yaakov and see what he had been up to since the time his family had been hounded out of Amsterdam in 1714.

Rabbi Yaakov Emden did not have an easy childhood. His father, Hakham Tzvi Ashkenazi, found it very difficult to maintain an easy relationship with communal lay leaders, whose gifts and favors he would never accept, and whose constant political maneuvering he abhorred. He was fearless in his opposition to any kind of misbehavior in the communities he led, and although this won him admiration and respect from his colleagues, and from ordinary folk whose hands were not on the reins of communal power, it landed him, and by implication his family, into hot water on numerous occasions. As a result he was unable to offer his children a solid education, and they were all home-schooled, usually without the benefit of private tutors. Rabbi Yaakov later wrote that he had studied privately with his father, but these study sessions were intermittent, as a result of the constant pressures and difficulties in his father's life.

This challenging background makes it all the more remarkable that Rabbi Yaakov turned out the way he did. Although there is no question that he was extremely bright to the point of being a genius, his intellect was amplified by his extraordinary motivation and superhuman self-discipline. From the youngest age no body of work was too daunting, and no intellectual pursuit too trivial. He taught himself to read and write Hebrew to perfection, and eventually became a master of the Hebrew language, as well as of Aramaic, understanding every nuance and feature of these languages in each era and record of their use. He finished the Talmud in his teens, and also mastered every detail of Jewish law.

Rabbi Yaakov also explored the complex world of Jewish customs and traditions, knowledge that he would later share in his monumental work on Jewish prayer. He taught himself public speaking and was considered a master orator. Being the eldest son of Hakham Tzvi also meant that he was respected simply because of who his father was. In short, Rabbi Yaakov possessed exactly the qualities that should have propelled him to one of leading rabbinic appointments of Europe.

But what Rabbi Yaakov did not possess was patience, nor the ability to suffer fools or crooks. He was utterly inflexible, refusing to compromise on his principles, nor would he ever massage egos in order to get something done. He considered compromise and flattery unseemly, inappropriate behavior for a religious leader. As a result of this attitude, and although his breeding and erudition might have resulted in a prestigious rabbinic appointment, his reputation as a no-nonsense rabbi meant that he obtained just one short-lived rabbinic position very early on in his career, after which he would never lead a community again. That rabbinic position was in a town with which Rabbi Yaakov later became synonymous – Emden, Germany, on the North Sea coast just north of the Dutch border, home to a small and fairly insignificant Jewish community.

His appointment happened unexpectedly in 1729, after more than a decade of turmoil and personal turbulence. In 1715 Rabbi Yaakov had married Rachel, the granddaughter of Rabbi Naftali Katz, in a union of two rabbinic dynasties. The marriage began badly, with him living in the home of his in-laws, a teenager far away from his family. To compound these difficulties he was badly mistreated by his wife's father, who took some of the young couple's wedding gifts for himself and refused to honor financial commitments made before the wedding, which in turn led to bitter acrimony between the newlyweds. For three years he endured this unhappy arrangement, burying himself in his studies and writing.

Then, in 1718, Rabbi Yaakov's father and mother died in quick succession, leaving him, as the eldest child, with the responsibility of looking after all his unmarried siblings. Financial problems dogged him at every turn. People with debts to his late father refused or were unable to pay up, and Rabbi Yaakov traveled far and wide trying to collect what was due to the family, all to no avail. Often those who offered to help him turned out to be swindlers, and on numerous occasions he was robbed or cheated. He became physically sick, and also went through several bouts of depression, the details of which he recorded frankly in an autobiography written many years later and published just over a century after his death.

With his family growing, the pressing need for financial security compelled him to find a steady job, despite his misgivings about working for the Jewish community. So when an offer came in 1729 to take up the vacant rabbinic position in Emden, he accepted immediately and settled there with his family. But his instinctive reluctance to become a community rabbi proved right, and the job was a disaster from the start. Rabbi Yaakov was unable to handle lay leadership insubordination, and he could not bear the sense of entitlement felt by wealthier members of the community. He also despised the mundane tasks expected of a communal rabbi, including the delivery of regular sermons. Rabbi Yaakov believed these tasks were a distraction from what a rabbi really needed to be doing – studying Talmud and Jewish law, writing and publishing beneficial books, and leading by example.

In 1732, after only three years in the job, he had finally had enough. The final straw was an altercation on Rosh HaShana, when the president of the community demanded that his clean-shaven unmarried son blow shofar for the community, and Rabbi Yaakov disapproved. The pettiness of the dispute and the uproar it precipitated made Rabbi Yaakov realize that he was simply not suited to be a community rabbi. He resigned and left Emden although, in spite of his disagreement with the president, Rabbi Yaakov not only made sure to reconcile with him but was even involved in defending him in a secular court case against accusations that could have caused the man great financial loss had he been found guilty.

FROM EMDEN TO ALTONA

The end of the Emden rabbinate experience was a turning point in Rabbi Yaakov's life. He would never again work for any Jewish community in any formal capacity nor, for the remainder of his life, would he ever be reliant on the whims of some wealthy backer. With his characteristic dry wit, he would later write that when he recited the daily blessing "*shelo asani aved*" – thanking God that he wasn't a slave – he would pronounce it "*shelo asani **abad***" – a play on words that made the Hebrew word for slave sound like the acronym for *av beit din*, the formal title of a communal rabbi.

And yet, although he was glad that he was no longer a rabbi who worked for a community, he was and always remained acutely aware of his standing as a rabbinic individual of unimpeachable integrity and distinguished ancestry, and was extremely conscious of the deficiencies and weaknesses of other rabbis, the worst examples of which he loathed with a passion.

After leaving Emden, Rabbi Yaakov decided to settle with his family in Altona, the town of his birth, which at the time was the main center of Jewish life in the Triple Community. This was comprised of six Ashkenazic synagogues scattered across Altona, Hamburg, and Wandsbeck, all under the auspices of one chief rabbi and a non-rabbinic lay leadership committee. The chief rabbi at that time was Rabbi Yehezkel Katzenellenbogen, a Lithuanian-born scholar who began his tenure in 1714, brought in by a wealthy philanthropist who had wanted to secure

Rabbi Yehezkel's previous rabbinic position in Kedainiai, Lithuania, for his own son-in-law.

Rabbi Yaakov, claiming that various physical ailments prevented him from walking to the nearest synagogue on a regular basis, sought and received permission from the Triple Community leadership to open up his own private synagogue at the home he was renting. While it was certainly true that Rabbi Yaakov had suffered from intermittent health issues while in Emden, and for many years previously, in all likelihood this request was also motivated by a desire for privacy, and to establish distance between himself and elements of the community and communal affairs with which he wished to have no contact. In particular Rabbi Yaakov had a very low opinion of the chief rabbi, whose scholarship and general demeanor did not meet his extraordinarily high standards.

During his first years in Altona Rabbi Yaakov did well in various business endeavors, and in 1733 personally funded the publication of his first book, *Lehem Shamayim*, a confident, scholarly work on *Mishnayot*. In 1738 he bought a house and remodeled it at great expense. This early period in Altona marked a peak; soon afterward things began to unravel. In 1739, Rabbi Yaakov's wife Rachel died shortly after giving birth to a daughter, who herself died after just a few months. Eight months after Rachel's death Rabbi Yaakov remarried, to Sarah, the daughter of a prominent communal personality from Halberstadt. But in 1743 she took ill, and died shortly afterward. A few months later Rabbi Yaakov remarried again, this time to his niece Batya Tzviya, daughter of his younger brother Rabbi Efrayim, rabbi of Lvov. But this marriage proved to be very challenging, particularly because Batya Tzviya found it difficult to get on with Rabbi Yaakov's daughters from his first marriage.

The financial situation had also taken a turn for the worse, as businesses went sour, and unscrupulous business associates took advantage of Rabbi Yaakov's trusting nature and distinct lack of business acumen. At the same time Rabbi Yaakov's contempt for Rabbi Yehezkel Katzenellenbogen rose to the surface when the chief rabbi consulted him about a controversial halakhic decision he had made that required the support of recognized scholars such as Rabbi Yaakov. Not only did Rabbi Yaakov disagree with the decision, he attempted to publish his dissenting view, causing a storm in the community. The community leadership supported Rabbi Katzenellenbogen, but it was clear that Rabbi Yaakov was a powerful force to be reckoned with.

When Rabbi Katzenellenbogen was stricken with his final illness in 1749 the community was rife with rumors that Rabbi Yaakov would replace him once he was gone. His late father had been the chief rabbi, he already resided in the city, and he was highly respected and amply qualified for the position. The scene was set for a drama that would haunt the Triple Community for decades.

THE TRIPLE COMMUNITY SEARCHES FOR A NEW RABBI

On Wednesday, July 9, 1749, Rabbi Yehezkel Katzenellenbogen passed away and was buried within a matter of hours. It quickly emerged that the late chief rabbi had requested that the community appoint his son, Rabbi David, as his replacement. Other names began to emerge as contenders for the coveted position, among them Rabbi Shmuel Hillman, who later filled the vacancy left by Rabbi Yonatan Eybeschutz in Metz, and Rabbi Arye Leib of Amsterdam, who was married to Rabbi Yaakov Emden's sister – as well as Rabbi Yonatan, and of course Rabbi Yaakov.

Rabbi Yonatan was certainly the most prominent of all the candidates. Almost sixty years old, and with an outstanding reputation as a rabbinic scholar and exceptional public speaker, he had many admirers in the Triple Community dating back to a two-year period, between 1713 and 1715, when he had lived in Altona with his wife's family. Murmurings that surfaced about his alleged Sabbatian leanings were dismissed as tittle-tattle generated by jealousy, or as tactical maneuvering by supporters of the other candidates. And while it was true that the other candidates, including Rabbi Yaakov, were free of any association with Sabbatianism, none of them could match Rabbi Yonatan's fame or acclaim.

Within the Triple Community there was a small but powerful group of individuals who considered it both appropriate and necessary to appoint Rabbi Yaakov as the new chief rabbi. In the first instance, they felt there was an unsettled "debt" owed to Hakham Tzvi, who had been forced to share the chief rabbinate position with another rabbi owing to communal politics at the time of his appointment. The dual chief rabbi idea had proven to be untenable, and had been the main factor that led to Hakham Tzvi's resignation and move to Amsterdam. The pro-Rabbi Yaakov faction felt it was only right for Hakham Tzvi's eldest son to reclaim the position his father would have bequeathed him had he remained in the position until his death.

More importantly, they saw Rabbi Yaakov as the kind of rabbi who would elevate the standards of Jewish observance in the Triple Community. In their opinion, Rabbi Katzenellenbogen had been far too easygoing, tolerating laxity and turning a blind eye to the inappropriate actions of those who were wealthy. If Rabbi Yaakov were appointed, he would be a very different kind of chief rabbi – the type who would ensure that any infraction of Halakha was acted upon immediately and appropriately, whoever the offender might be.

But the lay leaders of the Triple Community were not eager to appoint Rabbi Yaakov. While they respected his scholarship and were aware of his claim to the position, they felt that Rabbi Yaakov's disdain for the late chief rabbi – a feeling of contempt that on a couple of occasions had been expressed openly – made him an inappropriate replacement. Appointing him would show distinct lack of respect for the rabbi who had led their community for almost thirty-six years.

What was more, the community board perceived Rabbi Yaakov as a hothead with no political acumen, whose leadership of the community would inevitably result in a multitude of flashpoints and problems. Truth be told, Rabbi Yaakov himself was not eager to take on the chief rabbi role, despite the urging of his confidants. Nonetheless, he certainly believed that any other rabbi who accepted the job, knowing that he had the right of first refusal, would be guilty of perpetrating a grave insult and injustice against him and his late, revered father.

RABBI YONATAN IS APPOINTED CHIEF RABBI

Almost a year went by without a decision, as different factions within the community promoted their preferred candidates. Eventually, on May 14, 1750, the rabbinic selection committee sat down to make the fateful choice. A vote was taken and the winner declared. The Triple Community's new chief rabbi would be Rabbi Eybeschutz. An official letter was dispatched to Rabbi Yonatan, and he sent back word that he was delighted to accept the position and expected to arrive in the Triple

Community before Rosh HaShana. He left Metz as soon as he could and slowly made his way, town by town, to his new home.

One of those towns was Frankfurt, where he stayed for a few weeks. In the period immediately before he arrived there, several pregnant women had either died in childbirth or lost their babies at childbirth, or both. For several years, Rabbi Yonatan had been recognized for his expertise as a writer of amulets believed to help people in these kinds of situations. While in Frankfurt, he had several requests for such amulets from women who were pregnant. In an age before reliable medical care, requests like these were not unusual. People often sought amulets from an expert rabbi as protection against hazard.

But the use of amulets was a practice that was not welcomed by everyone. One of the major consequences of the Shabbetai Tzvi disaster was that any form of perceived kabbalistic "hocus-pocus" was automatically considered dubious. Only rabbis with the highest approval rating would dare to engage in practical kabbalistic remedies, as any lesser rabbi would run the risk of immediately being suspected of Sabbatianism. The fact that Rabbi Yonatan was willing to write and distribute amulets meant that he believed himself to be a rabbi whose reputation was so strong that no one would ever suspect him of being a Sabbatian, despite – or perhaps as a result of – his 1725 run-in with the anti-Sabbatian enforcers. He was widely acknowledged as a *gadol hador* – one of the select group of rabbis considered the greatest of their generation – and he therefore assumed that his kabbalistic amulets would never be called into question. He could not have been more mistaken.

Even before he had departed from Frankfurt, a number of Rabbi Yonatan's amulets were opened and reviewed by local rabbis. Their conclusion was that the amulets contained Sabbatian heresies and references to Shabbetai Tzvi through the use of cryptic kabbalistic codes. But rather than confront Rabbi Yonatan in Frankfurt, the rabbinic investigators instead sent letters to their friends in Hamburg and Altona to warn them that their new chief rabbi was not what he appeared to be. Although externally he behaved in complete conformity with normative Judaism, he was, they wrote, a crypto-Sabbatian who dispensed blasphemous amulets to unsuspecting folk seeking his help in difficult circumstances.

At this stage, Rabbi Yonatan was entirely unaware of these new accusations, and in the late summer he departed Frankfurt for the Triple Community. The numerous rabbinic students who had accompanied him from Metz had traveled ahead so that they would be there to welcome him when he arrived. His entrance into Hamburg in September 1750 was dramatic. A huge crowd gathered at the gates of the city to greet his carriage. As he drew close, his students formed a guard of honor. When the carriage windows opened and his face appeared, a huge cheer went up, as the community laid eyes on their new chief rabbi – the first new chief rabbi of the Triple Community many of them had ever seen.

A few days later, Rabbi Yonatan delivered his inaugural address at the main synagogue in Altona. The sanctuary was packed to the rafters, and people crowded in the aisles so that they could be present at this historic occasion. In the introduction to his oratorical tour-de-force, Rabbi Yonatan paid tribute to numerous community notables, including Rabbi Yaakov Emden. But Rabbi Yaakov was not there. He had decided that as the only rabbinic candidate in the selection process who lived locally, his attendance would turn into a distraction and might be very awkward, so he wisely chose to stay at home.

When Rabbi Yonatan finished his speech, the entire community danced him through the streets to his new house. As he walked through the front door, he kissed the mezuza and quoted a verse from Psalms (132:14): "*Zot menuḥati adei ad; po eishev ki ivitiha,*" "Let this be my resting place for ever; I will dwell here, for this is what I desired." It was a moment of high emotion, and many of those who witnessed it wept openly.

But even as the community celebrated Rabbi Yonatan's arrival, rumors circulated that he was a Sabbatian, and there were predictions that Rabbi Yaakov Emden was going to expose him. Local gossips quoted Rabbi Yaakov's wife, Batya Tzviya, as having declared before Rabbi Yonatan's arrival from Frankfurt, "Let the new chief rabbi come – my husband has already sharpened the knife to cut his throat." It is highly unlikely she uttered this statement, but the fact she was being quoted as having said it clearly indicated that Rabbi Yonatan's honeymoon was over even before it began.

Lurid stories about Rabbi Yonatan's affinity with Sabbatianism became the staple topic around every Shabbat table across the Triple Community. Rabbi Yonatan himself seemed completely unruffled, laughing off the rumors as a recycling of the accusations against him a quarter of a century earlier. He even continued to write amulets for those who requested them, and seemed to be of the view that firm denials would be enough to kill off rumors of his alleged heresy. After all, it had worked well for him twenty-five years earlier.

But this time it would not be so simple. In the anti-Sabbatian campaign of 1725, no one had been able to find the "smoking gun" to positively identify Rabbi Yonatan as a Sabbatian. Despite the numerous Sabbatians willing to take an oath confirming Rabbi Yonatan's commitment to their cause, and his authorship of the heretical tract "*Vaavo hayom el haayin*," it was entirely possible that their declarations were fantasy, and they were dreaming up the idea that a completely innocent rabbi was somehow their leader.

Alternatively, their assertions about Rabbi Yonatan's Sabbatianism could easily have been contrived, a web of lies deliberately disseminated as part of a dastardly conspiracy to besmirch a rising star of the rabbinate. Perhaps they hoped to sow confusion in the mainstream Jewish world. Whatever the truth actually was, Rabbi Moshe Hagiz had never been able to prove anything definitive against Rabbi Yonatan, and this lack of evidence coupled with Rabbi Yonatan's convincing denials had resulted in his complete exoneration.

Things were very different twenty-five years later. This time around there was physical evidence – the amulets. Rabbi Yonatan had been writing and distributing amulets for many years before he came to the Triple Community, and now, as the new accusations of heresy began to surface, his detractors started tracking the amulets down and opening them up. They discovered that the amulets were impossible to understand unless you were a kabbalistic expert. The resident expert on Kabbala in the Triple Community was none other than Rabbi Yaakov Emden. Consequently, at some point during the winter of 1750, a group of concerned Triple Community members brought one of the amulets to Rabbi Yaakov for an evaluation.

DECIPHERING THE AMULETS

It was this fateful meeting that would be the genesis of the raging controversy that ultimately engulfed the entire Jewish world, although at this stage no one would have dreamt that Rabbi Yaakov would emerge as Rabbi Yonatan's principal critic. As a matter of fact, although Rabbi Yaakov later became the person most identified with the anti-Rabbi Yonatan campaign, during the early stages of the controversy he was not the principal player. And while he may have had a reputation as a tough and demanding rabbi, Rabbi Yaakov had no history of battling those with whom he disagreed, nor had he ever played any role in an anti-Sabbatian crusade or previously tangled publicly or privately with Rabbi Yonatan Eybeschutz.

That fateful winter day the small group arrived at Rabbi Yaakov's home and was immediately shown in to his study. The mood was serious and pensive. One of the group explained the purpose of their visit, and handed Rabbi Yaakov a small handwritten amulet. Rabbi Yaakov shook his head and handed it back. They all looked at him, puzzled. He sighed.

"My dear friends, I have absolutely no desire to involve myself in this situation. Let me tell you why. Unless I completely exonerate Rabbi Yonatan I will be accused by everybody of harboring sour grapes. They will dismiss my opinion and claim that I hate Rabbi Yonatan for accepting the chief rabbinate position I wanted for myself – even though we all know that I had no interest in the position and do not want that job under any circumstances. I'm sorry to disappoint you, but I simply cannot offer you my help."

After a moment, the leader of the group, Yosef Prager, spoke up softly but with great determination. Prager was a long-standing friend of Rabbi Yaakov – an upstanding man whose devoutness and sincerity were indisputable.

"Honored rabbi," he began, "while I totally understand your position, please let me present you with another angle, for your consideration. If it is true – as many people are saying – that Rabbi Yonatan is a Sabbatian, how can we allow him to lead our wonderful community, and to guide us all down the wrong path? Rabbi Yehezkel, may he rest in peace, may not have been an ideal rabbi in every respect, but he was not a heretic. We all know that Sabbatianism is reprehensible heresy, and a grave danger to true Judaism. You must surely agree that as responsible members of our treasured community, we are compelled to either expose Rabbi Yonatan as a Sabbatian, or to confirm his claims of innocence. And, honored rabbi, you are the only one in this city who has the knowledge and expertise to guide us in this matter. So we have no choice but to ask you, and, respectfully, surely you have no choice but to honor our request for your guidance."

Rabbi Yaakov was quiet as he reflected on what Prager had said. After a few moments he nodded slowly and reached for the amulet – and then stopped.

"I have one condition," he said. "If I do discover that the amulet contains heresy, on no account can you mention that I was the one you consulted. I will show you what I see, and how I see it, and then it will be up to you to take things forward, without ever mentioning my name. Do we have a deal?"

They all nodded their consent.

Rabbi Yaakov took the amulet and carefully unfolded it. It contained a roughly drawn Star of David, with Hebrew letters inside and surrounding it. The letters seemed random, forming unintelligible words that only made sense to someone familiar with the craft of writing kabbalistic formulas. The rabbi was quiet as he turned the amulet this way and that. He held it up to the window to examine it in the light. Suddenly his face creased into a frown, and he gazed intently at one of the words on the amulet. He looked up.

"Are you absolutely sure this was written by Rabbi Yonatan?" he asked.

"We are completely certain," Prager replied. "It was received directly from the pregnant woman he gave it to."

"That is not good, not good at all. Come over here and let me show you something."

The men shuffled over to the window, and Rabbi Yaakov held the amulet up to the light, pointing to the handwritten word he had just closely examined. He looked at them, but they all shrugged their shoulders. They had no idea what the word meant.

Rabbi Yaakov's voice began to shake with emotion.

"This word is made up of an acrostic using a cryptic code known as ATBASH, where an *aleph* is a *tav*, a *beit* is a *shin*, a *gimmel* is a *reish*, and so on. What this word actually says is 'King Messiah Shabbetai Tzvi.'"

Everyone gasped in shock as they realized the magnitude of what Rabbi Yaakov had just told them. Here was the "smoking gun" Rabbi Moshe Hagiz had never managed to find. Here was actual proof that Rabbi Yonatan Eybeschutz, one of the greatest and most celebrated rabbis in Europe, was in reality a secret believer in the messianic mission of the charlatan messiah Shabbetai Tzvi. Rabbi Yaakov seemed lost in thought, and his visitors waited for him to say something. When he finally spoke, his words were slow and deliberate.

"This amulet is devastating, worse than anything ever produced by those cursed heretics Hayyun, Prosnitz, and Hasid. I'm begging you to please listen very carefully to what I am about to say. Whoever wrote this amulet is an extremely dangerous Sabbatian. For the moment I have no idea who wrote it, notwithstanding your certainty that it was written by Rabbi Yonatan. It's not that I don't believe you, but your affirmation of its authorship is only hearsay.

"My advice to you is to keep this discovery very quiet for the moment. Over the next few weeks gather up as many amulets written by Rabbi Yonatan as you can. Make sure to keep them closed and locked away. At some stage they will need to be opened in front of witnesses, or a notary, so that no one can ever claim they have been tampered with. You need to understand something very important: the only way anyone will ever believe Rabbi Yonatan is a Sabbatian is if you produce evidence – hard evidence! – that leaves him no room to deny it. My friends, you have a very hard task ahead of you. May God be with you."

Rabbi Yaakov solemnly shook hands with all his visitors and showed them out, totally unaware that he had just launched a process that would dominate the rest of his life.

A MEETING WITH THE COMMUNITY LEADERSHIP

Despite Rabbi Yaakov's request that his name be kept out of the matter, his involvement soon became an open secret. It seemed as if everyone in the community had expected his negative verdict on the amulet, and notwithstanding his reluctance to be associated with the investigation, particularly because he felt that his opinion would be immediately dismissed as biased, the talk in the Triple Community was that Rabbi Yaakov had uncovered Rabbi Yonatan's darkest secret and was ready to go public with what he knew.

It was only a matter of time before Rabbi Yonatan himself was informed of the rumors, and after discussing strategy with his closest advisers he decided to send a messenger to Rabbi Yaakov in an attempt to contain the matter before it spiraled out of control. The messenger arrived at Rabbi Yaakov's home bearing a friendly letter asking Rabbi Yaakov to disclose his views on the amulet, so that Rabbi Yonatan could offer an explanation. A rather surprised Rabbi Yaakov told the messenger that he was not quite sure why the chief rabbi was approaching him, as he had never expressed any opinion as to who the author of the amulet was, and had certainly never suggested that it was the chief rabbi who had written it. He had simply expressed his view that the formulation of the amulet was Sabbatian in origin, and whoever had written it was a dangerous heretic.

When this message came back to Rabbi Yonatan, he immediately called a meeting at his home of the community's most prominent lay leaders and informed them of his behind-the-scenes third-party dialogue with Rabbi Yaakov, and Rabbi Yaakov's insistence that the amulet contained Sabbatian heresy. The gathered dignitaries listened as Rabbi Yonatan recalled how he had battled accusations of Sabbatianism in the past, without anyone ever presenting a shred of evidence to prove anything against him. And now, once again, he was being accused. Rabbi Yonatan's voice quivered as he passionately denied that his amulets were Sabbatian or heretical in any way, and he requested that the community board intervene immediately and decisively to prevent his authority from being compromised by Rabbi Yaakov and others who were spreading rumors across the community.

The following morning there was a knock at Rabbi Yaakov's door. It was Tuesday, February 2, 1751. When Rabbi Yaakov came to the door he was shocked to find a full-sized horse-drawn carriage standing on the street outside his house. The man at the door informed him that he worked for the Jewish community, and was there to bring Rabbi Yaakov to the community's headquarters for an emergency meeting. Rabbi Yaakov was astonished. This was no ordinary invitation, and he realized this was not going to be an ordinary meeting. He asked the community employee if the chief rabbi was expected to be there, but was informed that only the executive committee of the lay leadership would be in attendance.

Rabbi Yaakov arrived at the meeting fearing the worst, but his apprehension was quickly dispelled. The three members of the executive committee – all personal friends for many years – were extremely respectful, and the atmosphere was amicable and benign. He sat at the head of the table and they explained apologetically how circumstances had forced them to act in this abrupt manner, but only because of the sensitivity of the matter at hand. After all, one of them said, it is not every day that a chief rabbi is accused of being a heinous heretic by another senior rabbi in the community. They all laughed heartily. But Rabbi Yaakov didn't even smile.

"Let me make one thing very clear," he began. "I have never made any public pronouncement suggesting that Rabbi Yonatan Eybeschutz is a heretic and nor do I want to. On the contrary, I have made it abundantly clear to the handful of people I have spoken to that I want to stay completely out of this matter, and not be involved in any way whatsoever. Frankly, I have no interest in getting into a fight with the chief rabbi and his supporters, nor do I wish to involve myself with sordid communal politics. In fact, as you well know, I despise community politics. So, unless you can give me a good reason to be here, I would like to leave immediately."

The atmosphere in the room shifted; suddenly no one was smiling. Rabbi Yaakov gazed at each member of the executive committee individually, looking to each one for a response, but they were all silent. So he reached for his hat and coat and began to leave.

"Hold on, hold on."

It was the president of the community speaking.

"Rabbi Yaakov, hold on, I'm begging you, please don't leave. We are in a crisis, and you are a part of that crisis, whatever you say."

Rabbi Yaakov eyed him intently. The president gulped, and continued.

"The chief rabbi is flatly denying the accusations of heresy, and yet we have heard from a number of people that you believe the author of the amulet – allegedly his amulet – is a heretic who believes in Shabbetai Tzvi. The entire community is in a total frenzy. You can't just walk away from this. We need to know why you said the amulet is heretical. And if you believe it is a Sabbatian amulet, you need to explain why we should be concerned. Rabbi, if we don't know the answers to these questions how do you expect us to deal with this matter adequately and properly? At the very least, we need you to help us navigate this emergency situation. After all, this is your community as much as it is ours. Who else besides you can we turn to? Surely you do not want to see our community destroyed."

POINT OF NO RETURN

Rabbi Yaakov slowly sat down. The president's plea had made a strong impact. It suddenly dawned on Rabbi Yaakov that he was in too deep to walk away. But at the same time he realized that whatever he said there would be terrible repercussions for him. If he belittled the Sabbatian nature of the amulet, and then at a later date Rabbi Yonatan was exposed as an insidious Sabbatian infiltrator with a mission to theologically destroy Judaism, how would he ever live that down? How would he forgive himself for having missed the opportunity to stop him in his tracks?

The alternative was no less scary. Everyone knew that Rabbi Yonatan had countless defenders who would never believe anything remotely bad about their hero. For them Rabbi Yonatan was the paradigmatic rabbi – learned, pious, and charismatic; a brilliant teacher, a gifted orator, a decisive halakhist, and a source of wisdom and advice. If Rabbi Yaakov openly expressed what he believed to be true, or his name became associated with an attack on Rabbi Yonatan's credibility, the consequences would be disastrous.

Rabbi Yaakov made one last attempt to avoid the inevitable storm.

"Gentlemen," he said, "you are making a big mistake. I am not the appropriate person to offer guidance. This problem needs to be brought to the attention of the greatest rabbis of our generation. Go and show them the amulets, and let them decide what to do. You know me – I want to lead a private, undisturbed life. That is why I chose to leave the rabbinate. Please leave me out of this, and use the appropriate channels to sort it out."

The president of the community looked at his colleagues and then back at Rabbi Yaakov.

"Rabbi, if only it was so simple. Unfortunately your name is already associated with the exposure of the amulet. You can't avoid that reality, and you cannot ignore our plea for help. We desperately need to understand why you believe the amulet to be Sabbatian so that we can take things further. And we really need to know from you how bad the amulet is."

Rabbi Yaakov looked at them, sighed, and reached into his pocket. He took out the letter received from Rabbi Yonatan only days earlier and passed it to the president, who immediately began to read it. Rabbi Yaakov then took out the amulet he had been shown. The amulet – now covered with Rabbi Yaakov's handwritten notes – was passed around in complete silence. After a few minutes Rabbi Yaakov spoke softly to the three lay leaders.

"My friends, I wish it wasn't true, but as you can see from my notes, this amulet is a sick and twisted example of Sabbatian heresy. Before I received the chief rabbi's letter I never told anyone the amulet was his, only that it was Sabbatian. So why did he write to me? What is he so nervous about? Draw your own conclusions, but one thing I can tell you for certain: the author of this amulet, and any amulets like it, is a highly dangerous man, a heretic of the worst kind. If it is Rabbi Yonatan, then his powerful influence over so many people across the Jewish world, not just in our community, presents the gravest danger to our faith since Shabbetai Tzvi himself, and maybe worse."

"But," he continued, "I don't expect you to believe me. Go to other experts, as many as you like, and check it out for yourselves. You need to, so that this controversy does not become framed as a personal battle between him and me."

The president stood up, shook Rabbi Yaakov's hand, and thanked him for coming. "Perhaps we can meet again on Thursday once we have discussed this with the whole community board." Rabbi Yaakov smiled and nodded, and the meeting was over.

The following morning the three members of the executive committee called the rest of the board for a full emergency meeting. Without embellishment they repeated what they had heard from Rabbi Yaakov and passed around the amulet and Rabbi Yonatan's letter. A discussion began, but there was no consensus. Several members of the board simply dismissed Rabbi Yaakov as a troublemaker, jealous of Rabbi Yonatan for having taken the rabbinic position he felt belonged to him. Others were furious that anyone was accusing their spiritual leader of being a heretic. And then there were those who felt that the mere hint of suspicion against the chief rabbi was a disgrace to their community, and the chief rabbi would have to go. The meeting descended into a screaming match, and despite hours of heated debate nothing was agreed or resolved.

Meanwhile Rabbi Yonatan was informed of the secret meeting between Rabbi Yaakov and the executive committee, as well as the emergency board meeting, and others whispered to him that there were plans afoot to see him deposed from his post. In a panic, he called an urgent meeting of his closest supporters to form a strategy to defend himself against the emerging storm. His supporters promised him a phased strategy to deal with the threat. First they would deal with Rabbi Yaakov. He would have to be neutralized. Then they would deal with the executive committee and the board. It wasn't going to be easy, but he had nothing to fear. The meeting ended with every one of Rabbi Yonatan's devotees pledging their full and unwavering support, and offering him their assurance to work tirelessly and ceaselessly to ensure his name would not be tarnished by this witch hunt.

THE FATEFUL ANNOUNCEMENT

That night, as evening services began at Rabbi Yaakov's private synagogue, Shmuel Hecksher, a longstanding friend of Rabbi Yaakov, rushed in, breathless and pale, and ran up to the rabbi.

"It's all over town," he gasped. "They are planning to come and kill you."

Rabbi Yaakov pulled him outside.

"Shmuel, what are you talking about? What's going on?"

"It's true, absolutely true. Rabbi Yonatan's supporters have let it be known that you are a *rodef* (dangerous individual), intent on destroying the chief rabbi's reputation by spreading malicious rumors. It is a sin punishable by death, they claim, and they are therefore permitted to kill you."

Now it was Rabbi Yaakov's turn to go pale.

Hecksher continued to talk, the words tumbling out in a torrent.

"These people are very powerful. They have friends among the gentiles. You will be murdered, money will change hands, and no one will be arrested." Tears were flowing down his cheeks. "Rabbi, I'm begging you, run away while you still can. This whole thing has gotten completely out of control."

A crowd had gathered at the door of the synagogue. Rabbi Yaakov spoke, his voice shaky but resolute.

"I'm not running anywhere. I was born here and have lived here for the past eighteen years. My home is here. My family is here. My friends are here. My library is here. My life is here. I have done nothing wrong, and everyone knows I am a man of integrity." He turned to Shmuel Hecksher, and put a hand on his shoulder. "Thank you, Shmuel, for your concern. But do not worry, I am at peace. God will protect me, and all of us, from all those who wish us any harm."

That night Rabbi Yaakov was unable to sleep, his mind at work weighing up his options. He still had the scheduled meeting with the executive committee the following day. Perhaps they would protect him, even though Rabbi Yonatan's supporters seemed to have the upper hand. Maybe he could work out a compromise solution with them. There had to be a way to avoid a full-scale communal war – especially if his life was in danger.

Suddenly Rabbi Yaakov sat bolt upright in his bed. What was he thinking? This wasn't about him! What was his own paltry life worth compared to the thousands of spiritual lives snuffed out as a result of some disreputable compromise? There was a Sabbatian heretic loose in the community! This was no time to worry about himself! The discussion needed to refocus on the amulet, and the dangers its author posed, a danger made infinitely greater if the author was in fact the chief rabbi. Hadn't his own father, Hakham Tzvi Ashkenazi, sacrificed everything in the battle with Nehemiah Hayyun? Now it was his turn to do the same. He would show them all that he was his father's true son, ready to risk everything to expose a Sabbatian infiltrator.

At Shaḥarit services the following morning, Rabbi Yaakov's private synagogue was packed with people. Everyone had heard about the incident the previous evening, and people were there from across the community to show their support and to find out what Rabbi Yaakov intended to do. There were also supporters of Rabbi Yonatan, including the messenger who had only recently brought the chief rabbi's letter. As the service concluded Rabbi Yaakov walked up to the podium at the front of the sanctuary. He raised his hand for everyone to be silent, and everyone immediately stopped what they were doing to hear him speak. Usually at this point Rabbi Yaakov would share some Torah thoughts, but not today.

"Last night," he began, "I was informed that my life is in danger. But rather then run away, as I was advised to do, I have decided to let you know what has been going on behind closed doors for the past few weeks. It was not originally my intention to do so, but in light of the unfolding situation I feel I am left with no choice.

"Some time ago I was approached by a group of people who asked me to examine an amulet and to give my assessment of its contents. After studying it carefully I confirmed that the amulet contained Sabbatian heresy. However, neither then nor since have I ever suggested that the author of the amulet was our community's chief rabbi, Rabbi Yonatan Eybeschutz. Just to be clear, I am not currently in a fight with Rabbi Yonatan, nor have I ever fought with him. The person I have a fight with is the author of the amulet, whoever he may be.

"And let me state for the record, so that no one can be in any doubt: the amulet that was shown to me, and that I was asked about, is entirely heretical, and the person who wrote it and gave it out for the purposes of healing is without question a heretic. Yes, you heard correctly, and I will say it again. There is not an iota of doubt in my mind that the man who wrote the amulet is an *apikoros* and has no share in the World to Come. If that person or any person can prove me wrong, I am ready to be proven wrong.

"I have one last thing to say, and this is very important. Although I have no idea if it was Rabbi Yonatan who wrote the amulet, many people believe that he was the one who wrote it. That being the case it is my view that he is obligated to vindicate himself and to save himself from suspicion. He has my word that if he explains himself properly, I will personally be his first and most vigorous defender. I will battle relentlessly to counteract the false rumors, and I will shut the mouths of those who are attacking him. What is more I will go to the Great Synagogue and – in front of the whole community – publicly beg for his forgiveness, even though I never meant him harm.

"Truthfully, I wish things had been different. I wish Rabbi Yonatan would have immediately and publicly explained the contents of all his amulets when this saga began. But that is now in the past. The facts are as they are, and we are where we are. All that matters now is that I am ready, with all my heart, to put this behind us – if it is proven that I have made a terrible mistake. But for that to happen Rabbi Yonatan needs to do what he needs to do."

With that Rabbi Yaakov stepped down and disappeared into his house. The synagogue was quiet for a moment and then erupted in heated conversation as the magnitude of what had just happened came into focus. Without saying it explicitly, Rabbi Yaakov Emden had accused the chief rabbi of being a Sabbatian heretic. What had until that moment been an unofficial rumor now had the backing of none other than Rabbi Yaakov Emden.

THE CONTROVERSY ESCALATES

Within hours the entire Triple Community had heard about the announcement, and so had Rabbi Yonatan. One of his supporters who had been present when Rabbi Yaakov spoke reported back to the chief rabbi. Rabbi Yonatan didn't waste a second; he immediately called the community's lay leaders to his home and informed them that Rabbi Yaakov had spoken out publicly about the amulets and had accused him of being a Sabbatian. Without attempting to hear what Rabbi Yaakov had to say about the matter, the community board decided they could not allow anyone, and particularly someone of Rabbi Yaakov's stature, to undermine the community in this way.

Rabbi Yaakov was informed by messenger that his second meeting with the executive board later that day had been canceled, and going forward he would no longer be permitted to hold daily prayer services at his home, as he had been doing for the past eighteen years. He was also placed under house arrest, forbidden to leave his home until further notice.

The following morning an announcement was made in the Great Synagogue that Rabbi Yaakov had been put into *ḥerem* (halakhic excommunication), and no member of the community was permitted to interact with him, or they themselves would be excommunicated. This same pronouncement was read to Rabbi Yaakov at his home later in the day. His response was simple and blunt: "Those who have excommunicated me are themselves excommunicated, as they have not followed halakhic protocol before putting me into *ḥerem*. They have acted outside Torah law and made a mockery of Judaism."

This defiant reaction only made the community leaders angrier, and they responded by arranging to have Rabbi Yaakov's rights of residence in Altona withdrawn by the local gentile authorities. On the following Sunday he was ordered to leave Altona within six months, and never to return. By Monday guards had been posted outside Rabbi Yaakov's home preventing him from leaving to walk the streets, and preventing anyone from the Jewish community from entering. Rabbi Yonatan's faction appeared to have won the day, with Rabbi Yaakov completely neutralized and the threat to the chief rabbi's authority and community peace essentially over.

But had anyone reached this conclusion over that cold February weekend, they would have been wholly mistaken. Rabbi Yaakov Emden was not a man to be trifled with. As far as he was concerned, the ferocity of the reaction to his Thursday announcement simply confirmed what he had suspected all along: Rabbi Yonatan Eybeschutz was a secret Sabbatian who could not possibly survive any objective investigation into his amulets, and he knew it. And so, despite the powerful forces mounted against Rabbi Yaakov, and probably because of them, his absolute conviction that he was right spurred him on, as did his belief that the truth would ultimately prevail.

With no one local willing to defend him or to take up his cause for fear of excommunication, Rabbi Yaakov decided to reach out to three rabbinic colleagues with a plea for help. In detailed letters he carefully described the recent events, and explained how his initially reluctant involvement had ultimately resulted in the draconian measures being implemented against him. The three colleagues he wrote to were Rabbi Shmuel Hilman, Rabbi Yonatan Eybeschutz's replacement as chief rabbi of Metz; Rabbi Arye Leib of Amsterdam, married to Rabbi Yaakov's sister; and Rabbi Yaakov Yehoshua Falk, chief rabbi of Frankfurt, and without doubt the most revered rabbi in Germany, and possibly all of Europe.

Rabbi Yaakov did not mince his words. Referring to his predicament as a "holy war," he accused Rabbi Yonatan – whom he now
referred to disdainfully as "Eybeschutz" – of "scandalous conduct" and
"Godless convictions." Rabbi Yaakov asserted he had long known of
Rabbi Yonatan's Sabbatian leanings, although he conceded he had not
objected to Rabbi Yonatan's appointment as chief rabbi so as to avoid
the inevitable communal strife this would have generated. His tolerance for Rabbi Yonatan had changed dramatically once the Sabbatian
amulets had emerged, and particularly because Rabbi Yonatan had been
unable or unwilling to come up with any kind of convincing explanation to exonerate himself.

The three letters all ended with the same unequivocal summary
that explained why Rabbi Yaakov was calling on his colleagues to act
immediately and decisively:

> If, God forbid, we remain silent, how will we answer future gen-
> erations when they ask, "Why did you allow this stumbling block
> to remain, and neglect your duty to excise it?" We must be coura-
> geous! We must be strong for our people and for God! We must
> publicize this abomination far and wide, so that the disease will
> not spread! And if we do, I am certain God Himself will repay
> us for this pious deed.

The letters were secretly dispatched and slowly wound their way across
Europe. Meanwhile, Rabbi Yaakov languished under house arrest with
local gentile police posted at his door to prevent any contact with the
outside world.

RABBI YONATAN DECLARES HIS INNOCENCE

Initially it seemed that the plan to isolate Rabbi Yaakov and his supporters and to impose the will of the lay leadership on the community at
large had been successful. As time passed, however, it became evident
that there was still an outstanding issue. Although the actions against
Rabbi Yaakov had silenced the opposition, they had done nothing to
address the fact that Rabbi Yonatan had been openly accused of heresy
by a distinguished and respected colleague, and had done absolutely

nothing to dispel the accusations. Even among the lay leadership there were those who felt that the speculation needed to end, and that there was only one person who could end it – Rabbi Yonatan himself.

A delegation of community notables met with Rabbi Yonatan and asked him to address a public meeting as soon as possible. He would have to unequivocally rebut Rabbi Yaakov's accusations, and also explain to the community how Rabbi Yaakov could possibly have reached such a devastating conclusion. But most importantly Rabbi Yonatan would have to use his appearance to publicly renounce Shabbetai Tzvi and Sabbatians, and to repudiate Sabbatianism. So far Rabbi Yonatan had been reluctant to respond in public to the accusations, believing it was below the dignity of his position, but after hearing from friends and colleagues how important it was to draw a line under the affair he agreed to give the speech on Sunday, February 21, 1751.

Signs announcing the speech went up all over the Triple Community. Sunday evening arrived and the synagogue was packed to the last seat. The chief rabbi sat at the front of the synagogue flanked by the city's *dayanim* and the executive board. After Minḥa prayers were over Rabbi Yonatan slowly made his way to the pulpit. Wherever he looked there were expectant faces. Even the women's balcony was full, and outside, in the lobby of the synagogue, hundreds more people were gathered, hoping to hear, however faintly, what Rabbi Yonatan was going to say.

The speech was outstanding. Rabbi Yonatan always spoke well, but on this occasion he was magnificent. He began with remarks about King David and his rebel son Avshalom, who in ancient Jewish history had tried to replace his father as king of the Jews – even though his father was the man designated by God to lead the nation. Weaving together an array of sources and ideas, all enhanced by the oratorical skill for which he was so famous, Rabbi Yonatan projected a vivid picture that depicted him as the suffering King David of his generation subjected to a vicious attack by a ruthless Avshalom. Having planted this powerful symmetry firmly into the minds of his audience, Rabbi Yonatan now turned to the central theme of his speech, and for the first time in more than twenty-five years directly addressed the disturbing topic of his rumored association with Sabbatianism.

"My friends, I didn't come here today to give you a sermon. I came here today because I have been slandered. Rumors are circulating that I am a member of the sect of Shabbetai Tzvi, may his memory be erased.

"If it was only about my honor, perhaps I would say nothing. But this matter involves the honor of my sainted forebears and teachers. It also involves the honor of my students, many of whom have become great rabbis and Torah scholars in their own right. How could I ever allow it to be said that the man who taught them and nurtured them is a fraud, that the spring from which they drank was contaminated? But more important than any of this is the honor of the Torah itself. How can I let the Torah be vilified? Would it not be the ultimate desecration of God's name if I allowed such a thing to happen?

"I must therefore call God Himself as my witness, and declare unambiguously that I am completely innocent of all the accusations against me! Neither now nor in the past have I ever been involved with the sect that believes in Shabbetai Tzvi!"

There was a collective gasp from the audience. The chief rabbi's statement was unequivocal. It was a complete denial. And yet, it still didn't make any sense! What about Rabbi Yaakov's accusations? Hadn't Rabbi Yaakov spotted clear Sabbatian references in the amulet he had examined? Why would these references be there if – as they had just heard – Rabbi Yonatan was not a Sabbatian?

Rabbi Yonatan seemed prepared for this question, and immediately addressed it.

"There may be those among you who are wondering how anyone can accuse me of being a heretic if I am not. The answer is simple – my accusers have no idea what they're talking about! I would be concerned if they were equipped with the knowledge needed to denounce me. But they are not. Don't be fooled just because they are Torah scholars. They have no background whatsoever in Kabbala, and have no idea how an amulet should be written.

"Only a real expert in Kabbala knows how the words and the letters in an amulet relate to each other. The composition of an amulet is a complex secret known to very few people, handed down by masters of Kabbala to a fraction of their students. Only fools would presume to know the meaning of amulets if they have never been trained or educated in their configuration. Letters and words that seem to say one thing can mean something else completely, and they would never know. Perhaps my enemies mean well, and I bear them no grudge if they do. But one thing I know – they are wrong, and I am innocent. It is as simple as that."

Then, with a voice that filled the synagogue sanctuary and could be heard clearly by those standing outside in the lobby, Rabbi Yonatan concluded his address with the following powerful words:

"May God judge me harshly if I have ever been any part of the Sabbatian sect. May fire and flames descend from heaven and destroy me if I have ever included Shabbetai Tzvi's accursed name in any of my amulets. May all the curses reserved for heretics befall me if I have ever attempted to entice people to heresy or to beliefs that run counter to our holy Torah. Because those who follow Shabbetai Tzvi are evil men, and their presence in our midst is a grave danger.

"I wholeheartedly join with all our greatest rabbis who say that these miscreants must be publicly identified and excommunicated. They are scoundrels and destroyers of our faith who can have no part in our redemption. Let us remain steadfast in our faith, and in our fervent hope for the true redemption, so that we will merit to be a part of it, speedily in our days, Amen."

The congregation all responded "Amen!" in unison and rose to their feet as Rabbi Yonatan slowly made his way back to his seat. People crowded around him eager to shake his hand and congratulate him on his stirring speech. Late into the night the synagogue continued to buzz with the energy his words had generated. At last it seemed that the saga was over, and that everyone could move on from the rumors and insinuations that had been plaguing the community for so many months.

THE FIGHT TURNS NASTY

Rather than slow things down, however, Rabbi Yonatan's speech created a whole new level of tension in the community. Rabbi Yonatan had asserted – without mentioning him by name – that Rabbi Yaakov Emden knew nothing about Kabbala or the composition of amulets. While those who didn't know him might have imagined this to be true, Rabbi Yaakov's close friends and associates knew him to be an accomplished kabbalist. The suggestion, therefore, that he was not "equipped" to examine an amulet, or that he had no "background" in Kabbala, was untenable and seemed glib. Rabbi Yaakov was certainly more than qualified to spot combinations of letters that contained references to Shabbetai Tzvi in an amulet and, notwithstanding Rabbi Yonatan's impressive oratorical presentation, to Rabbi Yaakov's supporters his defense was nothing more than an unconvincing attempt to present himself as uniquely qualified to understand the contents of amulets, so that any alternative explanation of the amulets could be summarily dismissed.

The division within the community began to intensify as these concerns were voiced. For Rabbi Yonatan's supporters there was nothing more to discuss. Rabbi Yonatan had publicly explained himself, he had satisfactorily dismissed his accusers, and he had explicitly denounced Sabbatians. But for those in the community who were skeptical, their concerns about Rabbi Yonatan only increased after his speech. They were also angry at Rabbi Yaakov's continued house arrest and the total shutdown of any conversation about the amulets. It seemed inevitable there would be an explosion. Tempers were short, and anger bubbled just below the surface.

The explosion came on May 7, 1751, during Shabbat prayers at the Great Synagogue as the head *ḥazan*, Moshe Kassewitz, who was a known supporter of Rabbi Yaakov, strode toward the *ḥazan's* lectern to begin leading the prayers. As he walked to the front of the sanctuary three of Rabbi Yonatan's supporters stood in the aisle to block his way.

"Excuse me," he said, and attempted to get past them.

"You're not going anywhere, young man," one of them said. "You are a disgusting individual, and disgusting individuals cannot lead our community in prayer."

"What are you talking about?" he asked. He glared at them, and they glared back.

"How dare you support the enemy of our chief rabbi, that trouble-maker Yaakov Emden? Do you really think we want someone like you to be the *ḥazan* of our community? We don't want you! Get back to your seat! Or better still – leave the synagogue, and never come back!"

Others now began to get involved in the altercation. They remonstrated with the three aisle-blockers, and tried to help the *ḥazan* push through to the front. People were shouting across the synagogue toward the scene of the incident and at each other. Suddenly one of the three men punched the *ḥazan* in the face. Kassewitz fell to the ground, his mouth bleeding.

"That's how one treats someone who insults the greatest Torah scholar of our generation!"

The attacker grinned nastily, and then spat at the dazed *ḥazan*.

Kassewitz was struggling to get up, blood dripping from his mouth. At that moment one of the *ḥazan's* friends, a big burly man, grabbed the attacker by the neck and began dragging him out of the synagogue, all the while slapping him around the face. Other people joined in the fight, and a violent riot ensued in the synagogue. Individuals who minutes earlier had been calmly praying in their seats were now yelling offensive insults, and kicking and punching each other. Children cried as they watched their wild-eyed fathers behave like animals. Elderly people huddled in the pews, afraid to move. It was complete pandemonium.

Within minutes the local police had arrived to break up the riot. They emptied the synagogue of people and locked the doors, insisting that the building would remain closed until the community executive could guarantee the peace. But there was no guarantee. The mood in the community was far too volatile. For the time being the local synagogues would remain empty as each faction prayed in small groups at people's homes. Even this separation was not sufficient to prevent outbreaks of violence. Time and again insulting remarks uttered in public would result in violent street brawls. The community was literally falling apart.

As the crisis intensified Rabbi Yonatan's supporters began to publicly threaten Rabbi Yaakov, who they believed was actively behind the unrest, encouraging his supporters to foment violence. As soon as Rabbi Yaakov heard this he reluctantly concluded that he had no choice but to leave Altona immediately and go to Amsterdam, where he could stay with his sister and brother-in-law until the situation had calmed down.

He informed the local authorities, but they warned him that leaving the city would not be simple. At least in his home he was somewhat safe, protected from harm by the local gentile police force. Once he ventured outside there was a real danger he might be attacked, or even killed. After intensive and secretive negotiations it was agreed that he would leave at midnight on a Saturday night, when the least number of people were on the streets, and, to further minimize any possibility of detection, his wife and children would stay behind.

The farewell to his friends and family was extremely emotional. Rabbi Yaakov blessed his crying children and then looked up at his house. Would he ever see it again? The situation seemed so bleak. How had he reached this low ebb? He shrugged and shook his head as he took his place in the carriage that would transport him out of the city. He took one last peek at his wife and children standing forlornly on the street in the pale moonlight. How would this nightmare ever end?

EXILE IN AMSTERDAM

Rabbi Yaakov arrived in Amsterdam both physically sick and very depressed – the result of months of confinement, his secret departure, and then a difficult journey. Rabbi Yaakov's sister and her husband tried everything to boost his spirits and health; in the weeks that followed his strength slowly improved, and so did his mood. Eager to salvage his reputation and the right to return home, he realized he would have to prove that his suspicions about Rabbi Yonatan were correct, and that the way he had been treated for voicing them was a travesty.

Now able to think more clearly, Rabbi Yaakov formed the opinion that there were only two reasons why so many people had supported Rabbi Yonatan and continued to support him – either there was a crypto-Sabbatian conspiracy to protect their leader at all costs, or Rabbi Yonatan was so charming and charismatic that he was able to mislead people into believing the accusations were false, even though they were not. Both scenarios were highly dangerous, as they allowed Sabbatian heresy to creep into mainstream Jewish life completely unchecked.

A third alternative – namely that Rabbi Yonatan was innocent and had been wrongly accused – was dismissed by Rabbi Yaakov as wishful thinking by naïve people who had allowed their respect for rabbis to undermine their critical faculties, and who simply did not appreciate that a guilty man can often convincingly present himself as innocent.

But would Rabbi Yaakov be able to counteract the powerful forces mounted against him? Rabbi Yonatan's influence was wide and deep, and particularly in the Triple Community he seemed unassailable. After reflecting on his options Rabbi Yaakov concluded that to win this fight he would have to do exactly the opposite of what he had originally suggested so many months earlier. When first confronted with the amulet evidence he had opted for a restrained, civil approach, on the basis that it would lead to a quiet solution – perhaps Rabbi Yonatan's discreet termination, and a minimum of negative backlash.

That strategy had failed miserably, and it was evident that forces loyal to Rabbi Yonatan would easily crush any such gentlemanly opposition. So Rabbi Yaakov decided that the only way to overcome the forceful defense would be to use equal force, and to publicize everything negative known about Rabbi Yonatan as widely as possible, so that the latter's position would become untenable, with no right-thinking person ever able to support him again.

In Amsterdam Rabbi Yaakov had no fear of repercussions and felt free to say and write whatever he wanted. He sent letters to all the rabbis he knew, recording in lurid detail every piece of information he had ever been told about Rabbi Yonatan that exposed the dark side of a man widely believed to be virtuous and without blemish. The aim was simple: to discredit his rival and to utterly ruin his reputation. He called him a liar, a sinner, a heretic, a phony, in each instance offering narrative support for these accusations. The upshot was that Rabbi Yonatan was clearly not the kind of man to lead a community, nor to teach impressionable young men. The counteroffensive had begun.

At the same time two other major developments began to unfold, one in Metz, Rabbi Yonatan's former city of residence, and the other in Frankfurt. In Metz, Rabbi Yonatan's replacement as chief rabbi, Rabbi Shmuel Hilman, had been one of the recipients of Rabbi Yaakov's desperate plea for help in the aftermath of his fall from grace after the fateful announcement on February 4, 1751.

The letter from Rabbi Yaakov came as no surprise to Rabbi Hilman, who had long been suspicious of amulets handed out by his predecessor, even before he had replaced him in Metz. In his response to Rabbi Yaakov's letter dated February 21, 1751, he wrote that he had decided soon after his arrival to confiscate all of Rabbi Yonatan's amulets and forbid their use by anyone in the community. He also offered to send notarized copies of the Metz amulets to the leadership of the Triple Community and suggested that they call in Rabbi Yonatan without warning him in advance, and ask for an explanation of the obvious Sabbatian references in the amulets, without giving him enough time to come up with a contrived meaning that explained them away.

Notaries were a fixture of Jewish communal life in those days, and could more accurately be described as court recorders. Present at any formal gathering, they would faithfully and accurately record all the proceedings at meetings of lay leadership and the rabbinate in an official record book that could later be used for reference when needed. In the city of Metz the two community notaries were Yitzhak Koblentz and Mordekhai Gumprecht, and on March 17, 1751, they carefully copied the contents of five separate amulets written by Rabbi Yonatan that had been given to five different individuals on five separate occasions.

Koblentz and Gumprecht then affixed their signatures to a declaration in which they stated:

> These five amulets were copied word for word, letter for letter, line by line, exactly as they appeared in the original amulets that were received by five different people from Rabbi Yonatan Eybeschutz who was our chief rabbi and is now chief rabbi of Hamburg.

A few months later, on November 17, 1751, the two notaries once again affirmed their original notarized document, this time in front of a local Christian judge, an act that gave their notarization official legitimacy in a gentile court of law.

Both notaries were known to be deeply devoted to Rabbi Yonatan, and no one could ever have accused them of being biased against him, nor of having deliberately misconstrued the notarized copies to show Rabbi Yonatan up in a bad light. Much later Rabbi Yonatan would accuse his enemies of having "forced" the notaries to sign the declaration against their will, essentially implying that the amulets had been deliberately reconfigured and the notaries threatened that they would lose their jobs if they didn't notarize the altered versions. The notaries themselves dismissed this claim, and it is clear from Rabbi Yonatan's later attempts to explain the notarized versions that even he considered the Metz copies to be accurate.

Meanwhile the amulets, all of which seemed to indicate a definitive Sabbatian obsession by their author, were widely disseminated by Rabbi Hilman, and within a few weeks, as rabbis and leaders across the Jewish world came face to face with the evidence, the accusations against Rabbi Yonatan could no longer be dismissed as representing the bitter resentment of a cranky competitor for the Triple Community chief rabbinate position. On the contrary, the evidence now seemed to show that Rabbi Yaakov had been right all along.

A RABBINIC ELDER ENTERS THE FRAY

Rabbi Hilman's devastating proof that the amulets were Sabbatian played an important role in the second development that began to unfold at around the same time, a development that was far more significant than a few notarized amulets. After having remained publicly silent for two months despite the desperate plea from Rabbi Yaakov for support, in late March 1751 the chief rabbi of Frankfurt, Rabbi Yaakov Yehoshua Falk, finally lent his backing to the growing group of people who felt that Rabbi Yonatan had a lot of explaining to do.

Clearly unaware that Rabbi Hilman had already notarized some of the Metz amulets, Rabbi Falk wrote to Rabbi Hilman on March 30 to advise him that any amulet reproductions would have to be accompanied by irrefutable evidence that they were genuine copies of the originals, otherwise "members of Rabbi Yonatan's community who are loyal to him will claim that his enemies are using falsified amulets to discredit him because of jealousy."

Rabbi Falk added: "I am in no doubt whatsoever that Rabbi Yonatan is guilty as charged, which makes your task all the more urgent."

Rabbi Falk was a savvy, experienced communal rabbi. He knew that even if Rabbi Yonatan was guilty, there was no way the Triple Community would ever fire him from his position, as this would amount to an admission of gross ineptitude – after all, it was they who had chosen him only the previous year, despite the not-so-secret information that their new rabbi had been dogged by suspicions of heresy for twenty-five years.

The only way to resolve the matter of Rabbi Yonatan's Sabbatian amulets once and for all was for Rabbi Yonatan to admit what he had done and publicly repent. At this stage Rabbi Falk felt that Rabbi Yaakov's strategy of totally delegitimizing Rabbi Yonatan would not be effective to convince those who adamantly refused to believe he was guilty, and the delegitimization strategy was certainly not pertinent to those who already believed he was a Sabbatian.

Rabbi Falk's strategy was to directly engage Rabbi Yonatan. At first he appealed to Rabbi Yonatan via messengers, asking him to be in touch. When this elicited no response, Rabbi Falk published a letter calling for the matter to be adjudicated by three rabbis, although he did not mention Rabbi Yonatan by name. Once again Rabbi Yonatan did not react, so Rabbi Falk then wrote a letter directly to Rabbi Yonatan exhorting him to do the right thing. When even this failed to get a reaction Rabbi Falk went public with that same letter so that his proposed solution would become widely known, in the hope that the publicity would force Rabbi Yonatan to accept his proposal.

When the published version reached Rabbi Yonatan he was livid. He claimed never to have received the original letter, and vigorously objected to Rabbi Falk's clear implication that he was guilty of heresy. Having decided to respond decisively to Rabbi Falk, he wrote a lengthy, angry reply in which, among other things, he dismissed Rabbi Falk's famous work, *Pnei Yehoshua*, as being full of mistakes. The letter also challenged Rabbi Falk to a "Kabbala contest," guaranteeing that any such contest would only prove that Rabbi Yonatan knew much more about this discipline than Rabbi Falk. The letter even accused Rabbi Falk of having harbored hatred toward Rabbi Yonatan for many years, making him an inappropriate person to suggest any method of rehabilitation.

Once Rabbi Yonatan finished writing the letter it seems his anger had subsided and, on reflection, he decided not to send it. Instead he left it on his study desk. Unfortunately for him, this fateful decision resulted in mischief. While he was away from his desk a group of his students sneaked into the rabbi's study and copied the letter word for word without telling him, and then began circulating it to a wide range of recipients. It was only a matter of time before a copy found its way to Rabbi Falk, who was understandably furious.

Rabbi Falk began to forcefully demand that Rabbi Yonatan appear before a panel of rabbis, but his appeals fell on deaf ears. Rabbi Yonatan's support in the Triple Community was still rock solid. Even in Rabbi Falk's own community of Frankfurt the leadership began to tire of their chief rabbi's involvement in the controversy, and before long it was he who was forced out of his position – the second major casualty of the Emden-Eybeschutz affair, after Rabbi Yaakov.

"INDEPENDENT" EXPERTS

Although Rabbi Yonatan felt safe, it had become apparent that the amulets were a burning issue, and he therefore decided to consult experts in Kabbala who would examine the evidence and publicly endorse his version of what they meant. The two experts he chose were Rabbi Shmuel Essingen of Muenster, a friend of Rabbi Hilman of Metz, and Rabbi Eliyahu Olianow, an elderly kabbalist who had spent time at the home of Rabbi Arye Leib of Amsterdam, Rabbi Yaakov's brother-in-law. Clearly these two rabbis were carefully and deliberately chosen to demonstrate how even friends of his enemies were willing to support his version of what the amulets said, rather than the version suggested by his enemies.

And so they did, both declaring that Rabbi Yonatan's amulets were completely fine, free of any Sabbatian references. Rabbi Olianow even suggested that banning the use of these amulets by insisting that the letter formulations were Sabbatian was highly dangerous, making Rabbi Yaakov and his supporters guilty of allowing those who really needed them to be subjected to illness and even death.

Rabbi Yaakov was unimpressed. In a pattern that would become familiar with regard to any supporters of Rabbi Yonatan, he accused both experts of being miscreants and bribe takers who had allowed money to influence them. Rabbi Essingen, he said, was someone who made money out of fake magic dressed up as Kabbala, while Rabbi Olianow was an immoral drunkard.

Meanwhile Rabbi Yaakov had not been idle. He had written dozens of letters to rabbis in Germany and Poland, informing them of Rabbi Yonatan's iniquities and trying to convince them to excommunicate Rabbi Yonatan and to demand that the Triple Community dismiss him from his position immediately. Using the notarized amulets from Metz as proof of his depravity and duplicity, Rabbi Yaakov added numerous other accusations and claims to boost his case against Rabbi Yonatan:

> With my own eyes I saw him throw out a Talmud student who traveled a great distance to study at his yeshiva in Hamburg, simply because he was poor and could not pay his way. Someone once asked [Rabbi Yonatan] why he eats wormy fruit, and he laughed, answering, "Worms and bugs have no power over me, so who cares!" His evil deeds in Prague could fill up a whole book, and all his followers are the same...immoral sinners who rejoice in transgressing against God!

The Jewish world was deeply divided into two camps: those who believed the accusations against Rabbi Yonatan and who were disgusted that a man with such a deep flaw could remain in a leadership position; and those who could not accept that a rabbi as great as Rabbi Yonatan could ever be a believer in the long-dead Shabbetai Tzvi and the ridiculous mystical system disseminated by his followers.

In fact, Rabbi Yaakov's rambling vituperative letters did not help the case against Rabbi Yonatan. On the contrary, those who read them and who might have been sympathetic to a case against Rabbi Yonatan based purely on the amulets dismissed any believable evidence once they read the exaggerated accusations coupled with ridiculous claims that Rabbi Yonatan was an ignorant fool.

THE KING OF DENMARK STEPS INTO THE FIGHT

With the controversy now raging full force across the Jewish world, it was inevitable that the gentile world would also become embroiled in the conflict. As the year progressed, incidents of public disorder increased in Hamburg and Altona, as arguments evolved into physical fights between supporters of Rabbi Yaakov and supporters of Rabbi Yonatan. One nasty fight on December 12, 1751 took place as a funeral was being conducted in the cemetery, and resulted in a court summons for Rabbi Yonatan, and on December 28 a violent fight broke out in the Hamburg Stock Exchange between a supporter of Rabbi Yaakov and a supporter of Rabbi Yonatan.

All the fights were the result of bitterness felt by Rabbi Yaakov's supporters at the success of Rabbi Yonatan's supporters in silencing and penalizing anyone who expressed any misgivings about the chief rabbi, or who expressed any interest in getting clarity on any aspect of the controversy.

In the fall of 1751 this animosity came to the attention of the young king of Denmark, Frederick V, whose kingdom included Altona, where Rabbi Yaakov owned his home and had resided for many years before running away. Rabbi Yaakov's close friend, Shmuel Hecksher, who was a member of the Triple Community board, had written a letter to his brother in Brunswick expressing doubt about Rabbi Yonatan's honesty, and also questioning why no major German rabbinic leaders had publicly supported the chief rabbi. Before the letter reached his brother it was intercepted and read by Rabbi Yonatan's supporters, who decided to punish its author.

Hecksher was humiliatingly deposed from the community board and expelled from Altona. He immediately appealed to King Frederick, and although the Hamburg City Council had no stake in his expulsion from Altona, which was in a different jurisdiction, it also demanded that Hecksher be readmitted into Altona, otherwise his antagonists would no longer be able to do business in Hamburg.

The main instigator in the Hecksher expulsion, Eliyahu Oppenheim, was forced to appear before the Hamburg authorities for his role in the affair, and after being fined a hefty sum he was ordered to present a list of all those who had formally joined the pro-Rabbi Yonatan faction in Altona. Oppenheim appealed to the Altona authorities for help, but they sided with Hecksher and their counterparts in Hamburg, and Hecksher was readmitted into Altona.

With this success in hand Rabbi Yaakov's supporters now formed the view that the gentile authorities could be the means for achieving Rabbi Yonatan's dismissal from office. In the first instance they appealed to the Hamburg City Council, alleging that Rabbi Yonatan had overstepped his legal rights by imposing punitive measures on his opponents. When this attempt failed to gain traction, a similar case was brought to the Royal Court of Denmark in Copenhagen, where both factions presented evidence to King Frederick himself. During the proceedings the king was also informed of Rabbi Yaakov's expulsion from Altona earlier in the year, and his ongoing exile in Amsterdam.

After a bitterly fought battle at the Royal Court, the king ruled that Rabbi Yaakov could return home to Altona and should be allowed to operate his printing press. The court also decided that Hecksher should be reinstated as a member of the Triple Community board. In addition, Rabbi Yonatan was ordered to appear personally before the king to explain his attempts to overreach his authority, and also the claims of heresy against him. It seemed, finally, that the tables had turned, although rather than the controversy being resolved by Jewish leaders, it would have to play itself out in a non-Jewish courtroom setting.

RABBI YAAKOV EMDEN RETURNS HOME

Rabbi Yaakov's supporters sent word to Rabbi Yaakov that the king had ruled that he should return home, but at first he was reluctant to return into the eye of the storm and instead hesitated in Amsterdam. Only after receiving an emotional letter from his wife begging him to come back did Rabbi Yaakov finally return to Altona, on August 3, 1752, having spent over fourteen months in exile.

Notwithstanding this triumph, Rabbi Yaakov's situation remained thoroughly unpleasant. Rabbi Yonatan was still the chief rabbi, and his defenders were defiant. And if this was not enough, Rabbi Yaakov's financial situation was in disarray due to his prolonged absence, and with each passing month, as more rabbis across the Jewish world declared their solidarity with Rabbi Yonatan, Rabbi Yaakov's prospects seemed bleaker than ever. Despite all this Rabbi Yaakov persisted with his unrelenting campaign against Rabbi Yonatan, whom he saw as epitomizing the dangers posed by Sabbatians, a group he believed were intent on insidiously inserting themselves and their perverse doctrines into mainstream Jewish life.

Rabbi Yaakov was petrified that unless he highlighted the threat, the uneducated Jewish masses, led by rabbis who dismissed the dangers of Sabbatianism as phantom nonsense, would sleepwalk into heretical oblivion, and particularly with someone like Rabbi Yonatan as a Sabbatian, this danger was heightened exponentially.

So rather than forcing him to reconsider his position, the more rabbis declared their support for Rabbi Yonatan, the more Rabbi Yaakov became convinced of the grave Sabbatian threat he represented. And the more people ridiculed the idea that someone of Rabbi Yonatan's caliber could believe in a long-dead messianic pretender, the more Rabbi Yaakov's mission to undermine Rabbi Yonatan in any way possible became his urgent priority.

SHOWDOWN IN COPENHAGEN

Meanwhile, King Frederick V of Denmark demanded that Rabbi Yonatan appear before him in Copenhagen and explain the controversial amulets. There was also official concern in the Royal Court about Rabbi Yonatan's position as chief rabbi. The king had been informed of a claim that Rabbi Yonatan's election to the coveted and much-contested chief rabbi position had been an absolute sham, with Rabbi Yaakov's supporters arguing that the number of people reported to have voted in his favor simply didn't make any sense.

Rabbi Yonatan was deeply disheartened by this turn of events, and wrote to friends and colleagues across Europe describing how disgusted he was that his opponents had resorted to the gentile court system, a tactic contrary to Jewish law. But although in isolation this may have been true, in reality the gentile courts had only intervened as a result of tactical moves made against Rabbi Yaakov's supporters by Rabbi Yonatan's allies, leading to repercussions that also affected local gentile businesses. And once the courts were involved, it was inevitable that each side would try to gain the upper hand. That being the case, Rabbi Yonatan's protestations, while not without foundation, were probably an expression of his disappointment that things had turned against him.

The protestations were also slightly disingenuous, as Rabbi Yonatan had consistently refused to appear before a *beit din* and be cross-examined by his accusers. In the final analysis, if there was no way to resolve the dispute equitably in a Jewish setting, surely the option of the gentile court, while regrettable, was the only alternative.

In anticipation of his upcoming court case, Rabbi Yonatan engaged the services of his former student, an apostate called Karl Anton. Anton was born Gershon Moshe Cohen, but after studying in Rabbi Yonatan's yeshiva he inexplicably converted to Christianity, changed his name, and eventually became the professor of Hebrew at Helmstadt

University, in Wurzburg, Bavaria. Rabbi Yaakov poured scorn on Rabbi Yonatan for hiring this outcast to assist him in his defense, although Rabbi Yonatan countered that he had no choice, as Anton was the only person he knew – perhaps the only person alive at that time – who was thoroughly familiar with rabbinic scholarship and could also conduct himself in formal German with ease, therefore allowing him to be comfortable in the official setting of the Royal Court while representing a rabbinic client accused of religious offenses.

Before approaching Anton, Rabbi Yonatan tried to hire a gentile called Rudolf von Neuendahl, an advocate with ties to the Danish judiciary. For whatever reason Neuendahl refused the brief, and Anton was the second choice. Months later Neuendahl agreed to discuss the case with Rabbi Yaakov, and he revealed that Karl Anton's spirited defense of his former teacher – a defense Rabbi Yaakov repudiated as a web of lies and evasion – had been entirely composed by none other than Rabbi Yonatan himself. Neuendahl knew this to be the case because he had seen the defense arguments before anyone else, when Rabbi Yonatan went through the file with him before hiring Anton.

After the court case was over Anton published his defense of Rabbi Yonatan, which revolved entirely around one particular amulet – an amulet Rabbi Yonatan accepted he had authored and had not been tampered with – in a German-language book titled *"Kurze Nachricht von dem Falschen Messias Sabbathai Zebhi und den neulich seinetwegen in Hamburg and Altona entstandenen bewegungen"* ("A short account concerning the false Messiah, Shabbetai Tzvi, and the events connected to him that recently took place in Hamburg and Altona").

Second choice or not, Anton performed very well in the courtroom. As a Hebrew professor at a gentile college he was completely comfortable explaining arcane rabbinic material to the uninitiated and, after being tutored by Rabbi Yonatan in the technicalities of mystical word formations of kabbalistic amulets, he totally mastered his brief before presenting the case. The trial attracted the attention of numerous journalists, religious scholars, and jurists from across Europe, all eager to find out more about the secretive world of Jewish mysticism and the details of its practical applications. Anton was undaunted by the packed courtroom. He took the obscure kabbalistic background that underpinned amulet authorship, and the detailed specifics of the particular amulet under examination, and submitted a compelling case on behalf of his client.

Words in the amulet that Rabbi Yaakov had claimed were coded references to Shabbetai Tzvi and his messianic mission, said Anton, were in reality coded acronyms for verses in the Bible, or were letter combinations that had appeared in kabbalistic works that were published long before Shabbetai Tzvi was born. It was simply preposterous, Anton claimed, to suggest that his esteemed client had been secretly referring to Shabbetai Tzvi when he inscribed these letter formations, if there was any other plausible explanation for the words and letters used in the amulet. After all, he said, there were so many different ciphers and cryptographs one could apply to the Hebrew alphabet that anyone who wanted to could easily force a Sabbatian connotation onto any text anywhere.

In a rousing closing speech Anton declared to the mesmerized courtroom that he had amply demonstrated, despite all the heated accusations, that his client had absolutely no case to answer:

"Everybody knows that Rabbi Jacob of Emden, despite his eminent lineage, is a sworn enemy of the chief rabbi. This is simply an undeniable fact. Moreover, Rabbi Jacob's knowledge of Kabbala is completely inferior to my client's familiarity with this ancient wisdom. All Rabbi Jacob knows are a few methods by which the Hebrew alphabet can be manipulated to mean this or that, or, indeed, anything.

"And the fact that he has rather cleverly insinuated heresy into the amulet that was composed by my client – the very same amulet we have studied so closely these past few days – has absolutely no bearing on my client's innocence or guilt. His spurious interpretations can be dismissed as the jealous rantings of a spiteful competitor, while my client's sterling reputation, and the love and devotion he is afforded by thousands of Jews both in his own community and in every European city, town, and village where Jewish communities exist, offer incontrovertible proof, beyond any reasonable doubt whatsoever, of my client's piety, his integrity, and his irrefutable dedication to the faith of his forefathers."

Anton now turned to the king, and unflinchingly looked him in the eye:

"Your Royal Majesty, it is my view that these proceedings have been a shameful waste of His Majesty's time. My client has on more than one occasion repudiated the false Messiah, Shabbetai Tzvi, along with any person or doctrine associated with that evil charlatan. May I respectfully request of His Majesty on my client's behalf – please do not permit this travesty against him to continue any longer. I implore His Majesty to declare my client innocent of all the charges so that he may be allowed to proceed with his duties as chief rabbi unhindered by unfounded rumors, lurid speculation, and groundless innuendo. Your Royal Majesty – surely enough is enough!"

With that final exclamation Anton bowed low and returned to his seat as the court erupted in excited conversation, overwhelmed by the fantastic drama that had played out there for day after day over a tiny scrap of parchment inscribed with a few Hebrew letters. Never before had the Royal Court of Denmark been witness to such proceedings. This was, after all, just a parochial dispute concerning an obscure religious matter – and yet it had been deliberated by the highest court of the land, and presided over by the king himself.

ROYAL VERDICT

The king retired with his advisers to consider the evidence. When they returned to the courtroom the verdict was unequivocal. In the first instance Rabbi Yonatan was completely exonerated of all the charges. Never again would anyone be allowed to cast any aspersions – neither spoken nor published – on the chief rabbi or his amulets. And secondly, so that Rabbi Yonatan's position as chief rabbi would no longer be in any doubt, the king ordered a new election to take place for the chief rabbinate position at the first available opportunity.

The election took place in December 1752, and Rabbi Yonatan was overwhelmingly reelected. But the unexpected victory and vindication were quickly diminished by other events. Almost immediately after his reelection as chief rabbi the Hamburg City Council – Hamburg was a "free" city not under the rule of the Danish king – rejected both the king's verdict and the election result, and a long, complex battle began to unfold over the formal definition of the chief rabbinate for the Triple Community, and about the powers the chief rabbi was legally entitled to. Simultaneous with this latest twist, the battle between rabbis across Europe over how to deal with Rabbi Yonatan's alleged Sabbatianism began to escalate, as positions hardened and enmity increased.

Rabbi Yonatan's strategy vis-à-vis his rabbinic accusers had been consistent throughout. He was only willing to present his version of what the amulets meant in a setting that did not include anyone qualified to challenge his version who would use the opportunity to defy him or disrespect him. This was his position throughout the controversy, and he resorted to numerous tactics to make sure that he would never be forced into any kind of hostile rabbinic hearing.

As far as Rabbi Yaakov was concerned, this evasive attitude alone proved that Rabbi Yonatan was guilty. Why would he not agree to a harsh cross-examination if he was as innocent as he claimed? Why was he so frightened of coming face-to-face with his opponents? Rabbi Yaakov believed he knew the answer. Rabbi Yonatan was acutely aware that if he was ever subjected to penetrating questions that he might be unable to answer, as opposed to the soft, respectful questions of deferential rabbis who held him in high esteem, his Sabbatianism would immediately be revealed for all to see. It was Rabbi Yonatan's unwillingness to appear before his accusers and the consequent presumption of guilt that underlined Rabbi Yaakov's ferocious attempts to destroy Rabbi Yonatan's reputation and see him unseated from his position.

It was inevitable that two distinct camps would emerge among the European rabbinate – one group that presumed Rabbi Yonatan's guilt but could not formulate an effective strategy to deal with it, and the other group that presumed Rabbi Yonatan's innocence but were seemingly unable to find any way to silence his critics.

THE FINAL RECONCILIATION ATTEMPT

It was at this point that Rabbi Yehezkel Landau stepped into the picture. Much later in his career Rabbi Landau would become famous as chief rabbi of Prague and as author of the scholarly work *Noda BiYehuda*, but in 1752 he was the relatively unknown thirty-nine-year-old rabbi of Yampol, a small town in Ukraine a thousand miles from Hamburg, who had never met Rabbi Yonatan Eybeschutz or Rabbi Yaakov Emden.

For some unknown reason Rabbi Landau felt compelled to resolve the epic dispute that had erupted between these two rabbinic titans, each of whom was old enough to be his father. To that end he wrote a long "letter of reconciliation" suggesting a compromise solution which allowed both Rabbi Yonatan and Rabbi Yaakov, along with all their supporters, to walk away with their pride and reputations intact.

The letter was diplomatically worded and cleverly constructed. It painted Rabbi Yonatan as one of the greatest rabbis of the time, whose understandable but misplaced mistreatment of Rabbi Yaakov had stained an otherwise unblemished reputation. It was a wrong that had to be put right, especially as Rabbi Yaakov clearly had grounds to behave as he did. To have publicly embarrassed Rabbi Yaakov by banning anyone from communicating with him and to then have him hounded out of town was simply not an appropriate way to behave toward a distinguished rabbi, and particularly Rabbi Yaakov, whose dedication to the most stringent Torah-observant life and whose positive influence on those around him were beyond question. Only rabbis who lead people astray can be placed under any kind of ban, said Rabbi Landau, and Rabbi Yaakov was certainly not in that category.

Rabbi Yonatan might propose that Rabbi Yaakov did lead people astray by suggesting he was a fraud, and I can see why he would say that. Rabbi Yonatan has been an exemplary teacher of Torah to thousands of students across the Jewish world, many of whom have their own students, making him the teacher of virtually every Torah scholar in Europe. If doubts are raised about him it would put the credentials of all those scholars into doubt, and Rabbi Yonatan might understand that as someone leading people astray. But in my opinion this would only be the case if Rabbi Yaakov deliberately led them astray, and this was not the case. On the contrary! We know that his intentions were to prevent people from going astray! That being the case he should never have been excommunicated, and never been expelled.

Rabbi Landau had clearly examined the notarized amulets from Metz, and was convinced they contained letter formations that referred to Shabbetai

Tzvi. But he had two superb observations to make – one that was a face-saving device for Rabbi Yonatan, the other a wise insight into the potential threat posed by the author of the amulets. In the first instance he questioned whether any notarized document that condemned a third party was valid under Jewish law, if that third party was not present when the document was notarized. He also noted that none of the amulets in question had been signed by Rabbi Yonatan, and it was therefore impossible to establish with any halakhic certainty that he had written them. In other words, he was providing Rabbi Yonatan with a graceful avenue to deny the authorship of any amulet that had a Sabbatian link.

His second point was even more astute:

> Although I made every effort to decipher the amulets in a way that would not lend support to the nonsensical teachings of the Sabbatian fools, I did not succeed in doing so. Nonetheless, I do not read them as heretical texts, for the heresy is not explicit.

With this remarkable proposition Rabbi Landau completely deflated the suggestion that Rabbi Yonatan posed any kind of threat to the future of Judaism, even if it was irrefutably true that the amulets attributed to him contained references to the false Messiah. As long as the amulets were destroyed, and Rabbi Yonatan visibly behaved in accordance with Jewish law and conducted himself according to the standards expected of a great rabbi, what difference did it make if he had surreptitiously inserted incomprehensible Sabbatian word puzzles into amulets that influenced nobody to believe in the messianic mission of the long-dead Shabbetai Tzvi?

To resolve the dispute Rabbi Landau proposed that all the amulets that had ever been attributed to Rabbi Yonatan should be handed over to the Jewish authorities and never used again, so that no one would be misled by their contents to believe in Sabbatian heresy. He also proposed that Rabbi Yonatan publicly declare that he would never write another amulet, so that no Sabbatian heretics would ever again be able to claim that he was partial to their cause. Rabbi Landau concluded his proposal with a forceful warning against any further mistreatment or criticism of Rabbi Yaakov for his campaign against Rabbi Yonatan.

Rabbi Landau's letter was widely circulated, and although it clearly implied that Rabbi Yonatan was the author of the amulets, the suggested compromise solution was nonetheless warmly welcomed by Rabbi Yonatan and his supporters, who clearly understood how Rabbi Landau's proposal set out a workable exit strategy that wiped the slate clean, and offered a way forward devoid of controversy, as long as no further associations between Rabbi Yonatan and Sabbatian heresy were ever discovered.

But Rabbi Yaakov was in no mood for a compromise of any kind. As far as he was concerned this was a holy war. Rabbi Yonatan had to be defrocked and humiliated. No other end to the dispute was acceptable. In a viciously worded pamphlet against the "letter of reconciliation" Rabbi Yaakov called Rabbi Landau every name imaginable, and even accused him of being a closet Sabbatian who desired Rabbi Yonatan's exoneration and rehabilitation.

AN INCONCLUSIVE CONCLUSION

The controversy had essentially reached a stalemate. Although Rabbi Yonatan remained chief rabbi of Altona, in Hamburg his powers were stripped away by the city council, and by the time they were reinstated some years later, the issue had become largely irrelevant. In the rabbinic world Rabbi Yonatan's opponents were unyielding in their antipathy toward him, and they continued to insist that he was an unrepentant heretic. Meanwhile, Rabbi Yonatan's supporters rallied to his cause, and hundreds of rabbis responded to his request for letters of support. He published them in 1755 as part of a book called *Luḥot Edut*, which also recorded his version of events.

Rabbi Yaakov continued to publish regular attacks against his nemesis, and in 1760 the controversy gained a new lease on life when Rabbi Yonatan's younger son, Wolf Eybeschutz, declared himself a Sabbatian prophet, and was then exposed as a close friend to a number of known heretics. As a result of this incident Rabbi Yonatan's yeshiva was closed down for good.

Rabbi Yonatan died in 1764, but even his passing did not end the controversy. Rabbi Yaakov continued to publish his attacks, and to maintain that Sabbatian heresy remained a very real threat to every

Jewish community. Rabbi Yaakov's death in 1776, and subsequent burial in close proximity to Rabbi Yonatan as a result of Rabbi Landau's halakhic ruling, finally brought the personal dispute to an end.

Ultimately it was Rabbi Landau's resolution that was the blueprint for future generations. Rabbi Yonatan's extensive scholarship was recorded in the numerous works, mainly published after his death, that are mainstays of Jewish learning to this day, principally as a result of Rabbi Landau's suggestion that if someone is in every sense a devout Jew and an exemplary rabbi, unverifiable aberrations ascribed to him must be completely disregarded.

Rabbi Yaakov is equally venerated as an exemplary rabbi who fought a valiant battle against a man he regarded as a dangerous heretic, and his works on Talmud, Halakha, and prayer continue to be widely used and respected.

In the final analysis, was Rabbi Yaakov right? Was Rabbi Yonatan really a Sabbatian? And if he was a Sabbatian, did he actually pose a danger to normative Judaism? There are multiple answers to these questions, but none is conclusive or definitive. What is absolutely clear is that Rabbi Yaakov truly believed Rabbi Yonatan was a Sabbatian, and he believed Rabbi Yonatan was a subversive who needed to be ousted from his senior rabbinic position and confined to the margins of Jewish life.

And Rabbi Yaakov was not alone. Even among those who ostensibly supported Rabbi Yonatan there were rabbis, like Rabbi Landau, who did not accept his protestations of innocence, although they still offered to support him in the belief that the belligerent campaign against him was ultimately very damaging to Jewish life, and that supporting him was therefore the lesser of two evils.

Throughout the saga Rabbi Yonatan was tactically very smart, bettering Rabbi Yaakov and his supporters at every stage, but his camp's overall strategy was not smart and was often counterproductive. In the belief that his reputation far outweighed any attempt to malign him, Rabbi Yonatan refused to take his interlocutors seriously, and he constantly sought to neutralize them without engaging with them directly, which only infuriated them more.

Of course hubris is not proof of guilt, nor can some of Rabbi Yonatan's more ridiculous claims vis-à-vis the amulets be used to condemn him. And yet it is a sad fact that he died without having conclusively shaken off the cloud of suspicion that hung over him. But ultimately, whether or not he was a Sabbatian sympathizer is a question that no longer has any relevance. Both Rabbi Yonatan Eybeschutz and Rabbi Yaakov Emden, despite the vicious *maḥloket* that so scarred the last years of their lives, are considered two of the most prominent rabbinic luminaries to have graced us with their presence and scholarship in the early modern era.

Chapter 4

The Infamous Case
of the *Get* of Cleves

Cleves, 1766

"*Why would you presume to write a legal opinion on the [Get of Cleves] case?... We are perfectly able to clarify this matter according to Jewish law without anyone's help, nor do we need to explain ourselves to anyone.*"

– *Frankfurt Rabbinate, January 1767, in response to a letter from Rabbi Shaul Lowenstamm, chief rabbi of Amsterdam*

꘎ כרוז ꘎

꘎ למען דעת כל עמי הארץ ꘎

שככל הדברים האלה הוכרז בקק פפ דמיין ביום א ג
אדר תקכ"ח לפק לעת ערב אחר תפלת מנחה
בבה"כ ישן וחדש:

שמעו גם עם כי המזידים על דבר • וזאת מיר ביכקהלין איזט וזמרטין אוֹז גו רופין כטם הקיק האלופי' קניטי'
פיז יין • נגירוף האלופי' קניטי' גובים יין • ונגירוף שני ב"ד יין • וכדאלטם הגאון תכ"ד גרלי' כאשר שהקהל
נשמע כרמה' • מהגודל המחולפש ורשעות מה שנעשלם לבתך בכתב לאחד להנאלתכ"ל גרלי טה"י רק מכורך בתכריך • וניכתב
כדרעם אלוח בכתב גלוחה' • וכתוך ההכריך כמאל כתב הג"ל מאזיה רבניס במדיכות פולין כגירוף אזיה אכשיס אשר
לא יד מש אדם מה טנעשב ומה שיחס' • רק לאחד מזוחד מהם מהם פעמו שלמה כהלמה מרככת המשכה רב הכולל דקק
זאמשט ונגיל ארדנגרייא יין • הוא לוֹש מפורסם לכל מי שהולך על יריד ליימפניג • ורווֹה קונפערטוין שפילין • אך תן
הרב הג"ל דאכרייא פינדן' • גם רגיל תתיד בשתוק שֹך כאכיל • והרמו בלגב הרנה ודכרי כזיאות וחטושב יהירה על
הפירדם של הגאלתכ"ד גרלי' ושני ב"ד יין • אשר הוסקב ג"כ זֵגֵת הגאלתן החקצי' החמ יכ אבד' דקק מנסיי' וז"ל עם צירוזפי'
האלופי' הדייניס ולומדיס מוכלניס ישכי בהד"ר דשם ' בדבר הנֵטַ הגידם לר' פיקב ג"ה מקק מנסיי' יע"א לכֹשתו
לאֵה בת הר"י יוקב ג"ה מקק כונב יע"א • תן קקק מנסיי' יע"א • וכרכו בגיוה כרוזיה קן קן קהלהינו יע"א • והם מכשירים אֹת הנֵטַ וכתב העשם כחתול
מהגב כאר • כי כודאי לא יצא מתחת יד הרב דקלֵויווֹש וזי' הצדק דבר שאינו מתוקן' • וכתב הג"ל הוא מקוים שהוֹב
התהתק אוֹת בלחום חגוף הכתב ע"י הרי נאפגניס קֵק כונב יע"א • הנקוניס כשמהוֹ' • שם האפר דוד ש"ן ונאמן פה
קֵק כונב' • שם השני ישֵככר כער שֵם ונאמן פר קֵק כונב' • והנב כעה מיטל עלינו לקייס מאמר מֵזל תפרסמין אֹת
הענוׂיפים וכי' • ולפרסם מי הוֹא הרב המקדר ר' ישראל דקלֵויווֹש הג"ל עם כדיה' • אשר סמכו עתה אזיה רבניס דמדיכות
תולין עם צירוֹתיהם אזיה אכשיס הג"ל ' וגם כבר סמכו אזיה רבני גאֹלוׂי הדור עליו הג"ל ועל חביריו **המסית ומדיח**
רישמעון קאפנהאנז אשר הוא מפורסם בסוד משחקים של לומברי
שפיֹלֵר • וכל אֹשֵר מיני שחוק אֹשֵר התחבר אֹל רעֹת הרב המקדר ר' ישראל בקלֵויווֹש הג"ל • אֹשֵר ה"י מקים הוֹי'
ליתוֹאה • וכאֹשֵר המקדר ר' ישראל הג"ל התיר מתחלה לאֹשתו לֵֹאֹת פנֵם שני אכשיס ע"פ נֵטַ נעֹל • כן התיר נ"כ ג לֵֹשֹת
שהֹי נשֹיס לֵֹאֹיס אֹחר הֹר בכפר הֹר התר בֹר הֹ וזמֹן מרדכי • ועורֹד מחֹיק בֹתֹי נֹסֹי' והֹלֵֹם תרֹדכֹי הג"ל כֹלֹא אֹשֹה אֹשֹה יֹקֹרה
על אֹשֹהֹ ע"פ היתר המקדר ר' ישראל בקלֵויווֹש הג"ל • כֹאֹשֹר כֹלֹא לֵֹדֹיֹנֹו דֹבֹרֹי שֹויֹש שֹלֹו • מתחֹת הֹסֹיֹהֹר של שֹהֹי נֹסֹים
הג"ל עם הכתוכיס שֹכֹהֹב לֹה לֵֹלֹוֹפֹיֹס דֹיֹיֹכֹים מֹוֹזֹמֹיֹס כֹל"י רֹכֹב דֹקֹק כֹרֹלֹין יֹע"א • והֹתֹשֹוֹבֹה הֹג"ל יֹפֹוֹרֹסֹם אֹלֹיֹך כֹרֹבֹיֹס
שֹם כֹאֹשֹר בֹכֹתֹבֹיֹם אֹלֹו • דֹם אֹר ט"ט הֹגֹרֹיֹם לֵֹהֹגֹדֹיֹר דֹקֹק כֹרֹלֹין דֹקֹק כֹרֹלֹין יֹע"א עֹם שֹפֹרֹתֹכֹם וֹזֹֹאֹן ג"כ מֹתֹיֹר וֹיֹרֹיֹן לֹאֹוֹתֹו אֹֹש
תֹרֹדֹכֹי הג"ל לֵֹאֹשֹא אֹשֹה אֹחֹרֹת על אֹשֹתֹו וֹכֹטֹבֹע על כֹל לֹקֹיֹס בֹכֹשֹמֹתֹו לֹיֹתֹן שֹכֹר מֹצֹאֹלֹב כֹלֹי גֹרֹעֹון אֹס וֹיֹכֹיֹהֹו עֹתֹו לֹהֹתֹר •
גֹם נֹאֹפֹר בֹכֹתֹבֹיֹם הג"ל וֹתֹקֹנֹש מֹכֹלֹדֹר דֹשֹם לֹהֹשֹקֹיֹס עֹמֹו לֵֹהֹשֹֹיֹר הֹגֹט נֹל שֹל רֹמֹ נֹל הֹג"ל • לֹוֹכֹד ג"כ שֹכֹר הֹסֹיֹהֹר פֹר שֹפֹרֹלֹכֹין

Public notice issued by Frankfurt rabbinate annulling the *Get* of Cleves, 1768

WEDDING IN MANNHEIM

In the late eighteenth century, a seemingly innocuous divorce in a provincial German town evolved into one of the most bitterly fought Jewish legal controversies of the era, involving the most famous rabbis of the day. The story of the *Get** of Cleves was an extraordinary episode involving intrigue, ego, and hubris. At the center of it all was a young couple whose personal lives were humiliatingly discussed and debated by rabbis and communities across Europe.

Modern secular law defines insanity as "mental illness of such a severe nature that a person cannot distinguish fantasy from reality, cannot conduct his or her affairs due to psychosis, or is subject to uncontrollable impulsive behavior." Insanity is normally used as a defense in criminal cases. The most common variety is cognitive insanity, which means that the alleged criminal was so impaired by insanity when committing a crime that he or she did not know that the crime committed was wrong.

Another form of insanity is volitional insanity, or "irresistible impulse," which refers to someone who is able to distinguish right from wrong, but has a temporary mental breakdown making him incapable of controlling his actions. This defense is commonly used in crimes of vengeance.

There is another condition that can affect a legal transaction, called "incompetency." Civil law requires a person to be legally competent in order to enter into a contract, or sign a will, or make any type of binding legal commitment. In contract law a person who agrees to a transaction becomes liable for duties under the contract unless he was legally incompetent at the time the contract was entered into. If someone does not comprehend the nature and consequences of a contract, he is regarded as having mental incapacity.

---

* A *get* is the official legal document that records the divorce between a man and his wife, and it is crucial that it is executed correctly, as the consequences of an invalid *get* would be a disaster. If the non-divorced wife remarries, she and her new husband are guilty of adultery, while any children would be considered *mamzerim* – halakhic bastards. For this reason, the rabbis who preside over a *get* take great care to do it properly, and the Talmud is extremely critical of those who retroactively question the validity of a *get*.

But how does Jewish law define insanity and incompetence, and what are the implications of an act carried out, or a contract entered into, by an insane or incompetent individual? The *Get* of Cleves saga was a watershed halakhic divorce case that brought all these issues into sharp focus.

In the late spring or early summer of 1766, a young man called Isaac Neiberg from Mannheim, Germany, became engaged to Leah Gunzhausen of Bonn, also a town in Germany. During the engagement period Isaac visited his fiancée and appeared to all to be perfectly normal and happy. On Friday, August 8, 1766, Leah and her parents arrived in Mannheim to join the groom and his family in anticipation of the wedding that was taking place the following Tuesday. Among the friends and family who joined them was their cousin, Rabbi Aharon Shimon Copenhagen, a rabbinic scholar who would later play a crucial role in providing the details of the strange story that unfolded over the next couple of weeks.

Friday night passed without incident, but on Shabbat morning something was not right. Without explanation Isaac became agitated and anxious. He paced up and down and muttered to himself, and no one could calm him down. His demeanor was so strange that Leah's parents began to worry about his mental state. They sat him down and asked him why he was so troubled. After some prompting Isaac explained that he was upset over a new apartment his father had promised to give him after the wedding, which his father had suddenly decided to instead give to his sister and her new husband. Although another apartment had been set aside for him, he claimed to be concerned that this smaller accommodation would not be sufficient for him and Leah once they were married and had children.

Leah's parents were satisfied that this explained Isaac's strange behavior and immediately went to confront Isaac's father, who, after a short negotiation, agreed to honor the original promise and allow Isaac and Leah to move into the larger accommodation.

With everything seemingly settled, the wedding took place as planned on the following Tuesday. Isaac addressed the wedding banquet, and acted in a composed and dignified way. But the following Shabbat morning Isaac was nowhere to be found. After a comprehensive search involving the local gentile authorities, it was discovered that not only had he disappeared, but he had absconded with a large sum of money. This was highly unorthodox behavior for an Orthodox Jew on Shabbat, and particularly strange behavior for someone in the midst of his own wedding week celebrations.

Both families panicked and hired a search party to look for him in the surrounding villages. Isaac was eventually discovered hiding under some hay in a farmhouse belonging to a non-Jew, about four hours' journey from Mannheim. He was brought back to Mannheim, but was very agitated and kept on repeating that he needed to run away to escape government agents who were intent on killing him.

Simultaneously, and perhaps as a result of what was going on, the two families began to bicker over financial support for the couple. A mediator was called in, and the dispute was settled. As part of the settlement it was agreed that the couple would not stay in Mannheim as originally planned, but would instead move to Bonn with Leah's family, at least for the immediate future. Everyone was happy with the new arrangement, especially Isaac, who was delighted to be leaving.

DIVORCE IN CLEVES

On August 19, 1766, exactly one week after the wedding, the young couple left Mannheim and began their journey to Bonn, together with Leah's family and the friends from Bonn who had attended the celebrations. The following night, at a Jewish inn near Mainz, an innocent conversation involving the innkeeper that touched on the story of the groom who had run away the previous Shabbat resulted in Isaac becoming completely hysterical. The family eventually calmed him down, but once again his strange behavior had become a cause for concern.

The journey toward Bonn continued, and the family arrived on Friday just before Shabbat. The following morning Isaac attended prayers and was called up to say the blessing over the Torah. Notwithstanding the outburst in Mainz his demeanor throughout Shabbat was serene and relaxed.

But beneath the surface Isaac was in total turmoil. On Saturday night straight after Shabbat he sent for Rabbi Copenhagen and begged for his help to arrange a divorce. Rabbi Copenhagen was dumbstruck.

"What are you talking about? Why would you want to divorce Leah?" he inquired incredulously.

Isaac responded that he had begun to feel that Leah disliked him, and he could not live with someone who disapproved of him. He then added that his life was in grave danger, for reasons he could not divulge, and he needed to leave Germany immediately. His abrupt departure would mean that Leah would still be his wife and be unable to remarry, he said, particularly if his enemies caught up with him and killed him without anyone knowing. For this reason he wanted to divorce her while he still could, rather than cause her and her family the anguish associated with a missing husband unable to provide his wife with a *get*.

Rabbi Copenhagen was a wise and worldly man, and he told Isaac to consider the matter overnight while he conferred with the family. Having thereby created a breathing space, he ran to Leah's father and reported his conversation with Isaac, and the two of them agonized through the night trying to figure out what to do. The following morning Rabbi Copenhagen told Isaac that he had no solution to suggest as yet, but was happy to continue discussing options and ideas.

But Isaac was adamant and responded that he was not interested in any solution. Having reflected carefully since his conversation with the rabbi, he had decided to divorce Leah without delay so that he could escape the mortal danger he faced. If Leah or her family would not agree to cooperate, that was their choice, but meanwhile his bags were packed and he was ready to leave for London, where he felt he would be safe.

After an intense conference, Leah's family concluded it was best to just go ahead with the divorce and put an end to the matter. Isaac was itching to leave, which meant that they could not execute the divorce in Bonn, so the family decided to accompany him on the first part of his journey and arrange for the *get* to be given in Cleves, a small town on the German side of the border with Holland. The rabbi of the provincial community was a respected scholar called Rabbi Yisrael Lipschuetz, who everyone was satisfied would be helpful in the unusual circumstances, and would do what was necessary in an efficient and proper way.

So, on Sunday morning, Isaac, Leah, Rabbi Copenhagen, Leah's brother, and another relative left Bonn and headed toward Cleves. The hundred-mile journey took them a couple of days, and they arrived there on Tuesday, August 26 – exactly two weeks after the wedding. Rabbi Lipschuetz was understandably taken aback when this unexpected delegation arrived at his door, particularly when he heard what they wanted. Isaac explained what had happened and why he wanted the divorce, albeit without mentioning his Shabbat disappearance. He was lucid and composed throughout, though, and articulated perfectly why he felt the need to end his marriage. The rabbi explained the divorce process to him, and he seemed to understand every aspect, as well as the implications of the detailed asset separation that had been agreed between him and Leah's relatives.

Isaac was insistent that they press ahead with the divorce as quickly as possible. He also asked that the divorce not be publicized in Cleves, as he had heard there were people there from Mannheim, and he did not want them to hear about what had happened and report back to his parents.

As the scribe wrote out the divorce document, Rabbi Lipschuetz took Isaac aside and tried to talk him out of what he was doing. Explaining that he found what was happening extremely upsetting and puzzling, he added that he was concerned that Isaac's parents would be devastated when they found out what he had done. Isaac was unyielding and replied that it would be too dangerous for him to go back to Mannheim, claiming that if he returned there he would be executed on the spot, although he still refused to elaborate. The divorce proceedings went ahead, and the *get* was given to Leah in front of witnesses, as required by Jewish law.

THE CONTROVERSY BEGINS

The following day Isaac and Leah parted ways. She returned to Bonn with her family, and he left for London. Within days Isaac's parents discovered what had happened, and after the shock had worn off, rage set in, prompted by the belief that Leah's family had taken advantage of their vulnerable son. In addition, Isaac's parents were upset that the asset separation had been decided so heavily in Leah's favor. Isaac's father insisted on an emergency meeting with the local rabbi, Rabbi Tevele Hess, who knew Isaac well and had attended the wedding. At the meeting he told Rabbi Hess the story as it had been conveyed to him and insisted that the rabbi find some way to annul the divorce, which as far as he was concerned was a complete sham.

Although Rabbi Hess was a distinguished rabbinic scholar in his own right, he did not feel sufficiently qualified to perform an annulment. Instead he did something that would turn this parochial story into an international controversy – he wrote a detailed letter, co-signed by nine other rabbis, that described the situation, to one of the most famous rabbinic courts in Europe, the illustrious *beit din* of Frankfurt.

The Frankfurt *beit din* was headed by Rabbi Avraham Abish Feld, author of the authoritative halakhic work *Birkat Avraham*. Rabbi Abish, as he was known, was one of the most eminent rabbinic authorities in Germany, renowned not only as an exceptional expert in Jewish law, but also for his piety and dignity.

The letter from Rabbi Hess ended with a simple request – on the basis that Isaac had not been competent at the time of the divorce, Rabbi Abish and his colleagues should annul the *Get* of Cleves, which would mean that Isaac and Leah were still married. This request was a sensation, and the response of the Frankfurt *beit din* would reverberate around the Jewish world in a controversy that embroiled rabbis far and wide.

CAN A JEWISH DIVORCE BE ANNULLED?

There were two questions that hovered in the background as the controversy gathered pace: Can someone who is mentally incompetent divorce his wife according to Jewish law? And if such a man does divorce his wife, what is the legal status of the divorce after it is executed? The Mishna in Tractate Gittin, which records the laws of divorce, states that "if a man is seized with *kordiakos* and says, 'Write a *get* for my wife,' it is as if he has said nothing. If he says, 'Write a *get* for my wife,' and is only then seized with *kordiakos*, during which time he says, 'Don't write it,' his latter words are considered null and void."

According to the Gemara that explains this mishna, *kordiakos* is a form of mental illness with symptoms that are similar to the behavior of someone who has become completely incapacitated through inebriation, after he has drunk a potent wine directly from a fermentation barrel. Such a person cannot be taken seriously, as he is not lucid, which would mean that when he issued the command to write a *get*, even if the *get* was written properly, and even if he later recovers from his mental episode and says he wants to divorce his wife, the *get* written while he was incapacitated is not valid and cannot be used for the divorce.

The doubt concerning the *Get* of Cleves centered over Isaac's sanity at the time he had instructed that the *get* be written and given to Leah. Was he suffering from a chronic mental illness that diminished his competence? Or were the strange incidents at the time of his wedding just a temporary mental breakdown, and did he then recover? Perhaps it was possible, however remote such a possibility may have been, that Isaac's life was really in danger at the time of the *get*, for reasons he could not reveal, and indeed never revealed. Even if he was in the throes of a mental breakdown, did it invalidate his instructions to Rabbi Lipschuetz for the *get* to be written?

Isaac's father was insistent that his son had been in the midst of a severe mental breakdown when he issued the instruction in Cleves to write the *get*, and on this basis lobbied frantically and relentlessly for the divorce to be annulled, even if it could be proved that Isaac had since recovered and wanted the divorce to stand. Isaac's father cited the various episodes of Isaac's strange behavior before and after the wedding, and claimed that when Rabbi Lipschuetz of Cleves had agreed that the *get* be written, he had been unaware of the full history, and therefore the *get* had no legal status.

Those who advocated for the *get*'s annulment were also disturbed by the underhanded way in which it had been obtained. Isaac's parents had not been informed in advance, they argued, and no attempt had been made to inform them subsequently. According to them this was extremely suspicious behavior. They also questioned why the divorce had been executed in Cleves, which was a remote and insignificant community. There were larger cities with more substantial communities closer to Bonn, such as Dusseldorf and Koblenz, both with outstanding rabbis who were perfectly capable of arranging a proper *get*. Why had Leah and her family traveled the greater distance to Cleves? And finally, why had the *get* proceeded before the couple had even had time to establish their physical relationship, which had ceased after the marital act on the night of the wedding?

The advocates for the annulment drew the conclusion that Isaac was crazy, or had been at around the time this had all happened, and

Leah's family had consequently arranged for the *get* to be executed in a secretive manner, to ensure that Leah did not become encumbered for life with a crazy husband. The claim was that the family had manipulated Isaac into divorcing Leah, and arranged for it to happen in a remote location with no oversight, without informing the rabbi who arranged the divorce that Isaac was not competent to execute it.

Those opposed to the *Get* of Cleves also cited the talmudic dictum which states that no one spends a large sum of money and wastes time getting married, only to then divorce his wife immediately afterward. It was well known that Isaac's family had invested an enormous amount of time and money into his marriage to Leah. Isaac himself had borrowed a large sum of money to pay for his marital wardrobe. Thus it was inconceivable that Isaac would have divorced his wife a couple of weeks later unless he was clinically, and therefore halakhically, crazy.

Despite their arguments that the divorce should be annulled, the rabbis and others who supported Isaac's parents were in a distinct minority. The majority view was that the only thing Isaac had done to put his sanity into question was his unexpected and unexplained disappearance with the money on Shabbat morning after his wedding. Since he had only acted abnormally on that one occasion, he could not be judged as someone who had descended into madness.

Some rabbis even felt that the Shabbat incident could not be defined as "insane," as Isaac genuinely believed that he was being targeted by some person, or group of people, and assumed his life was in danger. Although he had no proof this danger was real, or at least he had not offered any, that did not mean his story was a fabrication or simply a figment of his imagination. It was perfectly possible that his life had been in danger, in which case his Shabbat disappearance was perfectly reasonable.

In any event, the definitive arbiter of Jewish law, the *Shulḥan Arukh*, states unequivocally that "a man who fluctuates between lucid and crazy – when he is lucid he is to be regarded as completely normal in everything he does, and if he divorces his wife in that time, his *get* is considered valid." Rabbi Lipschuetz of Cleves maintained unequivocally that Isaac had been completely lucid throughout the divorce proceedings. Six members of the Cleves Jewish community who were present at the proceedings also testified that Isaac had behaved completely normally – not just during the proceedings, but throughout his stay in Cleves. Rabbi Copenhagen, who had accompanied Leah and Isaac to Cleves and was present throughout the divorce, also confirmed that Isaac's behavior had been reasonable the entire time.

THE FRANKFURT RABBINATE
AND RABBINIC JURISDICTION

Another relevant issue began to emerge as more rabbis and community leaders became involved in the dispute and the controversy grew. Many people felt that it was entirely out of place for the Frankfurt rabbis – however distinguished and respected they were – to interfere in an affair that was beyond their jurisdiction. The *get* had been granted by Rabbi Lipschuetz, and was therefore his sole responsibility. It had always been the custom in Germany that a *beit din* in one location did not interfere with or intervene in the decisions and activities of a *beit din* in another location. It was therefore felt that the Frankfurt *beit din* was out of line in expressing an opinion on a matter that was essentially none of their business.

Despite the eminence of the Frankfurt rabbinate, numerous rabbis across Germany announced their full support for Rabbi Lipschuetz. Furnished with the details of the story, and knowing him as a man of unimpeachable integrity, and as a rabbi well versed in the laws of Jewish divorce who knew the implications of a non-divorced woman marrying another husband, they simply refused to believe that he would allow such a travesty to unfold simply to protect his reputation.

The man who had originally triggered the controversy by writing to the Frankfurt rabbinate, Rabbi Tevele Hess of Mannheim, unexpectedly died shortly after the controversy began. His plan had been simple, if somewhat naïve. He had wanted the rabbis of Frankfurt to nullify the *get*, and then have Isaac interviewed by a panel of experts upon his return from London to Mannheim. If he was found to be perfectly sane – as all those who supported the *get* claimed he was – he would simply be asked to issue a new *get* and the problem would be resolved.

When Rabbi Hess died, however, the matter was taken up by the *dayanim* of Frankfurt, and their agenda was totally different from his.

They believed that they had to take a stand against sloppy rabbinic practices, and it was their opinion that the only reason Rabbi Lipschuetz of Cleves had not realized that Isaac was suffering from mental illness was because he had not been given all the details of Isaac's strange behavior. This exposed his lack of professionalism, a failing that had resulted in an untenable and unsupportable *get*.

Rabbi Lipschuetz himself was incredulous at the obstinacy of the Frankfurt *beit din*, and in the fall of 1766 wrote a formal ruling validating the *Get* of Cleves and dispatched a copy of his ruling to Frankfurt. In a subsequent letter to Frankfurt he included witness statements from several residents of Cleves who had come into contact with Isaac. Some of these witnesses had even participated in the divorce proceedings. They all agreed that Isaac had acted normally throughout. But despite this, and the halakhic arguments presented by Rabbi Lipschuetz, the Frankfurt *beit din* did not even acknowledge receiving the documents or reply to Rabbi Lipschuetz.

This refusal to engage with Rabbi Lipschuetz was extremely unorthodox. It also reflected badly on the Frankfurt rabbinate in light of the way another rabbi whom Rabbi Hess had approached had reacted to his original letter. When Rabbi Hess had sent his missive to Frankfurt requesting the annulment, he had sent an almost identical letter to Rabbi Naftali Hirsch Katzenellenbogen of Pfalz. The first thing Rabbi Katzenellenbogen had done was to ask Rabbi Lipschuetz about the exact details of the divorce. Rabbi Lipschuetz responded immediately with a comprehensive timeline. Upon receiving Rabbi Lipschuetz's letter, Rabbi Katzenellenbogen wrote to Rabbi Hess to tell him that the *Get* of Cleves was perfectly valid, and the divorce stood. He also castigated Rabbi Hess for having written to anyone else before contacting Rabbi Lipschuetz, describing this as an unforgivable breach of protocol.

Rabbi Hess had also asked Rabbi Katzenellenbogen to consult with his brother and brother-in-law, both of them rabbis. They concurred that the *get* was valid. Rabbi Katzenellenbogen's brother-in-law, Rabbi Yosef Steinhardt of Fuerth, was evidently so incensed by the behavior of the Frankfurt rabbinate that he wrote a strong letter to Rabbi Abish, the chief rabbi of Frankfurt, to make his feelings clear, but his pleas to Frankfurt to cease their involvement were to no avail.

As the months rolled by it became evident to Rabbi Abish and his rabbinic colleagues that Rabbi Lipschuetz was not going to concede, and that they needed to counteract his efforts against them. So they summoned Rabbi Copenhagen to Frankfurt, along with members of Bonn's Jewish community, on the pretext that they needed to thoroughly investigate the events surrounding the divorce. Rabbi Copenhagen, believing they were now looking for a face-saving way to reverse their position, agreed to come to Frankfurt and gathered together a delegation of senior community figures to accompany him. The delegation arrived in Frankfurt during Ḥanukka of 1766, and stayed there for three weeks. At hearing after hearing they were questioned and cross-examined by the Frankfurt rabbis about every detail of the episode, including the divorce itself. Every word was faithfully recorded by the court scribe, and Rabbi Copenhagen was convinced the evidence provided was conclusive in favor of the *get*.

But within a couple of weeks the Frankfurt *beit din* sent a letter to Bonn curtly informing the community leadership that after having carefully considered the testimony presented, the Frankfurt rabbis had concluded that their original view was correct, and the *get* could not be used – meaning that Leah was forbidden to remarry, and if she did remarry, her children would be *mamzerim*.

Despite being so belligerently confident, the Frankfurt rabbis were clearly conscious that their position was controversial, and so they also wrote to a former Frankfurt rabbi, Rabbi David Tevele Schiff – who was now chief rabbi of London – and asked him to interview Isaac in London to find out if he was sane, or whether he was in fact suffering from mental illness, as was being claimed by his father. They were also interested in hearing Isaac's version of events. Rabbi Schiff met with Isaac and they spoke for some time. In a letter back to Frankfurt he described how he had found Isaac to be completely sane, although Isaac had admitted that his behavior around the time of his marriage and divorce was objectively irrational. In terms of Jewish law his admission was irrelevant, though, as even had he insisted he was totally insane at the time of the divorce, if the presiding *beit din* did not think so, all his protestations to the contrary – and certainly at a later date – would be ignored.

Another senior European rabbi, Rabbi Shaul Lowenstamm of Amsterdam, hearing about the London interview with Isaac, wrote to his cousin, Rabbi Meshulam Zalman Emden – also a resident of London and the rabbi of a community there – and asked him to meet Isaac and report back. Rabbi Emden met Isaac and wrote back that his meeting had gone well, and that he seemed lucid and rational. This new "evidence" came to the attention of the Frankfurt *dayanim*, and they demanded that Rabbi Lowenstamm send it to them immediately, on the basis that they were the sole arbiters of the validity of the *Get* of Cleves.

Rabbi Lowenstamm agreed to send them a copy of the transcript, but queried their claim of sole jurisdiction. He also expressed his view that on the basis of what he had seen and heard he was satisfied that the *get* was valid, irrespective of their contrary opinion. The Frankfurt *dayanim* were not cowed by his forthright rejection of their self-proclaimed role, and replied that they were entirely within their rights to claim sole jurisdiction, as they were the only ones who were painstakingly collecting testimonies about the episode. They added that notwithstanding their view that the *get* was invalid, Rabbi Lipschuetz's reputation was not in any danger, as he had clearly been deliberately kept in the dark about Isaac's history.

Although they seemed to be resolutely adhering to their position, the tone of their letter did indicate that they were conscious of the fact that their high-handed approach – which they had perhaps imagined would bolster their reputation as serious and impartial jurists – had in fact resulted in the perception that they were just arrogant, dismissive, aloof snobs.

SUPPORT FOR THE *GET* OF CLEVES

As all this was happening Leah's father was busy writing to all the rabbis he knew to ask them to support the divorce. He was extremely concerned that if the Frankfurt ruling was accepted, his daughter would never be able to remarry. Meanwhile, Rabbi Lipschuetz was becoming increasingly agitated with each passing week at how his reputation was being called into question, and he also began to write letters to rabbis everywhere asking them to consider the details of the story and to support his position.

In March 1767, Rabbi Yaakov Emden, the elder statesman of the German Jewish rabbinate, declared in response to a letter from Rabbi

Lipschuetz that in his view the *get* was completely valid, and Leah was free to remarry. That same month Rabbi Arye Leib of Metz, author of *Shaagat Aryeh*, wrote an open letter stating that Leah was free to remarry, despite the objections of Frankfurt.

Incredibly, despite the universal support for the *Get of Cleves* from every rabbinic authority apart from Frankfurt, the Frankfurt *dayanim* remained unrepentant, and even began to issue public declarations voiding the *get*. Rabbi Yaakov Emden sent a message to the Frankfurt rabbis suggesting that they stand down, as they were making fools of themselves. He told them that a minority opinion must always give way in the face of an overwhelming majority, and it was evident that the vast majority of rabbis supported the *Get of Cleves*. But the Frankfurt *beit din* was in no mood to listen to him, despite his seniority, nor would it heed anyone who did not concur with its view. And so, despite the avalanche of opposition to Frankfurt's inflexibility, the campaign against the *get* and all its supporters continued unabated.

At around this time, Rabbi Yehezkel Landau of Prague, author of the acclaimed *Noda BiYehuda*, intervened in the controversy. Still quite young, and not nearly as well known as he would be ten or fifteen years later, Rabbi Landau was by nature a leader and a man of action. In his opinion the *Get of Cleves* was without doubt a legally viable document, but nevertheless he felt that Rabbi Lipschuetz of Cleves, who had presided over the divorce, should try and negotiate a face-saving compromise with the Frankfurt *beit din* so that everyone could walk away from the controversy with their pride intact.

Despite this conciliatory approach, after making a number of approaches to the rabbis of Frankfurt Rabbi Landau concluded with regret that they were in no mood for a compromise of any kind. Once this became evident to him, he immediately issued a public ruling validating the *Get of Cleves*. In his pronouncement he rebuked the Frankfurt *dayanim* for their obstinacy and for claiming sole jurisdiction in the case, and suggested forcefully that they immediately reverse their decision in accordance with the majority view of all the other rabbis who had ruled on the case.

In an effort to appear somewhat neutral, he wrote that as he was sure the Frankfurt *beit din* had initially acted in good faith and in accordance with its religious convictions, its refusal now to comply with the majority view was understandable. But, he said, it was a grave violation of Jewish law to question the legitimacy of a valid *get*, and therefore, although he did not wish to offend the Frankfurt rabbinate, his duty to justice and Torah law compelled him to declare that Leah was free to remarry immediately. He nevertheless suggested that she should wait a full year from the date of the divorce, to give the Frankfurt rabbis a chance to reconsider their position.

Frustratingly for all concerned, Rabbi Abish of Frankfurt and his *dayanim* totally ignored Rabbi Landau's suggestion. They were not looking for any exit strategy. In fact, it seemed that they were determined to force the entire rabbinic world to fall in line with their way of thinking. When he realized this, Rabbi Landau decided to act, and to act decisively. Exactly one year after the dispute had initially erupted he called together the entire Prague community into the city's main synagogue, and in a rousing public address announced that Leah was free to remarry, and that he would perform the wedding if called upon to do so. He also launched a powerful attack on the Frankfurt rabbis, calling them to task for allowing pride and vanity to color their judgment.

"Even the greatest Jewish legal minds can occasionally make mistakes," he thundered, and with the packed synagogue listening in stunned silence, he closed his dramatic speech with these devastating words: "When there is a desecration of God's name it is my duty to defend the honor of Heaven, the honor of the Torah, and the honor of laws relating to the daughters of Israel. How sad that this story so perfectly demonstrates how careful one must be to ensure that the evil inclination does not gain control over us."

Rabbi Landau was far from done. He wrote to Rabbi Aharon Shimon Copenhagen, who had attended the wedding of Isaac to Leah, and later the divorce, and asked him to publicize the Prague speech as widely as possible, and also to send printed copies of the validation of the *get* to as many rabbis and communities as he could. Even at this juncture he made an attempt to get the Frankfurt rabbis to back down. But it was to no avail – not only were they in no mood to listen, in March 1768 they took his published letter and publicly burned it in front of the whole Frankfurt community.

Rabbi Landau was not alone in defending the *Get* of Cleves. In the early fall of 1767, Rabbi Yosef Steinhardt went public with his ruling in favor of the *get*. The following month Rabbi Yehoshua Heschel Lvov of Ansbach did the same. Toward the end of the year ten rabbis from Brody in Poland validated the *get*. Rabbi Shlomo of Chelm, a renowned and respected halakhic expert, was next to come out in support of the *get*, and he was followed by Rabbi Arye Leib of Hanover, son of the former chief rabbi of Frankfurt, Rabbi Yaakov Yehoshua Falk, author of *Pnei Yehoshua*, whose students included the *dayanim* of Frankfurt.

IMPASSE AND CONDEMNATION

In Frankfurt the mood remained belligerent and unrepentant. Copies of the avalanche of rulings by the various rabbis were publicly burned, and a stream of pronouncements were published, all of them restating that the *Get* of Cleves was not worth the paper it had been written on, and Leah was forbidden to remarry without a new *get*. Although they never explained their inflexibility, it seems that the Frankfurt *dayanim* were of the view that sanity and insanity had to be judged contextually and holistically. If the behavior leading up to the *get* process indicated that the husband was insane in some way, then his instruction to give the *get* could also be considered part of that same trend. Isaac's disappearance with the money on the Shabbat after his wedding was a clear indication that he was mentally ill, and therefore any subsequent act – including his instruction to write a *get* – had to be treated as part of his mental breakdown, even if he appeared rational when giving the instruction.

Rabbi Lipschuetz of Cleves, and every single other rabbi who weighed in on the matter, disagreed profoundly with this viewpoint. The Shabbat disappearance incident was totally irrelevant, and what mattered was whether or not Isaac was lucid and coherent at the time the *get* was given, which Isaac had certainly been.

It had also become a matter of great concern among the rabbinic community that the Frankfurt *dayanim* had refused to publish their legal arguments, or to publish refutations of the reasons published by those who opposed them. Especially because their stance was so contentious, it seemed odd, at best, that they refused to back up their views with solid evidence and source-based material.

Their complete refusal to concede to the majority view was by far the most problematic aspect of all. Had they been involved with the actual divorce, their obstinacy might have been excusable. But as their involvement had only begun after the fact, and even then only as representatives of one side, they really had no standing. Even had they been completely right, Jewish law dictates that the majority has priority, which meant that the *Get* of Cleves had to be treated as a valid legal document.

There was a view that the Frankfurt rabbis and community had closed ranks to defend their esteemed chief rabbi, Rabbi Abish. This view seemed to be borne out when the community leaders in Frankfurt entered the following decree into their official community rulebook a few months after Rabbi Landau's speech to the community of Prague:

> Since Rabbi Landau publicly insulted our chief rabbi we decree that he, his children, grandchildren, sons-in-law, and grandsons-in-law, and any of his descendants shall never hold an official position in our community. If a member of his family ever visits Frankfurt, he will not be allowed to speak publicly, nor be given any communal honors. Any document signed by the rabbi of Prague alone, without any additional rabbinical signatures, shall be completely disregarded by our community.

Interestingly, it was never Rabbi Abish who was the driving force in the fight back by the Frankfurt rabbinate. The leading protagonist in Frankfurt was Rabbi Nathan Maas, author of the scholarly work *Binyan Shlomo*. A charismatic and forceful personality, he was regarded as a very wise man, and was undoubtedly the most influential *dayan* in Frankfurt. It was Rabbi Maas who composed all the letters and public pronouncements, and it was Rabbi Maas whom rabbis outside of Frankfurt accused of misleading Rabbi Abish and forcing him to adhere to his position, by convincing him that he was fighting a holy war.

Tragically, Rabbi Abish died the day after Yom Kippur in 1768. His death shocked the Frankfurt Jewish community to its core. The belief was that his death had been caused by the anguish he had suffered as a result of the controversy. At his funeral it was announced that no rabbi who had opposed him in this case could ever be elected to replace him. It took four years to find a replacement, due to the huge numbers of rabbis who had publicly defended the *Get* of Cleves against Rabbi Abish's opinion.

Eventually, Rabbi Pinhas HaLevi Horowitz was hired to take up the position as chief rabbi of Frankfurt. It emerged much later that he had in fact written a letter to Rabbi Lipschuetz to support the notorious *get*. But as he finished writing the letter he reached for the container of sand to scatter some of it on the letter to blot the still-damp ink. Instead of picking up the sand container he mistakenly picked up the ink container and spilled it over the paper, ruining the entire letter. He began writing the letter a second time, but someone who was with him told him not to bother. Rabbi Lipschuetz already had the support of so many other rabbis, the man said, and Rabbi Horowitz's letter would not add anything extra, so it was not worth wasting time to write the letter a second time. Inadvertently, it was that advice that got Rabbi Horowitz the position in Frankfurt a few years later.

WHAT HAPPENED TO ISAAC AND LEAH?

In the course of this incredible tale we have been so caught up with the epic battle between the rabbinic luminaries of Europe that we have lost touch with the original characters – Isaac and Leah. Whatever happened to them? As it turns out, the story's conclusion is almost too fantastic to be true, and considering the source of the story, it could well be a fanciful fabrication.

In the late nineteenth century a book was published that described the history of the Frankfurt rabbinate over the previous centuries. The story of the *Get* of Cleves was included in the book, for the first time from the perspective of the Frankfurt rabbinate. The book claimed that in early 1768 Leah and her family decided that they would accept the decision of the Frankfurt *beit din*, and she would not remarry, despite the numerous rabbis who had validated her divorce. Then, without warning, Isaac suddenly returned to Germany from London, and came to visit Leah and her family in Bonn.

After a long heart-to-heart talk, the couple announced that they had decided to "remarry." As far as the Frankfurt rabbinate was concerned they did not need a wedding, as the divorce had never been valid to start with. But just to be sure, the couple took part in a strange pseudo-wedding ceremony in Frankfurt, presided over by the Frankfurt rabbinate, during which Isaac put a ring on Leah's finger and said, "*At od mekudeshet li betabaat zo kedat Moshe veYisrael,*" "You *remain* betrothed to me with this ring in accordance with the laws of Moses and Israel."

The author of this extraordinary version of events was a man called Rabbi Marcus Horovitz, who was Orthodox chief rabbi of Frankfurt during the latter half of the nineteenth century (although by this time the Orthodox community had split into two separate communities, with the strictly Orthodox group that would have nothing to do with the reform Jews headed by Rabbi Samson Raphael Hirsch). Rabbi Horovitz claimed that his account of events was based on previously unseen source material taken from the archived files of the Frankfurt *kehilla*.

The rabbinic world once more erupted in uproar over the *Get* of Cleves, especially as Rabbi Horovitz had declared in a published work that the *Get* of Cleves had been invalid, echoing the controversial views of the rabbis of Frankfurt a century earlier. This opinion had been dismissed for a century or more, and that it had now resurfaced caused no end of consternation. Rabbi Horovitz also claimed to have found a manuscript authored by Rabbi Maas in which he had explained why he and his colleagues had remained silent in the face of mounting rabbinic opposition.

According to Rabbi Horovitz, Rabbi Maas wrote that the Frankfurt rabbinate had simply been asked to endorse the view of Rabbi Tevele Hess of Mannheim, who had himself witnessed Isaac's curious behavior during the wedding week culminating in his Shabbat disappearance, and who believed therefore that the *Get* of Cleves was worthless. With no reason to doubt the veracity of Rabbi Hess's opinion, as it was based on first-hand knowledge of Isaac and his state of mind, the Frankfurt rabbis were under no obligation to change their minds once they had ruled on the matter, nor to relinquish the jurisdiction of the case, which had been granted to them by Rabbi Hess.

But this statement of Rabbi Maas, as reproduced by Rabbi Horovitz, raised more questions than it answered for those who knew the ins and outs of the story. Concerned that the confusion caused by Rabbi Horovitz's account would have real repercussions for Halakha, many rabbis publicly condemned the Horovitz book and dismissed it as fiction.

Their views were later summarized and published by a man called Rabbi Yehuda Lubetzky, the Lithuanian-born Ashkenazic chief rabbi of Paris, in a pamphlet called *Kevodan Shel Rishonim*. In a long introduction he repeated the view of his predecessors in the late eighteenth century, namely that a halakhic decision such as the one reached by the rabbis of Frankfurt about the *Get* of Cleves did not occur in a vacuum, and if a majority of senior rabbis decide that a halakhic opinion is wrong, it is simply untenable to persist in defending that position.

Rabbi Lubetzky's main criticism was directed at Rabbi Horovitz for concluding that the Frankfurt rabbinate had got it right. He accused Rabbi Horovitz of being disingenuous and sloppy in his presentation of the facts of the case, and even of being deliberately misleading in his eagerness to exonerate the Frankfurt rabbis. If the Rabbi Maas manuscript even existed – and he questioned whether it actually existed, and if so, whether it was genuine or a later forgery – the most likely reason why it had never been published or seen was because Rabbi Maas himself had probably realized how foolish he would appear if he attempted to defend the indefensible. There was no doubt at all, said Rabbi Lubetzky, that Halakha in such cases had been firmly established in favor of those who had supported Rabbi Lipschuetz.

Just before closing the door on this incredible tale, it is worth noting that both Rabbi Lipschuetz and Rabbi Copenhagen published books recording their personal experiences of the controversy in which they demonstrated the halakhic basis for their views, and reproduced the prolific correspondence generated by the whole saga.

LITERARY DUPLICATION

There is quite a curious side story with regard to Rabbi Lipschuetz's publication. In 1770 he published his work, which he called *Or Yisrael*. On pages 31 and 32, after he had accused the Frankfurt rabbis of spreading lies about him, and of being utterly dishonest, he included the text of a public declaration he had made in Cleves that described the "wickedness of these men" in explicit detail, even referring to Rabbi Maas as "the evil and corrupt *dayan* of Frankfurt."

But this incendiary version of *Or Yisrael* was quickly withdrawn from circulation, possibly following negative feedback by the rabbis who were behind the campaign to validate the *Get* of Cleves, and whose support Rabbi Lipschuetz needed. The invective against the Frankfurt rabbinate was clearly a step too far. And so, a new version was published in which page 31 was rewritten, page 32 was removed, and the text reworked so that it flowed seamlessly from page 31 to page 33. The first version of *Or Yisrael* is exceedingly rare, and perhaps there are a couple of dozen copies in the world, most of them in private hands. The second version is less rare, although it is also a prized collector's piece.

The *Get* of Cleves controversy set the precedent for defining incompetence and insanity in divorce cases according to Jewish law. The obstinacy of the Frankfurt rabbinate forced the rabbinic community of the eighteenth century to crystallize around a more lenient understanding of the relevant definitions and to enshrine them in Halakha, making it easier to ensure that women in failed marriages could not be held to ransom by husbands who feign "madness" and then claim they are not competent to issue a *get*.

Chapter 5

Lord George Gordon:
A Most Unlikely Convert

London, 1780

> *"The prisoners [at Newgate Prison] bemoaned his loss, and missed him; for though his means were not large, his charity was great, and in bestowing alms among them he considered the necessities of all alike, and knew no distinction of sect or creed.*
> *There are wise men in the highways of the world who may learn something, even from this poor crazy lord who died in Newgate."*
>
> *– Charles Dickens, on Lord George Gordon,* Barnaby Rudge, *chapter 82*

Lord George Gordon before his conversion to Judaism

BORN INTO ARISTOCRACY

Lord George Gordon is most often associated with the violent riots that raged across London for several days in 1780. This period of civil unrest, which became known as the Gordon Riots, was so named as a result of the widespread belief that Gordon had instigated them. Gordon was born into privilege; his family was a well-established ducal dynasty that began in Scotland. The first duke, also called George Gordon, was originally known as the Marquess of Huntly. As a Catholic, he supported James II, the last Catholic monarch of Great Britain. His grandson, the third Marquess of Huntly, was Cosmo Gordon, Lord George Gordon's father. Cosmo was married to his first cousin, Catherine Gordon, a feisty woman whose behavior often raised eyebrows, and indeed the entire Gordon family was considered somewhat eccentric. George was Cosmo and Catherine's fourth son, born in 1751. Cosmo died the following year and Catherine soon remarried, to someone seventeen years her junior.

The young George was unsurprisingly a neglected child, and at the age of eleven his mother packed him off to boarding school at Eton. He would never return home. After Eton his mother arranged for him to become a commissioned officer in the British Navy, and within a year he was at sea. By nature a social activist, and also very outspoken, the new young officer quickly made himself unpopular with senior officers when he began to agitate for an improvement in the general conditions of ordinary sailors. Soon afterward, when he attempted to raise his rank, the admiralty board rejected his application, noting on his record that he was "wholly unsuitable for promotion."

On shore leave in the American colonies he became fascinated by the social conditions of blacks, both slaves and freed slaves, who he concluded were generally very badly treated by white colonists. Gordon would prove himself to be a tireless fighter for the causes he believed in, and he was full of energy, initiative, and innovation, with an inexhaustible capacity for hard work and long hours. At the age of twenty-two he left the navy and soon afterward set his sights on becoming a member of the British Parliament. At first he campaigned in Scotland, for the parliamentary seat associated with the Inverness-shire constituency. He endeared himself to the local population by learning to speak Gaelic and playing the bagpipes. He also regularly threw lavish and quite raunchy parties to which he invited all of the registered voters, of whom there were less than a hundred, and it seemed inevitable that the seat would easily fall to him at the next election.

But it was not to be. The sitting MP for that constituency was General Simon Fraser, who was unhappy at the prospect of losing a seat that he and his family had held onto since 1754. Fraser pressured George's eldest brother, the Duke of Gordon, to remove his brother from the race, and George was forced to withdraw his candidacy. Instead, he stood, unopposed, for another constituency located in southern England that was bought for him by Fraser. He took his seat in the House of Commons in 1774.

It didn't take too long for George to become embroiled in controversy. In speech after impassioned speech he railed against what he saw as the British government's obsession with subduing restless American colonists through military force. Bitterly opposed to the lack of real democracy in Great Britain, the result of direct involvement in government affairs by the unelected monarch, King George III, Gordon became a vocal supporter of the colonists in their fight against British imperialism. He quickly established a reputation as a great parliamentary performer, a role he truly enjoyed. Unfortunately, although he was a fierce critic of the administration, he could be equally critical of the opposition. As a result, despite his independent and refreshing approach to politics, his outspokenness was not an effective strategy for political advancement; in an echo of his stalled career in the Royal Navy, Gordon failed to advance his political career beyond the most basic level, as in politics you need allies, and he had none.

THE GORDON RIOTS

As the 1770s drew to a close, the most hotly debated political issue was the proposal for longstanding anti-Catholic laws to be repealed. It wasn't that Catholics were particularly persecuted any more, but the law needed to be changed so that the mandatory oath taken by soldiers entering the army – which was in desperate need of soldiers for the war in the American colonies – could be changed in such a way that Catholics could also take it. The law was drafted, proposed, and quietly passed in the late spring of 1778. As the details emerged, however, radical Protestants began to vigorously protest the repeal, claiming that all Catholics had dual loyalties and that their primary allegiance was to Rome and the Pope.

Gordon became the leading campaigner against the repeal, mainly as a consequence of his opposition to continued war in the American colonies. He realized, correctly, that the repeal was not a victory for social justice; instead it was a charade, passed so that the government of George III could ensure more men would fight in the American War, to which he was so opposed. His notoriety and family ties were considered extremely valuable to radical Protestants, and they appointed him president of the London Protestant Association, a position he gladly, if somewhat ill-advisedly, accepted. This marriage of convenience soon set off a chain of events that would prove a disaster for Gordon personally, but also for the stability of the still-immature democratic system of British government.

In early 1780 the association began to compile a petition to bring back the anti-Catholic laws by quashing the repeal. Notices went out inviting the public to come and sign the petition at Gordon's home in Central London. Despite numerous warnings that he was being used by dishonorable people, Gordon categorically refused to resign his position as head of the Protestant Association.

Although the petition soon had thousands of signatures, the prime minister, Lord Frederick North, refused to present the petition to King George III, forcing Gordon to exercise his right as the son of a duke to demand an audience with the monarch. Gordon met the king on three separate occasions to discuss the petition, but by the third meeting his behavior had become so offensive and unpleasant that when he attempted to arrange a fourth meeting he was politely but firmly turned away.

King George III was by nature a tolerant man who was perfectly at ease doing away with England's outdated laws against British Catholics, and he adamantly refused Gordon's request to recommend the petition to Parliament. But the petition just kept on growing, and eventually it had over 100,000 names. The political establishment began to sense danger. Prime Minister North called Gordon in to a meeting and attempted to bribe him with a significant sum of money, as well as a senior government position, on condition that he resign from leadership of the association. But Gordon could not be bought. Instead he began to call for a public protest meeting on the morning of Friday,

June 2, 1780. Remarkably, fifty thousand people turned up that morning to march toward the Houses of Parliament.

At first the rally was peaceful, but the weather that day was unusually hot and the streets were extremely crowded. After a few hours of peaceful demonstration the carnival atmosphere began to dissipate, and the mood changed from peaceful to disorderly. Within a short period of time the protesters were out of control. Government officials leaving Parliament were forced out of their carriages and beaten, and their carriages destroyed. Demagogic speakers ranted against the Catholics and against the government that tolerated them.

As all this was going on Gordon was in attendance at the House of Commons, and as he rose to speak the noise of the demonstrators was clearly audible inside the chamber. With a dramatic flourish he produced rolls and rolls of paper containing the signatures of the petitioners, and insisted that fellow members of Parliament immediately adopt the petition's demands. A heated debate ensued. Without exception every speaker opposed Gordon's suggestion to adopt the petition and criticized him for the unseemly protest in the streets below. The contentious debate lasted for over six hours, and when a vote was finally taken in the late evening, Gordon's motion for the petition's demands to be adopted and the anti-Catholic laws reinstated was soundly defeated 190–8, with no abstentions. Troops were then called in to disperse the demonstrators outside, and everyone went home thinking that the saga was finally over.

But by midnight gangs of drunken, violent men had begun a rampage across London. The violence would last an entire week, and as each day progressed the anarchy increased and the carnage escalated. The homes of leading politicians were burned to the ground. Catholic churches and homes of leading Catholics were attacked and looted. Prisons were broken into and prisoners freed. Eventually, as it became clear that ordinary law-enforcement measures were not working, the military was mobilized with a shoot-to-kill dispensation. Within hours hundreds of rioters had been killed, and hundreds more wounded.

While the riots raged, Gordon came to the realization that his plans had badly backfired. He desperately attempted to quell the demonstrators as the week progressed but was totally ignored by the mobs marauding through London. He had become completely irrelevant. On Friday, June 9, exactly one week after the original demonstration, Gordon was arrested and incarcerated in the Tower of London. Several of the leading rioters were also arrested that day and summarily tried and executed for treason. Gordon's trial did not materialize for months. Finally, in late December, he was charged with high treason, a crime punishable by the gruesome execution of being hung, drawn, and quartered. But Gordon was no common criminal. Although not a respected politician, his aristocratic origins and wealthy family meant that he would have the benefit of being properly defended, despite the grave misgivings over his role in the affair.

With financial help from family, friends, and sympathizers, Gordon hired the top trial lawyer of the day, Lloyd Kenyon, and his brilliant assistant, Thomas Erskine, to defend him at the trial. Erskine, later 1st Baron Erskine, was a devout Protestant and a gifted orator. Nevertheless he later wrote that he had told Gordon his acquittal was unlikely. The attorney general himself led the prosecution team and the judge was the Lord Chief Justice, William Murray, 1st Earl of Mansfield (1705–1793), whose house was one of those that had been burned down in the riots. The odds were not in favor of Gordon walking free.

A TALE OF TWO TRIALS

The trial began on February 5, 1781. Gordon was accused of "maliciously, traitorously, and unlawfully planning to execute a war against the King," and of then personally launching that war with a mob of armed men on June 2, 1780. Both sides presented their evidence, and the witnesses were cross-examined. The principal defense lawyer at the trial was Erskine. He was a brilliant trial performer, which later on in his career resulted in his appointment as lord chancellor.

Erskine's closing speech is purported to have been the best he ever gave. He argued that Gordon's intentions had been peaceful, and he could not be held responsible for the actions of rioters, many of whom were not even members of the Protestant Association. Ideology was not treason, nor was advocacy for the repeal of a pro-Catholic law. The fact that there were those who had resorted to violence was not his fault, nor a crime that he had committed, even if it was a fact that they had committed violent crimes. There was no evidence he had ever incited or encouraged them, and it was well known that he had tried hard to disperse them. If he was guilty of anything, it was of a lack of foresight and of gross naïveté, but neither of these was high treason. The jury was mesmerized.

Despite a highly biased summing up by the judge, who endeavored to undermine Erskine's arguments in any way that he could, the jury returned a unanimous "not guilty" verdict, and Gordon was immediately released. But strangely enough this stunning turn of events did not seem to affect Gordon. Instead of being euphoric he seemed unmoved.

It turned out that the nine months of incarceration in the Tower of London had changed him. He had become deeply attached to religion and the Bible. His life of wild parties and loose women was abandoned for one of introspection and prayer. Although he remained outspoken and his views remained extreme, he was more reflective and serious. In the months that followed his acquittal he attempted to rejoin the political world a couple of times, but was quietly prevented from doing so. The world had moved on, and before long Gordon disappeared from sight.

So it remained until 1786, when out of the blue Gordon was arrested and charged with two criminal offenses. Suddenly London was abuzz with Gordon's name once again. It turned out that an ongoing investigation into two anonymously published incendiary republican pamphlets had uncovered information that proved beyond any doubt they had been authored and published by Gordon. One of the pamphlets viciously libeled the French queen, Marie Antoinette, a popular target of republicans, while the second pamphlet contained a startling attack on the judiciary.

Gordon now found himself in the spotlight for all the wrong reasons. This time there was no support from family and friends, and Gordon was forced to undertake his own defense at two separate trials. His handling of the cases was brave but ultimately farcical, and in June 1787 he was found guilty of all the charges. The judge retired to consider the sentence overnight, and Gordon, who had been bailed until sentencing, left the court that evening, apparently to sort out his affairs before submitting himself to an inevitable prison sentence. The next morning the court reconvened for the sentencing, but Gordon was nowhere to be found. Sightings were reported, but not followed up. It seemed the authorities were unable or unwilling to make the effort to find him. Weeks turned into months, and life moved on. The mystery of Gordon's disappearance became nothing more than the subject of dinner-table discussions and bemused speculation.

Seven months later, in January 1788, the news broke that he had finally been located in Birmingham and arrested. Except that this wasn't the same Lord George Gordon of the House of Commons and the Gordon Riots. The person the police found in a shabby rented room in a grubby area of the city was a full-bearded Orthodox Jew, dressed in a Polish kaftan and black broad-brimmed hat, who proudly gave his name to the arresting officers as Yisrael bar Avraham. Lord George Gordon – aristocrat, socialite, and political activist – had converted to Judaism.

At first he refused to accompany the arresting officers back to London, as it was a Saturday, which he insisted was his Sabbath, but a magistrate was hastily summoned to rule that he must be transported immediately. With no alternative, Gordon was hastily shipped off to London, but not before he had obtained a package of kosher food from his Jewish landlady.

SECRET CONVERSION TO JUDAISM

It didn't take long for the whole strange story to emerge. On the fateful night of his disappearance, Gordon took a boat to Holland, but upon his arrival the Dutch authorities refused him entry and immediately repatriated him. When Gordon arrived back in England he slipped into the country unnoticed and vanished from sight. His ability to disappear was enhanced by a new fraternity of friends and a new mode of dress that masked his real identity. Apparently, a year earlier he had converted to Judaism, and he now adopted the religious garb and appearance of an Eastern European Jew – a kaftan and hat, and a full beard. Within a matter of weeks he was completely unrecognizable.

The conversion was the final chapter in Gordon's evolving religious metamorphosis. Some years earlier Gordon had come to see Christianity's rejection of the Hebrew Scriptures as hypocrisy and sacrilege, and it was at that time that someone introduced him to the Jewish community in London. He was overwhelmed. He regarded this as the pinnacle of his life, getting to meet the "People of the Book," living relics of the Hebrew Scriptures who adhered closely to the word of God as delivered by Moses and the prophets. Within a short period of time he had begun to keep kosher and study Torah with Jewish commentaries.

His actual conversion was not easily achieved. Initially he approached the distinguished and widely respected chief rabbi of London, David Tevele Schiff. But Rabbi Schiff turned him away and refused to consider converting him under any circumstances. Gordon was far too prominent and controversial, and it was the considered opinion of the chief rabbi and his advisers that welcoming Gordon into the Jewish community would not reflect well on the Jewish community and would lead to negative repercussions.

Undeterred, Gordon went to Aaron Barnett, the learned *hazan* of the Hambro Synagogue breakaway community. Barnett was also reluctant to preside over such a controversial conversion, but having been convinced of Gordon's sincerity, he sent him to the Jewish spiritual leader of Birmingham, a man called Rabbi Jacob, who arranged for Gordon's circumcision and a *mikve* immersion, and also taught him to read Hebrew. After the conversion was done, Gordon returned to London and was called up to make a blessing on the Torah at the Hambro Synagogue. In gratitude for his inclusion and Barnett's readiness to help him he presented the synagogue with a generous donation. And although everyone knew who he was, Gordon's conversion remained a secret, confined to the insular Jewish community which had no interest in attracting attention to itself via its latest recruit.

It was evident to his new Jewish friends that Gordon's love of Judaism and Jews was sincere. He sat for much of the day in tefillin, praying, studying the Hebrew language, and learning *Mishnayot*. But the conversion had to be kept a secret. His family was completely unaware of it, as were his political acquaintances. In any event, he was a fugitive from the law, and his newfound coreligionists were concerned that revealing his change of faith would not serve the best interests of the community, so he was able to maintain his anonymity. But after his arrest, Gordon's conversion to Judaism and his new appearance were thrust into the public eye, and Gordon soon became the focus of ridicule and scorn.

Aside from the negative impact of his change of faith, his escape and disappearance resulted in the full weight of the law being brought to bear against him. The court was in no mood for leniency and handed down a harsh sentence – five years in jail – and he was fined an astronomical sum of money, well beyond his means. He was brought to Newgate Prison to serve his sentence, although after his family intervened he was given a private cell in a slightly more salubrious part of the prison facility.

CELEBRITY PRISONER OF NEWGATE

Gordon soon emerged as a celebrity prisoner, and found himself entertaining a constant stream of visitors. He held regular dinner parties with only kosher food, and even had full-scale balls at which he played the bagpipes accompanied by musicians on other instruments. One regular visitor was Prince Frederick, Duke of York, second son of King George III. The duke was fond of Gordon, and often sent over his chamber orchestra to Gordon's cell to play at the regular parties held there which, by all accounts, were the most popular events in town.

Gordon's prison cell was strictly kosher and he engaged both a Jewish and a non-Jewish maid to cook and clean for him. The prison authorities allowed him to hold a *minyan* on Shabbat and festivals, and he made arrangements for Polish Jewish immigrants also imprisoned at Newgate to make up the ten men required for the *minyan* together with him. He was extremely tolerant of people of all persuasions, with the exception of lapsed Jews. On one occasion a Jewish beggar arrived at the jail asking if he could see the famous prisoner to ask for his financial help. After consulting Gordon the guards refused the man entry, as he did not have a full beard and his head was not covered as required by tradition. The man in question, Angel Lyon, was deeply hurt, and wrote Gordon a letter to express his disappointment. In the letter he cited God's statement to the biblical prophet Samuel that He judged people by what was in their hearts, not by their appearance.

Gordon replied at length, and his letter was later published in a celebrated pamphlet. He argued that God had not suggested that appearance was immaterial, only that ultimately it was not an indicator of what was in someone's heart – even if that person appeared devout. The statement to Samuel was "not intended to abolish or contradict the laws of outward appearance among the Jews, but to teach that God sees through all outward appearances." On the importance of retaining the appearance of a devout Jew if one was Jewish, he wrote that those Jews who shaved and dressed like Gentiles were "ashamed of the outward and visible signs, given unto them by God Himself, and commanded to be preserved by Moses, because it distinguishes them as Jews, in public, from the nobility and gentry of these lands. But this is serving man and despising God."

When Gordon's mandated sentence was over in early 1793, he was brought before the court. The judge demanded that he pay his as-yet unpaid fines, warning him that otherwise he would have to continue his incarceration. Gordon was unfazed and accused the court of using the astronomical fines as a ruse to ensure his imprisonment for life. During the entire proceedings he refused to acknowledge that the court had any jurisdiction over him, as he had served his jail sentence, and on a number of occasions his acerbic wit, mainly directed at the judge, saw the gathered spectators reduced to fits of helpless laughter. His brother, the duke, had indicated the family's willingness to pay the fines, but Gordon refused the offer on principle, and after a long and unproductive day at court he was sent back to Newgate Prison.

As it turned out this was a fateful decision. The prison was in the midst of an outbreak of typhus, and prisoners were dying daily. Despite his isolation from the other prisoners, Gordon contracted the deadly disease and began to sink rapidly. He was visited by hundreds of well-wishers, but was soon close to death. On November 1, 1793 – coinciding with 26 Ḥeshvan – Yisrael bar Avraham Gordon, *Ger Tzedek*, died at the age of forty-two.

As a final indignity, despite his desire to be buried in the Jewish cemetery of London, his family had him buried in a Christian burial ground at St. James's Church on Hampstead Road in Euston, Central London – a site that was ultimately turned into a public park.

For some time after his death Gordon retained the notoriety he had attracted in his lifetime, particularly as his previously perceived extreme views on liberty and democracy had become the mainstream political ideology in both America and France, and he was now viewed as a pioneer champion of libertarianism.

In 1795 a book was written and published by the fierce anti-Catholic Gordon acolyte Robert Watson, called *The Life of Lord George Gordon*. Watson was a Scot by birth, slightly older than Gordon, and had fought in George Washington's army against the British. From 1780 he was Gordon's secretary. The book was an apologetic work, extremely sympathetic in its portrayal of Gordon, although its author was clearly not a lover of Jews, and he spuriously claimed that had Gordon been released he would have given up Judaism and returned to Christianity.

Shortly after Gordon died, a one-penny coin was issued in London depicting his profile. In the 1790s the lack of copper coins in Britain and the need for small change as a result of the Industrial Revolution led to numerous private token issues that could be used as legal currency. Some issuers used these coins to praise the achievements of the Industrial Revolution; others used them for political propaganda, such as those issued by the left-wing publicist Thomas Spence. The Gordon penny was one of the coins issued by Spence, who decided to depict Gordon as a Jew, with a hat and beard.

As the years went by, Gordon receded from public consciousness, and if he was remembered at all it was only for his role in the Gordon Riots, and as a marginal political figure of the late eighteenth century. But for Jews he remains one of the most enigmatic converts to our faith in the early modern era – a true revolutionary, and at the same time a mitzva-observant Jew who was willing to sacrifice everything for his newfound faith.

Chapter 6

The Maharal Haggada: A Confused Tradition and Literary Forgery

Warsaw, 1905

"Even aside from the dictates of rationalism, what militates against the notion that the Maharal created a golem is the fact that nowhere in his voluminous writings is there any indication that he created one."

– Professor Shnayer Leiman

"By calling the stories [about the golem] factual accounts by Rabbi Isaac Katz, and by using such a notable figure as [the Maharal], Rosenberg sought to magnify the importance and reception of his own work, and to provide validity to the narrative and to its implications."

– Reynolds Nelson Hahamovitch

Rabbi Yehuda Yudel Rosenberg, rabbinic scholar and literary forger, c. 1914

THE MAHARAL HAGGADA IS PUBLISHED

One of the most prominent rabbis in sixteenth-century Europe was Rabbi Yehuda Loewe (1527–1609), the chief rabbi of Prague, usually referred to as the Maharal of Prague. His numerous works on Torah were famous and widely disseminated even during his lifetime, and after his death his many students continued to propagate the Maharal's deep and insightful ideas, until they became the fundamental theology underpinning the essence of Jewish life in Europe. His influence continued to grow with each century that passed, and it continues to grow even today.

So imagine the joy and excitement that greeted the publication of his *Haggada Shel Pesaḥ* in Warsaw, Poland, at the beginning of the twentieth century. The text was apparently based on a long-lost manuscript that had lain undiscovered in an obscure French library and that the publisher claimed had been put together by the Maharal's son-in-law, Rabbi Yitzhak Katz of Nikolsburg (1550–1634), who had recorded all the Haggada-related material taught to him by the Maharal during his lifetime. The manuscript also included information about the Maharal's customs during the Seder itself, observed by Rabbi Katz during his father-in-law's lifetime.

The most remarkable new piece of information contained in the Haggada was that the Maharal had included a fifth cup of wine at his Seder, a cup that only he drank and over which he recited a unique proclamation. Maharal devotees began to introduce this practice into their own Pesaḥ Seders, and the revelation of this fifth-cup custom, purportedly practiced by such a prominent rabbinic authority, generated enormous excitement across the rabbinic fraternity.

THE NEED FOR A FIFTH CUP AT SEDER NIGHT

One of the enduring mysteries of Seder night is the confusion over the need for a fifth cup of wine. Rabbinic tradition records the requirement to drink four cups of wine at the Seder, based on a talmudic explanation that matches each cup of wine with a particular expression of redemption in the Exodus narrative (Ex. 6:6–7). There is also a fifth cup of wine at the Seder, always referred to as the "Cup of Elijah." This is a solitary cup of wine poured toward the end of the Seder, but not drunk by anyone. Some people have the custom to pour the wine from this cup back into the bottle after the Seder, while others use it for Kiddush the following day.

The origins of this "fifth cup" custom are shrouded in mystery. There seems to be no explanation for pouring a cup of wine that no one is going to drink, while its identification as the "Cup of Elijah" seems unconnected to the Exodus narrative.

The Mishna at the beginning of the tenth chapter of Tractate Pesaḥim instructs that one must ensure that no member of the community is without four cups of wine at the Seder, even if it means charitable funds must be used to pay for them. Later on in the chapter we are informed exactly when to drink the four cups, with the fourth one coinciding with the conclusion of Hallel, after the meal. The Gemara adds a further, mystifying piece of information: "R. Tarfon says that the fourth cup coincides with the end of Hallel, and one [also] says the Great Hallel."* Although the text of the Gemara does not mention a fifth cup of wine, Rashi and *Tosafot*, the two primary medieval Talmud commentaries, intriguingly point out that the text of the Gemara should be amended so that it does not include any reference to a fifth cup, as it is impossible that R. Tarfon would have mandated a fifth cup at the Seder. *Tosafot* does mention one opinion that permits anyone who "needs" to drink a further cup of wine to do so. Evidently these early medieval rabbis had a different Gemara text in front of them, and based on their own knowledge and experience of Seder customs they concluded that any mention of a fifth cup was an error and needed to be removed from the text.

Meanwhile, Rabbi Yitzhak Alfasi, known as the *Rif*, who preceded both Rashi and *Tosafot* and was the author of an authoritative halakhic distillation of Talmud, clearly had quite a different view. His version of the Gemara text clearly states that R. Tarfon mandated a fifth cup over which one should recite the Great Hallel.

Rabbi Alfasi is not alone. The Rambam (Maimonides) mentions a fifth cup, although he concludes that it isn't mandatory. The Rambam's greatest critic was the French rabbi, Rabbi Avraham ben David of

---

* *Hallel HaGadol*, or the Great Hallel, is Psalm 136, which consists of thirty-six declarations of praise to God, all of them ending "*ki le'olam ḥasdo*," "His kindness is eternal."

Posquières (known acronymically as Rabad). But on this occasion he totally concurs with his *bête noire*, confirming that R. Tarfon obligates a fifth cup to match up with a fifth expression of redemption in the Exodus narrative: *"veheveiti"* – "and I shall bring you [to the land that I promised to Abraham, Isaac, and Jacob]."

Similarly, Rabbenu Asher ben Yehiel (known as Rosh) dismisses the claim that the Talmud text talking about a fifth cup is wrong, as it is clear R. Tarfon considered a fifth cup obligatory, even if contemporary practice had reduced it to a voluntary custom.

Later rabbinic authorities understood this confused picture to have been a result of the destruction of the Temple in Jerusalem. All Seders during the Temple period had included five cups of wine, not just four, allowing Jews to commemorate all five expressions of redemption. But once the enduring reality of the Second Temple's destruction had sunk in, the custom to drink a fifth cup of wine became less common, and then slowly receded into the background. After all, how could one celebrate Jewish dominion over *Eretz Yisrael* if that dominion no longer existed, and Jews had been dispersed across a far-flung diaspora?

And yet, despite this depressing reality, the custom to drink a symbolic fifth cup of wine prevailed in at least some communities as a hopeful reminder of a future return to *Eretz Yisrael* under messianic leadership. Rashi and *Tosafot* either did not have this custom or believed it to be misconceived. Rabbi Alfasi, Rambam, Rabad, and the Rosh may have had this custom, or at least felt it was too important to be entirely dismissed.

At some point during the late medieval period, the custom of drinking a fifth cup of wine morphed into pouring a fifth cup of wine that was not drunk by anyone, which became known as the "Cup of Elijah," possibly a reference to the traditional idea that the prophet would be the first person to inform us of the Messiah's arrival and of the Jews' imminent return to *Eretz Yisrael*.

RABBI YUDEL ROSENBERG AND THE MAHARAL

Rabbi Yehuda Yudel Rosenberg of Warsaw was a fascinating individual, a rabbinic scholar who claimed to be descended from the Maharal. Born in 1859, in a town called Skaryszew, Poland, he was recognized as a prodigy at a very young age. He married aged seventeen and was appointed rabbi of a town called Tarlow at the age of twenty-five. Much later he would style himself as the "Tarla Rebbe," although there was no Tarlow hasidic dynasty, and he never ran a hasidic court when he was the rabbi there.

From Tarlow, Rabbi Rosenberg moved to Lublin, where he served as a *dayan* on the *beit din* of Rabbi Shneur Zalman Fradkin, a Hasid of Chabad and the author of an acclaimed halakhic work, *Torat Ḥesed*. Although Rabbi Rosenberg was an exceptional scholar, he began to attract criticism when his fondness for Russian literature was revealed, and eventually he moved to Warsaw, where he opened a tiny synagogue and acted as a community *dayan*, resolving local disputes and answering halakhic questions for payment.

Clearly this work did not provide him with sufficient income to look after his family, so in 1902 he published a book on the talmudic tractate Nedarim, an unusually complex volume that is unaided by Rashi's commentary, as it seems to have been lost or was possibly never written. *Yadot Nedarim*, as Rabbi Rosenberg's book was titled, was an excellently written and erudite work and was welcomed and widely used by Talmud scholars and yeshiva students alike, and it continues to be utilized by those studying Nedarim to this day.

Perhaps sales were slow, or perhaps Rabbi Rosenberg needed more money, or maybe Rabbi Rosenberg was not content with the publication of an ordinary book that would be lost in a sea of other similar publications. Whatever the reason, in 1905 Rabbi Rosenberg published the Maharal Haggada in Warsaw. On the title page he asserted that this was the first time this Haggada commentary had ever been published, and he claimed it was based on an old manuscript originally held at the Royal Library in Metz, a small town on the border of France and Germany, and home to a well-established, centuries-old Jewish community.

In his foreword to the Haggada, Rabbi Rosenberg wrote how it had been extremely difficult for him to bring the manuscript to print, particularly because its current owner had refused to part with it under any circumstances. As a result of these difficulties he did not include what he claimed was a long and rambling introduction by its author, the Maharal's son-in-law, Rabbi Yitzhak Katz, but instead focused on the Haggada commentary itself.

Below Rabbi Rosenberg's foreword was a letter addressed to him written by a man called Hayim Scharfstein, and dated 15 Av 5664 (July 27, 1904). Scharfstein wrote that he was sending Rabbi Rosenberg an accurate handwritten copy of the original manuscript previously held in the Royal Library, and he assured Rabbi Rosenberg that no one else would get a copy besides him, as had been agreed between them.

THE ROYAL LIBRARY IN METZ AND THE *GOLEM* OF PRAGUE

In the years that followed, the Hayim Scharfstein manuscript collection would go on to play a significant role in Rabbi Rosenberg's literary output. In 1909 Rabbi Rosenberg published another book called *Niflaot Maharal* based on a manuscript from Metz purportedly also authored by the Maharal's son-in-law. This time the contents of the manuscript described the Maharal's creation of a *golem* – a mythical and powerful humanoid creature animated by kabbalistic formulas – who was used by the Maharal to protect the Jewish community of Prague against the evil conspiracies of local anti-Semites. The Maharal *golem* myth had first emerged into popular culture in 1832 when a German-Jewish poet and author called Berthold Auerbach wrote a fictional account of what must have been an ancient oral legend that described a series of stories involving the *Golem* of Prague. There were some other limited literary references to the *golem* in the years before that. In the years that followed Auerbach's version a number of similar accounts were published, all of them folklore-style literature that made no claim of authenticity.

Niflaot Maharal was quite different. The title page described how the stories it contained were originally written down by Rabbi Katz, the very same Rabbi Katz who had recorded the Maharal's commentary on the Haggada. And just as the Haggada manuscript had lain undiscovered for centuries in the Royal Library of Metz, so too had the *golem* manuscript. The title page also claimed that the Metz library had been destroyed during a war approximately a century earlier, perhaps a reference to the Napoleonic wars, and as a result many Jewish manuscripts had found their way into the possession of some wealthier members of the local Jewish community.

The 1909 publication was very well received, and was followed in 1913 by another publication, *The High Priest's Ḥoshen Mishpat* [Heb.]. This book was based on yet another manuscript from the Metz library, this one written by Rabbi Manoah Hendel, a well-known student of the Maharal who died in 1612. Rabbi Hendel had apparently devoted many years attempting to catalog the whereabouts of any sacred utensils that survived the 70 CE Roman destruction of the Holy Temple in Jerusalem, and this new manuscript documented that quest in great detail.

One of the most arresting parts of the manuscript was an incredible story that Rabbi Hendel claimed to have heard from the Maharal himself, about his involvement in the recovery of the twelve precious stones which had been a part of the *ḥoshen mishpat* – the bejeweled breastplate worn by the Temple's high priest, and originally worn by the very first high priest, Aaron, brother of Moses.

Evidently the twelve precious jewels of the *ḥoshen mishpat* had somehow made their way to England, where they were kept at the Belmore Street Museum in London. In the year 1590, the Maharal discovered that the precious gems had been stolen from the museum, and he went to London to locate them so that they could be returned to the museum for safekeeping. Once he was in London the Maharal pretended to be an antiques collector, and in that guise met someone called Captain Wilson, who turned out to be the thief who had stolen the gems. The Maharal offered to buy them from Wilson, and they agreed on a price. They also agreed that the actual transaction would take place two weeks later, giving the Maharal enough time to come up with the astronomical sum of money he needed to buy them.

The transaction never took place. During the prescribed two-week period the Maharal generated constant mayhem for Wilson through the medium of kabbalistic miracles; by the time the two weeks were up Wilson agreed to give the Maharal the precious jewels for nothing, and the Maharal was able to return them to the museum.

A CASE OF PLAGIARISM

The problem with this riveting story was that it had nothing to do with the Maharal, nor with Rabbi Manoah Hendel – nor, indeed, with Rabbi Yehuda Yudel Rosenberg. This remarkable tale was a piece of contemporary fiction, written and published in 1899 by the famous British author of the Sherlock Holmes mysteries, Sir Arthur Conan Doyle, as a short story titled "The Jew's Breastplate."

Rabbi Rosenberg must have been familiar with the story in a Russian translation, and must have also been pretty certain that nobody who read his Hebrew translation, or his later Yiddish version, would be remotely familiar with this English-language literary vignette. He was so convinced of this that he did not even change any of the names used by Doyle in the original version! The only thing that Rabbi Rosenberg bothered to change was the main character in the story, who was no longer the first-person narrator but instead was the Maharal of Prague.

As it turns out, the entire backdrop to these Metz manuscripts was fiction. There was never a Royal Library in Metz. Neither Rabbi Yitzhak Katz nor Rabbi Manoah Hendel left us with any manuscript material relating to the Maharal in the form claimed by Rabbi Rosenberg. Even Hayim Scharfstein was a fictional creation, produced by Rabbi Rosenberg to generate the impression that his Maharal material was authentic. Whether the Maharal ever created a *golem* is a question for scholars to debate, but it is certainly the case that Rabbi Rosenberg's stories about the mythical man-beast were the fanciful creations of his literary imagination, and bear no relationship to what may have really happened.

In 1913, shortly after publishing his *Ḥoshen Mishpat* forgery, Rabbi Rosenberg moved from Poland to Toronto, Canada. In 1919 he moved to Montreal, where he became one of the most prominent rabbis in the city. For the remainder of his life – he died in 1935 – Rabbi Rosenberg regularly published books and pamphlets on Jewish subjects, although he never again published any Maharal-related material.

It is unclear whether Rabbi Rosenberg thought that his fictional Maharal stories would be taken seriously, or whether he cared. It is certainly the case that the Haggada was taken seriously, something Rabbi Rosenberg must have been aware of during his lifetime. But at no time after he published the Haggada, or any Maharal-related material, did Rabbi Rosenberg ever disavow its authenticity, nor admit that his spurious claims about its authenticity were nothing more than a hoax.

Much of the material in the Maharal Haggada can be found in Maharal commentary on the Torah that is authentic; Rabbi Rosenberg simply adapted existing material for Seder night. The Maharal also wrote a genuine commentary on the Haggada in his work titled *Gevurot Hashem*, chapters 48–65. But anything that cannot be sourced in the Maharal's reliable body of work must be dismissed as fantasy. Rabbi Rosenberg had mixed this genuine material with his own imaginary material to produce a Maharal Haggada. This means that the Maharal never drank a fifth cup of wine at the Seder, and that Rosenberg's claim to the contrary was fake, concocted by him to generate wider interest in his new publication, and no doubt to boost sales. Of course there was this ancient tradition to drink a fifth cup of wine at the Pesaḥ Seder, but the loss of our Temple in Jerusalem resulted in the abandonment of this custom, and it eventually disappeared completely, replaced with the custom of the "Cup of Elijah."

Chapter 7

Ignatz Timothy Trebitsch-Lincoln: Adventurer, Agitator, and Conman

Shanghai, 1943

> *"Trebitsch-Lincoln died in Shanghai in October 1943. Yet, even in death, he retains a capacity to astound, and I suppose it is possible he may yet rise from his grave in the Shanghai Municipal Cemetery, in the form of a posthumous cache of papers, to contradict everything I have found out about him."*
>
> *– Professor Bernard Wasserstein*

Ignatz Trebitsch-Lincoln, political agitator and international
adventurer, c. 1915

INTERVIEW WITH A FORGOTTEN LEGEND

It was sultry afternoon in the summer of 1943, and a young Jewish journalist, Anna Ginsbourg, gingerly entered the imposing YMCA building on Bubbling Well Road in Shanghai, China. The YMCA was by far the largest building in Shanghai, overflowing with European refugees who had found themselves in the Far East while war raged across the world. Ginsbourg informed the receptionist she had come for an appointment with one of the residents, a Buddhist monk called Chao Kung.

Ginsbourg was a feisty woman in her early thirties, and had been seeking an audience with this monk for many months, desperate to interview him for the local Jewish refugee newspaper. Eventually she received word that he had consented to meet with her, and the day of the meeting had finally arrived. After a short wait in the chaotic reception area, Ginsbourg was shown into a quiet side room. Chau Kung was already sitting there waiting for her, dressed in his ceremonial robes and a black cloth skullcap that almost completely covered his shaven head. He eyed her up and down, and then motioned for her to sit down.

"What language would you like to use for this interview?" he asked her in English, his voice high pitched, but soft. "English, German, or Yiddish?"

His crinkled face broke into a smile, and Ginsbourg smiled back at him. For Grand Abbot Chau Kung of Shanghai, the Japanese government-recognized Dalai Lama of Tibet, was none other than Ignatius Timotheus Trebitsch-Lincoln, the notorious Hungarian-born Jewish fraudster and fugitive, erstwhile Christian missionary, Liberal member of the British Parliament, German spy, and infamous political agitator, who had over the previous fifty years been arrested and imprisoned numerous times in multiple countries, and whose life story was more remarkable than the most imaginative fiction.

The interview with Ginsbourg that balmy summer's day was the last interview Trebitsch-Lincoln ever gave, after a lifetime of desperately seeking notoriety and fame. Just two months later he was dead, struck down by a mysterious stomach ailment. There were those who believed he had been poisoned by the Nazis, who had only recently contemplated using him in a scheme against the British. Others believed that his unhealthy and frenetic lifestyle had ultimately caught up with him and hastened his untimely death. Whatever it was, on that July afternoon in the peaceful setting of the YMCA building side room, as Ginsbourg scribbled notes and sipped green tea, Trebitsch-Lincoln presented her with his final version of his own life story. And although his fanciful version to her that day was undoubtedly more fiction than fact, the true account of his life story is so dramatic, and so unbelievable, that even the most imaginative author of fiction would find it challenging to come up with a narrative so varied and improbable, for fear that his work would not be taken seriously by any reader.

TROUBLED EARLY LIFE

Ignatius Timotheus Trebitsch-Lincoln began his life as Yitzhak Trebitsch, born in the spring of 1879 to a devout family that belonged to the breakaway "Status Quo" Orthodox community of Paks, Hungary. The Paks Jewish community was tiny, barely exceeding one thousand souls. Breakaway communities in Hungary were extreme and inflexible, refusing to belong to any government-recognized organ, even if it was Orthodox, in the belief that official recognition inevitably led to assimilation.

Trebitsch's father, Nathan, was a successful businessman who owned a fleet of barges transporting grain to cities across the Austro-Hungarian Empire. Nathan's wife, Julia, hailed from the distinguished Freund family. Nathan was a dogmatic and forceful personality fully supported in his strict application of Orthodox Judaism by Julia, who bore him fourteen children, or possibly sixteen, several of whom died in infancy. Trebitsch was the second son, of six who survived. The oldest, Vilmos, was a child genius who later descended into mental illness and never recovered. The other boys went in multiple directions, none of them retaining the Orthodoxy of their youth into adulthood.

The rabbi of Paks during this period was a renowned talmudic scholar, Rabbi Eliezer Zussman Sofer (1830–1902), devoted disciple of Rabbi Avraham Shmuel Binyamin Sofer (no relation), the *Ketav Sofer* of Pressburg (Bratislava), and an uncompromising traditionalist who rejected any contact with the outside world. Perhaps at Rabbi Sofer's urging, Nathan sent his second son to Pressburg at a young age to study at the renowned Pressburg yeshiva. The experience was formative, not because it brought the young Trebitsch closer to his Judaism, but because it exposed him to the German language, which he mastered quickly and comprehensively, enabling him to widen the scope of his exposure to non-Jewish culture and studies.

In the early 1890s the Trebitsch family moved to Budapest so that Nathan could turn the provincial family business into something more substantial. But in 1893 the stock market crashed, and he suffered a substantial loss of money. Desperate to rebuild his financial capital, he cashed out his shares at a loss and invested the money in various business ventures, all of which ultimately failed.

The once-prosperous Trebitsch family was suddenly reduced to struggling for its survival. This change of circumstances had a profound effect on the young Trebitsch, resulting in a lifelong distaste for capitalism, a system that had so dramatically destroyed his family's life. But rather than turn him into a socialist or a communist, as was common during that period, the tragic circumstances of his father's financial ruin turned him into a cynical, amoral crook with an insatiable desire for money.

In early 1897 Trebitsch was accused of stealing an expensive gold watch in Budapest. At around the same time accusations of petty theft emerged in the Italian port of Trieste, where he spent a few months. In both instances he evaded arrest, as by the time the accusations were made he could not be found. His restless nature had by now resulted in his traveling frequently from one country to another, but not so much because he was heading toward a particular destination; rather he seemed to enjoy the constant journey. He restively flitted around Europe, and possibly North and South America, never staying anywhere for too long. Indeed, the nomadic fervor would become a lifelong hallmark, and he always seemed to be on the move.

CONVERSION TO CHRISTIANITY

In the summer of 1897 he arrived in England, probably to attend the widely advertised Diamond Jubilee celebrations for Queen Victoria. There he fell in with Christian missionaries through the efforts of an indefatigable Jewish convert to Christianity, Reverend Hayim Lypshytz of the Barbican Mission to the Jews. The missionaries in London's East End district were extremely active among foreign Jewish immigrants, offering them free lodgings and food in exchange for attending classes in Christian theology.

Whether Trebitsch had any interest in conversion at the time, or whether he was simply looking for a free place to stay, is hard to determine. What we do know is that some months later he left the hostel simultaneous to the disappearance of a gold watch and chain belonging to Mrs. Lypshytz, along with a passport that belonged to a fellow resident.

Trebitsch reappeared in Hungary, but didn't stay there for long. With his family in disarray as a result of Nathan's financial problems, he tried unsuccessfully to find work. Accused yet again of stealing a gold watch, in late 1898 he left Hungary and went to Hamburg, where he found refuge in the Irish Presbyterian mission house. This was a Christian facility run by another convert from Judaism, a former bank clerk turned pastor called Arnold Frank. Under Frank's influence Trebitsch began studying for conversion to Christianity, and in December 1899, a few months after the sudden and unexpected death of his father, Trebitsch was formally baptized into the Christian faith.

The conversion idea was no doubt enhanced by his introduction to a young German gentile woman called Margarethe Kahlor. She was an unlikely match for the restless young Trebitsch. The daughter of a retired sailor, she was two years older than him, and had given birth to an illegitimate child in 1897. Perhaps it was this that made the idea of Trebitsch courting Margarethe more acceptable to her parents. Whatever it was, he became a frequent visitor to their home. Every visit would apparently end with Trebitsch leading the family in passionate prayer, on their knees, eyes closed, arms raised, as he cried out, "Deliver us from all sins and purify our hearts!"

The Kahlors were fairly wealthy and this was certainly an important factor for Trebitsch, whose desire for money was boundless. It was agreed that the young couple would marry once he found a way to make a living, and the plan was for him to become a Christian minister after having trained at a theological seminary. After his conversion, Trebitsch joined a Lutheran college in a small town called Breklum, near the Danish border, to train for the ministry, but he found college life exceptionally boring and was soon back in Hamburg.

For some reason, Trebitsch now boarded a boat and sailed to Canada, where he spent a few weeks at an ailing missionary church in Montreal before traveling to New York. Within a couple of months, following an intense exchange of correspondence, Trebitsch had convinced the presiding minister of the Montreal mission, Reverend John McCarter, to engage him as his assistant, upon which he returned to Montreal and began trying to convert Jews to Christianity.

Among his Christian friends Trebitsch could not have been more popular. They found his enthusiasm infectious, and his zeal inspiring. But the Jews of Montreal found this opinionated, insidious convert, who regularly knocked on their doors to missionize, and who tried to hand out Yiddish translations of the Gospels on the streets of the Jewish neighborhoods, repulsive and annoying. Not that the hostility toward him diminished Trebitsch's commitment to his new calling. He frequently gave public speeches on street corners, and was ready to debate any Jew who engaged with him. At the same time as he continued with his missionary work, Trebitsch also concluded his theological studies at McGill University, and within a year he had graduated as a fully-fledged Lutheran cleric.

In the early summer of 1901 Trebitsch wrote to Margarethe and asked her to join him in Montreal. Within weeks she had arrived, and in July of that year they were married by Reverend McCarter. But all had not gone according to plan. Although Margarethe's father had made promises of a dowry, the amount of money he sent with his daughter was woefully insignificant in Trebitsch's eyes, especially as it was evident that no more money was on the way.

FROM CANADA TO ENGLAND

For a couple of years, Trebitsch desperately tried to build up his own Christian mission and use his activities to solicit church funds and missionary society funds. But although he seems to have been a very popular public speaker, and was well regarded for his effervescent enthusiasm, his admirers failed to deliver the financial support he needed for even his family's most basic needs. When Margarethe's sister died in early 1903, Trebitsch abruptly gave up the Montreal mission and, without saying goodbye to anyone, returned to Hamburg with Margarethe.

Trebitsch then left his pregnant wife with her parents and traveled to London, where he attempted to get a job with the London-based parent organization of the missionary society. But between Reverend Lypshytz's undisguised disdain for the man who had stolen his wife's watch, and slowly emerging information of financial irregularities perpetrated by Trebitsch in Montreal, the London missionaries were reluctant to engage him and turned him away.

Trebitsch was unfazed by his failure with the missionaries, and he now took a job as a pastor in Appledore parish, a sleepy village in the southwest of England. How he got the job is unclear, as he was not authorized as an Anglican minister by Randall Davidson, the Archbishop of Canterbury. It was some months before he took the basic priesthood entry test, but he failed, getting miserable scores, even in the Hebrew section.

In July of that year, Margarethe gave birth in Hamburg to their second son, their first having died shortly after birth in Montreal. They named the baby boy Ignatius Emanuel, and Margarethe joined her husband in Appledore soon afterward. Things were not going well there. Trebitsch's superficial knowledge of the Gospels and of basic church practice were slowly catching up with him, and had it not been for a lucky break that allowed him to leave the priesthood, he would have been defrocked and fired from his job within a short period of time.

Suddenly, totally out of the blue, Trebitsch had what might be termed a lucky break. This was the unexpected death of Margarethe's father, Captain Johann Kahlor. For the first time in his life, Trebitsch came into some significant money. He immediately moved to Hampton-on-Thames, a suburb of London, and began to live like a country squire. Around this time he began using an English last name: Lincoln. He bought a large house, furnished it, and started to buy books on economics and politics, as his focus shifted away from spiritual pursuits to these more temporal interests. Within eighteen months he was actively looking for employment in the political sphere, and eventually applied for a job as director of the Temperance Society, an organization that fought against the evils of alcoholism and against the distilleries and breweries that underpinned this social problem. Trebitsch did not get the job but, as fate would have it, as a result of the interview he came to the attention of one of the society's principal funders, a wealthy industrialist called Benjamin Seebohm Rowntree.

EUROPEAN ROAD TRIP

Rowntree was a decent man who would later regret that he had ever met Trebitsch. He was born in York into a wealthy Quaker family. His father, Joseph Rowntree, started the famous cocoa and chocolate company bearing his name, which by the end of the nineteenth century was one of the largest employers in Great Britain. Benjamin was an indefatigable social activist who over the years funded and was involved in various research projects whose aim was to reveal the true extent of poverty in Britain at the time by demonstrating how many thousands of families and individuals were living below what he referred to as the "poverty line," a term he invented to define the minimum amount of money required for people to house themselves and keep themselves warm, clothed, and fed at a basic subsistence level.

For some reason, Rowntree took a liking to Trebitsch. He was fascinated by his ability to speak multiple languages, flowing seamlessly from one to another. Trebitsch also impressed him with his wide, if not deep, knowledge of numerous subjects. For Rowntree, Trebitsch's value lay in the fact that he could conduct research for him in European countries, and then convey that information back to him and his team in flawless English so that it could be examined and analyzed together with similar British data.

Rowntree appointed Trebitsch as his personal private secretary and awarded him a generous salary plus a travel allowance that paid for any expenses associated with travel on his behalf. How he could have been so naïve is hard to understand. Perhaps it was Trebitsch's obsequious middle-European charm, or perhaps Trebitsch was just the right person appearing at the right time, when Rowntree had a specific need for a linguist for this particular project. Either way, Rowntree's connection with Trebitsch, although it would last for several years, proved to be a disaster from the very beginning.

Trebitsch's job description was simple. Rowntree wanted him to collect and collate information about the social and economic conditions in rural Europe. To facilitate this Trebitsch requested that his well-connected boss enlist the help of the British Government Foreign Office so that he could gain entry to all the British embassies in the various countries he intended to visit. Rowntree unquestioningly arranged for Trebitsch to receive a letter of introduction from his close friend Captain John Sinclair MP, later 1st Baron Pentland, at the time a senior cabinet minister in the British administration, then in the hands of the left-leaning Liberal Party. Bearing this letter, Trebitsch confidently strode into the Foreign Office in London on March 20, 1906, and purposefully sought and obtained letters of introduction for him to show senior British diplomats at the embassies in France, Belgium, and Switzerland.

Initially things went well. Trebitsch arrived in Belgium and was the recipient of generous assistance from the British embassy staff in Brussels, who brought him into contact with Belgian government officials and other people who could furnish him with the information he was looking for. In Switzerland he received similar help from British officials. Full of confidence, and clearly enjoying the extravagant hotels and high living afforded by his lavish travel allowance, Trebitsch wrote to the Foreign Office for more letters of introduction, asking that they be addressed to a variety of British diplomats across Europe. They were sent out, but soon things were going wrong. An indignant letter from the vice-consul in Copenhagen complained of Trebitsch having "borrowed" books and not returned them.

Slowly a pattern emerged. In each new city Trebitsch's demands would escalate. He inexplicably began to see himself as an instrument of the British government, researching statistics that would contribute to his adopted country's economic success, both at home and abroad. In reality he was just a private individual on an idiosyncratic research mission on behalf of a wealthy patron, and no British official was obliged to help him in his quest for information. That being the case, his ill-mannered demands for assistance were wholly misplaced.

While most of the British embassy officials he encountered diplomatically ignored his obnoxious behavior, in the summer of 1907 Trebitsch met his nemesis, in the form of the British ambassador to France, Sir Francis Bertie. Bertie was notorious for his arrogance and eccentricity, and seems, with the benefit of hindsight, to have been an unlikely candidate for the post as principal British diplomat to such an important European country. Notwithstanding this anomaly, his revulsion for Trebitsch was well placed. It seems that the intrepid researcher had arrived in Paris and marched into the embassy brandishing his introduction letter, demanding that the staff arrange for him to obtain a collection of official publications from the French Foreign Ministry that would cost them two thousand francs.

In the scheme of things this was not a huge sum of money, but Bertie was unwilling to spend a penny of the embassy's budget on this rude, self-important upstart, even if he was working for a leading British industrialist.

Bertie's refusal to cooperate with Trebitsch resulted in a bitter exchange of correspondence. Trebitsch threatened that unless his request was met he would take his complaint to the "highest quarters." The ambassador forwarded the offending letter to his superiors in London, in the expectation that they would support him. He could not have been more wrong. In a saga that epitomized the indecision and weakness of government bureaucracy and ability to waste time on trivialities, this matter of no importance spiraled into a full-scale diplomatic crisis, involving multiple diplomats, civil servants, elected officials, and representatives of a foreign government. In the end Trebitsch got his books, which he insisted should be sent via an expensive courier to Rowntree's home in England. They were probably never read, and the victory was in every sense meaningless. But Trebitsch was not someone concerned with meaningful victories.

MEMBER OF PARLIAMENT FOR DARLINGTON

By 1909 Trebitsch had concluded his research for Rowntree. The book based on the collected data was not published until 1911, but in the meantime Trebitsch went in a new direction, using his connection with Rowntree to launch one of the most extraordinary political careers in British parliamentary history. There is no historical record to explain how he obtained the nomination as Liberal Party candidate for the Darlington constituency, but the facts speak for themselves. In April 1909, the Darlington Liberal Association unanimously decided that their designated candidate for member of Parliament would be Ignatius Trebitsch-Lincoln.

What was particularly strange about this decision was that Trebitsch was not naturalized as a British citizen until May 1909, which meant that at the time of his selection he was still a foreign national. In truth, his selection was to all intents and purposes academic. The next general election was not expected for several years and, in any event, the seat in question had been solidly Conservative for many years, in the hands of the Pease family, whose influence permeated the local scene at every level. Trebitsch's chances of being elected to Parliament were limited to the point of being non-existent.

Then, in the fall of 1909, the House of Lords – the unelected upper chamber of Britain's Parliament – soundly rejected the "People's Budget" proposed by Liberal Prime Minister David Lloyd George, precipitating a political crisis that led to an unexpected general election in January 1910. Suddenly Trebitsch was up for election, thrusting him into the spotlight, a situation he embraced with characteristic relish. His opponent was Herbert Pike Pease, later 1st Baron Daryngton, whose credentials were impeccable, and whose record was unsullied by watch thievery and reckless controversies. In addition, the Pease family had held the Darlington seat for decades, and would continue to hold the seat long after Trebitsch had disappeared from the scene. More significantly, there was a local distaste for foreigners, which in Trebitsch's case was further augmented by an undercurrent of anti-Semitism. But Trebitsch was not concerned by these impediments; indeed, they seemed only to spur him on.

As usual, he desperately needed money, having already burned through a very generous loan granted to him by Rowntree when he left his employment. Shamelessly he turned to an old acquaintance, Reverend Hayim Lypshytz, and asked him for a loan of a few hundred pounds to help fund his election campaign. Incredibly, Lypshytz loaned him the money, an act of generous-spiritedness that defies explanation, particularly in light of the disappearance of his wife's gold watch coinciding with Trebitsch's departure from his mission in 1897. It goes without saying that the loan was never repaid.

With money in hand Trebitsch began to stage public meetings to inform bemused voters why his opponent would be a terrible choice to represent Darlington, despite years of honorable service. He also used Lypshytz's money to produce a squalid pamphlet titled "Powder and

Shot," in which he attacked Pease and the Conservatives for their intention to introduce trade tariffs to protect British manufacturers. According to the pamphlet, similar policies in Germany had forced many Germans to eat their own horses, and even their pet dogs. This remarkable claim was attributed to the lack of any serious competition from abroad – the inevitable result of strict trade controls – which meant that local suppliers were able to raise the prices of staple goods, forcing thousands of Germans into dire poverty.

The residents of Darlington began to fall for Trebitsch's exotic charm, as he entertained them with shrill political speeches peppered with outlandish stories and bizarre slogans. "You are Britishers by a mere accident of birth," he declared in his thick accent at one meeting, "while I am a Britisher by choice." Asked how he could ever expect to win such an uphill race, he confidently predicted that he would win "by thirty votes."

Conservatives were understandably irritated by his nerve and by his nefarious tactics. Pease supporters began to attend his public meetings, purposely drowning out his speeches by chanting "Cocoa! Cocoa!" – a reference to his former paymaster, Rowntree, whose money everyone assumed was funding his campaign. Trebitsch later wrote that at one meeting "we had the unpleasant experience of being pelted with banana skins, stones wrapped in paper, and rotten eggs." But he was undeterred, having experienced the same hostility and worse during his time as a missionary to the Jews of Montreal.

One of the most astonishing aspects of Trebitsch's campaign strategy was the decision to play up his Jewishness. The same man who had unceremoniously discarded his Jewish faith the moment his father had died, declared to a meeting of Liberal Party supporters, "I am a Jew and I am proud to belong to that race. I am a Jew with all the ability of a Jew. I have the will power, the lofty ideas, and I will show the Tories of Darlington that I can fight like a Jew." This was a perfect example of Trebitsch's self-serving audacity. Rather than remaining silent on the subject of his origins, he responded to persistent anti-Semitic murmurings by highlighting his roots, proclaiming them a great advantage in his fight to win the seat.

Another remarkable feature of the campaign was the endorsements he received from some of the most prominent politicians of the day. Herbert Samuel, later 1st Viscount Samuel, a senior minister in the administration who was to become famous as the first British high commissioner in Palestine, joined Trebitsch as he campaigned in Darlington, telling the residents that they were "fortunate in having so able and active a champion." Even Winston Churchill sent a message wishing Trebitsch every success "in the fine fight you are making for Free Trade, Land Reform and Popular Government."

The day of the election arrived, and Trebitsch had himself driven around Darlington in an open-top car while he stood in the back waving dramatically at startled pedestrians. A remarkable ninety-five percent of the electorate came out to vote. In the evening more than two thousand people crowded into the town hall to hear the result. The vote count was so close that both candidates agreed to a recount. This delayed announcing a winner, and the crowd began to get rowdy. Finally, at 10:30 p.m., the mayor of Darlington strode up to the podium to declare who had won.

"A deafening shout from the multitude below quite drowned the voice of the mayor," the local newspaper later reported, "but the fact that Mr. Lincoln stood at his right hand and was the first to step forward was a plain indication that he was the victor." The result was indeed a stunning victory for Trebitsch. He had predicted winning by thirty votes. He was off by one. The margin was a twenty-nine-vote lead over his opponent, with 4,815 votes to 4,786. Even fellow Liberals were shocked, with one senior party member referring to the result as an "electoral freak."

BANKRUPTCY

Trebitsch was overjoyed at his spectacular triumph. After a brief visit to Hungary to see his aged mother, he returned to England, settling in London. On February 23, 1910, he delivered his first speech to the House of Commons. Bemused MPs were treated to a detailed analysis of trade statistics, lengthy personal anecdotes, and a series of stale jokes. The press devoted far less attention to the content of his speech than they did to the thickness of his Hungarian accent. As the year progressed Trebitsch addressed Parliament several more times. But his contributions were unexceptional, and the initial interest in his unexpected election victory fizzled out as he drifted out of the spotlight.

Meanwhile Trebitsch was going through a profound financial crisis. Members of Parliament were not salaried or given any financial support; rather they were expected to be of independent means. Trebitsch had no income, save for money borrowed from an array of hapless lenders. But his reckless overspending was on a scale that far outweighed what he was able to borrow. In the fall of 1910, Rowntree realized that the significant sums of money owed to him by Trebitsch would never be repaid, and that his former protégé was hopelessly in debt.

Rowntree acted swiftly and decisively. The Darlington Liberals were informed that on no account was Trebitsch to stand for reelection. Rowntree's concern became more urgent when it became clear that the government was about to collapse and a new national election was imminent. On November 30, 1910, Trebitsch startled his constituents by announcing his retirement from the Darlington seat, abruptly concluding one of the most extraordinary – if short-lived – political careers in the history of British politics. In the election that took place a week later, Herbert Pike Pease, Trebitsch's election opponent only a few months earlier, easily retook the Darlington seat, which he held onto until 1923.

The following month, in January 1911, Trebitsch attended a formal meeting with his numerous creditors to agree on a way forward. The creditors eventually decided to reduce his overall liability by seventy-five percent, although even as they signed the terms of the deal they must have known that their money was lost for good. Trebitsch, by now the father of four children – a fifth child was born in May 1911 – did not seem in the least bothered by his predicament. He moved his family from Darlington to Watford, just north of London, and embarked on a series of speculative high-risk business enterprises that revolved around Eastern European oil exploration.

Using his toxic mixture of charm and lies he convinced an impressive array of large and small investors to put their money into two shell companies – Amalgamated Oil Pipelines of Galicia and The Oil & Drilling Trust of Romania – both of which were predicted by him to produce massive returns as soon as crude oil began to flow across Eastern Europe. But the dream of massive oil discoveries and extraction in that region never materialized, and within a short time Trebitsch knew that his continued exaggerated promises to investors were fraudulent. But he needed the money to fund his lifestyle, so the charade continued.

Even as the earlier investors realized they had been conned, he managed to find new ones who fell for his extravagant promises and magnetic personality. Meanwhile, one after another the nominal directors whose names Trebitsch had used to attract investment resigned, not wanting to sully their names by association. The entire enterprise was heading toward a spectacular disaster. In September 1913 the High Court in London appointed an official receiver to take over the business to sort it out. The receiver was a former Liberal parliamentary colleague of Trebitsch, John McDonald Henderson. Henderson waded through the opaque financial affairs of the various arms of the business and discovered liabilities exceeding £150,000 – more than fifteen million pounds in today's values.

At a hastily called meeting of shareholders and banks Trebitsch was asked to explain the deep financial problems. In an impassioned defense of his activities he dismissed the financial issues as meaningless, claiming that the oil exploration and pipeline business in Eastern Europe was "on the verge of success." But his luck had run out. Investors demanded that any saleable assets be liquidated immediately so that at least some of their money could be salvaged. The receiver was put in complete control and Trebitsch marginalized. In December he resigned in protest, but his departure was, by this time, completely irrelevant. It would take almost a decade for the mess he had left in his wake to be sorted out, and the vast majority of the shareholders never saw a penny of their investments returned.

By now Trebitsch was desperate. His lavish spending had continued unabated and his hunger for money knew no bounds. But left without anything to sell to investors he was forced to find friends who would loan him money to help him out. Even this proved difficult. Rowntree flatly refused to lend him any money, and others were also understandably reluctant. Eventually, in the early summer of 1914, John Goldstein, a seasoned financier who had known Trebitsch for several years, agreed to lend him money if he could find a reliable guarantor. A few days later, Trebitsch informed him that Rowntree had agreed to guarantee the loan. Goldstein was a little incredulous and wrote to Rowntree at the

National Liberal Club, where he resided while in London, to get written confirmation. A few days later he received a reply from Rowntree confirming the guarantee. With this letter as security, Goldstein advanced Trebitsch £750 to be repaid in three months. But the letter from Rowntree was an elaborate hoax, forged by Trebitsch, whose own frequent attendance at the National Liberal Club had enabled him to interfere with Rowntree's mail.

This brazen fraud was the twisted result of Trebitsch's indomitable optimism. He was still convinced that some Romanian oil concessions he had held onto were worth money and could be sold, enabling him to repay Goldstein and a host of other creditors. He made plans to travel to Bucharest to arrange for their sale, but on August 1, 1914, the First World War broke out, dashing any hopes of travel to Romania. By this time the house in Watford was gone, and the Lincoln family resided in a grubby boarding house in East London.

With no viable options to repay his debts Trebitsch was beyond desperate. He begged Goldstein for an extension to the loan. He then forged another letter from Rowntree to underwrite the extension. It was too late. In late November Rowntree discovered the deception, and immediately wrote to Goldstein to deny any association with Trebitsch or the loan. In a furious showdown Goldstein informed Trebitsch that he was going to involve the police if his money was not returned immediately. Perhaps in the hope that Trebitsch would somehow find the money to repay him he waited a full three weeks before carrying out his threat. But by then Trebitsch had fled to Holland, where his torrid life was about to take another extraordinary twist.

INTERNATIONAL SPY

In December 1914, Trebitsch contacted the British War Office and presented officials with an outrageous plan to help beat the Germans in the horrific war that was gathering pace with each passing week. As a fluent German speaker, and a former member of Parliament, he suggested he might present himself to the Germans as a traitor and gain their trust, and meanwhile he would report back to the British if he came across any useful information. His ultimate goal would be to gain their complete trust so that he could inform the British of any plans involving the German war fleet, enabling the Royal Navy to surprise and destroy German warships in an epic naval battle that would change the course of the war.

It is fair to say that Captain P. W. Kenny at the Secret Service Department in the War Office (if that was his real name) did not take Trebitsch too seriously. He suggested that Trebitsch travel to Holland to find out how much cocoa Germany imported via Rotterdam. Perhaps Kenny was being facetious, or maybe he was telling Trebitsch politely that his services were not required, but either Trebitsch didn't get the joke or he was so desperate for a formal role that he chose to treat the ridiculous quest as an official mission. He would later claim his discussion with Kenny was a double bluff, and that he had always intended to lead the Royal Navy into defeat against the German war fleet, not the other way around. In reality, his desperation had allowed him to drift into a world of wild fantasy and make-believe, a one-way trip from which he would never return.

On December 18, 1914, Trebitsch arrived in Rotterdam, where he arranged to meet with the German consul-general, Carl Gneist, to offer his services as a double agent. Gneist considered Trebitsch odd, but in times of war even the strangest people can become an asset, so he decided to give him some innocuous information to take back to London. Although Gneist was only testing the waters, Trebitsch saw this mission as official validation and, of course, a financial opportunity. He rushed back to London where he met with Kenny, who immediately sent him to the director of British Naval Intelligence, a formidable man called Admiral Sir William Reginald Hall (1870–1943), later an admiral and a member of Parliament. Hall was extremely suspicious of Trebitsch, and after hearing him out, and taking copies of the German information, told him he would be in touch to discuss payment and future missions in due course.

But the wait was unbearable for Trebitsch, who was under huge pressure. At any time he could be arrested for fraud, and within a matter of weeks several loans would come up for repayment and angry creditors would be at his door demanding money. A fugitive from the law, and completely broke, he tried to put pressure on Hall by getting in touch with contacts from his parliamentary days. One former parliamentary colleague owned a popular Sunday newspaper. Trebitsch met him and presented his story as a complaint about Hall, who he said was missing a unique chance to end the war. He also wrote to Sir Winston Churchill, who as First Lord of the Admiralty was directly responsible for the Royal Navy.

Neither of these approaches produced results, so Trebitsch began peddling the story of his espionage experiences to a number of newspapers in the hope they would pay him. But the idea that any newspaper would pick up the story was ludicrous. Any war-related news story needed to be cleared by the censors, and publishing a story without going through the censors was a criminal offense.

Predictably, Trebitsch's frantic efforts came to the attention of the War Office, and Hall decided that a line needed to be drawn. He summoned Trebitsch to his office, and in an uncomfortable meeting informed him that he would not now, nor ever, be required to work for the British government in any capacity, and that the papers he had brought with him from Holland were worthless, and he would not be paid for having obtained them. As if this was not shocking enough, Hall told him that he was also fully aware of Trebitsch's financial situation and criminal activities, and that it was not the habit of the British authorities to engage felons as secret agents.

The meeting was nothing less than a bombshell. It was clear Trebitsch had reached the end of the line and had no place left to turn. He rushed back to his wife and informed her he would need to leave the country immediately. In the early hours of January 30, 1915, Trebitsch slipped out of the shabby boarding house where they lived, and made his way to the southern coast of England, where he boarded the ocean liner *Philadelphia*, bound for New York. When he arrived in New York he made contact with his three brothers, who all lived there. But none of them was in any position to support him, or even offer him a place to stay. Unperturbed by this setback, Trebitsch turned to some fellow passengers whom he had befriended while on the ship to New York to ask them for financial assistance. Remarkably he was able to obtain loans to keep himself going while he worked on finding a source of income that would propel him back to the lavish lifestyle he desired.

He contacted the German embassy in Washington DC to offer information he claimed to have about British war plans, but a telegram from Berlin informed the embassy staff to "have nothing to do with Trebitsch." In truth, espionage was not at the forefront of Trebitsch's mind. His negative experiences with the War Office in London had more than convinced him that the secret service was not financially lucrative. Instead, he decided sensational news stories were where the money was. In May, the widely read magazine *New York World* ran a screaming headline: "Revelations of I. T. T. Lincoln, former Member of Parliament, who became a German Spy."

The story that followed in two separate articles saw fantasy embrace fiction, with nuggets of truth used as a launch pad for dramatic and self-aggrandizing escapades involving Trebitsch and an entire cast of dubious characters. Trebitsch claimed he had tried to gain the trust of the British authorities by bringing them secret codes from the Germans, but somehow his intentions were discovered and he had been forced to escape for his life. Incredibly, he defended his hatred for the British as a natural reaction to their arrogant prejudice toward foreigners, and particularly those originating from the Austro-Hungarian Empire – this from a man who had not only been elected to Parliament by British citizens, but who had systematically defrauded every British individual with whom he had ever come into contact.

A SPELL IN JAIL

For a few weeks after the articles appeared Trebitsch found himself in the limelight, as his incredible "exploits" were reported around the world. But his triumph was short lived. The British government may have allowed a fugitive from the law to remain at large while it was involved in a major military effort, but the embarrassment caused by the articles, particularly when they were delightedly used as propaganda by the Germans, meant that this irksome troublemaker had to be caught and silenced. Hall at the War Office made arrangements with the famous Pinkerton Detective Company to apprehend Trebitsch, which they did on August 4, 1915. The following morning he was arraigned in front of a judge in Brooklyn.

Trebitsch claimed the accusations of fraud were false, insisting his crime was espionage, and he tried to claim political asylum. But the judge dismissed his protestations, and he was remanded at the infamous

Raymond Street Jail in Brooklyn while the court awaited papers from London. For the next few months the British authorities struggled to organize Trebitsch's extradition, even sending a senior police officer to New York to accompany the prisoner back to London. But the judge was in no hurry to comply, and the disgruntled British policeman was forced to return to London empty-handed. Meanwhile, Trebitsch had managed to charm the prison authorities and gain their trust. He became a celebrity prisoner and was granted privileges that allowed him to leave and reenter the jail almost at will.

In January 1916, as the extradition process worked painfully slowly through the justice system, Trebitsch published a scurrilous book titled *Revelations of an International Spy* in which he made the fantastic claim, among others, that his espionage exploits had begun long before the onset of war, and had included his European work for Rowntree, going back almost a decade. More startling than this "revelation" was the fact that by the time the book hit the bookstores Trebitsch had escaped from jail and completely disappeared.

Some days after his escape, he made an unannounced visit to the offices of the *New York American* newspaper, where he gave an impromptu press conference to the astonished editorial staff before disappearing again. As the police desperately sought his whereabouts, journalists from multiple media outlets received letters from Trebitsch on an almost daily basis. Each letter contained ever more incredible claims and threats. With the police looking clumsier and more inept with each passing week, it became evident that his escape and incessant agitation were nothing more than a remarkable publicity stunt. The entire run of his book sold out, and his notoriety grew exponentially.

Trebitsch was eventually recaptured on February 20, 1916, after being betrayed by an acquaintance whom he had arranged to meet. He was thrown back into jail, this time with stringent supervision. His extradition was still not finalized, and his lawyers appealed for clemency to the United States Supreme Court. The court was in no mood for leniency, however, and on May 8 issued a ruling that Trebitsch be extradited back to England at the earliest opportunity. Once again, a police officer was dispatched from London to accompany him back to England, and after sailing back across the Atlantic, Trebitsch finally appeared for his arraignment at Bow Street Police Court in East London on June 6.

Within a month he was on trial, and although he presented an impassioned defense on his own behalf, the jury found him guilty of all the charges without even retiring to consider their verdict. Bearing in mind that he was being tried for petty fraud, his sentence was unusually harsh – three years' high-security incarceration at Parkhurst Prison on the Isle of Wight. The decision to treat him so severely was unquestionably influenced by his anti-British activities in New York, activities that had caused enormous embarrassment to the British during this period.

In the summer of 1919, Trebitsch was released, and, with his British citizenship revoked, arrangements were made for his deportation. At first there was a reluctance to let him go, with senior British officials inexplicably concerned that he would join forces with the new Communist government in Hungary, but when that government collapsed Trebitsch was unceremoniously deported to mainland Europe. Instead of making his way back to Hungary, however, he journeyed to Berlin, where within weeks he had joined forces with an extreme right-wing group, for which he wrote anti-British articles in the *Deutsche Zeitung*, a disreputable publication that ranted against anyone who was thought to have contributed to the humiliation of Germany's defeat in the recently concluded world war.

It was at around this time that Trebitsch got to know a man called Colonel Max Bauer, a former senior German military strategist with a bitter resentment of the German political class, which he blamed for Germany's capitulation and surrender. Bauer was deeply involved in revolutionary agitation against Germany's new leaders, although he remained widely respected by huge swathes of the German public. He was also a vicious anti-Semite, but strangely enough this does not seem to have affected his relationship with Trebitsch, even though he must have known that Trebitsch was born a Jew.

THE KAPP PUTSCH

Bauer, like so many others before him, was taken in by Trebitsch's charm and intelligence and adopted him as his protégé. In the fullness of time – again, like so many before him – this was a decision he would live to regret. By October 1919, Trebitsch had become Bauer's closest adviser, and also his principal public representative. Very soon Trebitsch was caught up in various intrigues involving every kind of unsavory political character engaged in trying to reestablish the German monarchy under the rule of Crown Prince Wilhelm, son of the recently abdicated and exiled Kaiser Wilhelm II.

In March 1920, Trebitsch took a leading role in one of the most remarkable of all the interwar national insurrections – the notorious Kapp Putsch. This five-day chaotic and ultimately abortive coup lasted between March 13 and March 18, 1920, and was led by a right-wing East Prussian bureaucrat, Wolfgang Kapp. It was an abject disaster from the very beginning. Although initially the recently installed German Weimar government was frightened enough to flee to Dresden, within a couple of days a general strike was declared by the unions, and it became clear that most of the military had not sided with the plotters, leaving them utterly powerless on every front. As a result, the coup collapsed in shambles.

During the five days of frantic activity, however, at least one person seemed to revel in every moment – Trebitsch. Appointed by Kapp as his "Minister of Public Information," Trebitsch became the official spokesman of the revolution, and its censor. No telegram could leave Germany without his permission, and no information could be published unless he had personally approved it. The foreign correspondents in Berlin reacted angrily and vehemently, but to no avail. Trebitsch took particular delight in ripping up the telegrams of British correspondents in front of them. Within a couple of days the "revolution" had started to unravel, and on March 17 Kapp, seeing that the game was up, summarily resigned and fled to Sweden. Other conspirators also fled, or were arrested, as law and order was reestablished and the Weimar government took back the reins of power.

One of the last senior Kapp conspirators to leave the Reich Chancellery building at the end of the coup, on March 18, was none other than Trebitsch. On his way out he encountered two men who had flown in especially from Munich to join the now-defunct revolution. One was fifty-two-year-old Dietrich Eckart, a poet and journalist, who had recently established the *Deutsche Arbeiterpartei*, forerunner of the Nazi party. The other was a young former corporal from Austria and future Chancellor of Germany, Adolf Hitler. Many years later Hitler's press secretary referenced this chance meeting in his memoirs, noting that Hitler would recall that Eckart had prevented him from talking to Trebitsch on account of his Jewish origins.

Trebitsch himself never mentioned the meeting, and was possibly not even aware that it had taken place. As he rushed out of the Chancellery building that day he was probably so absorbed in planning his survival following yet another catastrophe that the sight of a middle-aged journalist accompanied by a scruffy ex-military sidekick would not have caught his attention. One can only speculate what might have happened had they met under different circumstances.

When the Kapp Putsch collapsed, most of the principal instigators went into hiding or left Germany to avoid arrest. Trebitsch obtained a false identity but remained in Berlin, while the authorities argued among themselves whether or not to arrest him. Eventually he left Berlin for Munich where he joined the other conspirators who had taken refuge there, protected by the right-wing sympathetic local government of Gustav Ritter von Kahr. He reconnected with his new friend, the right-wing reactionary and former military commander, Colonel Max Bauer, who had written a pamphlet defending the Putsch and its intentions. Trebitsch returned to Berlin to try and find a publisher for the pamphlet, but he came to the attention of the Berlin police, who were now looking to arrest him, and was forced into hiding.

Soon afterward, Trebitsch returned to Munich, where he took refuge in a house in which some of Germany's most notorious right-wing extremists were in hiding. These included Bauer and General Erich Ludendorff, the commander of Germany's military forces during the First World War, and a bitter opponent of postwar peace arrangements. Although there were many Germans who felt bitter about postwar arrangements, what the Kapp Putsch had proven to both Ludendorff and Bauer was that there was not yet a critical mass of people who could effectively oppose the British and French influence over Germany and take control. But instead of giving up and moving on, they came up with an audacious plan to form alliances with similarly disenchanted groups in other countries, so that the right-wing reactionary forces in Europe could return the continent to its prewar arrangements. German militarists, Russian czarist sympathizers, Austro-Hungarian conservatives, and a range of anti-Communists and malcontents would unite together in an unbeatable force to liberate Europe from the weak and ineffective governments that had emerged after the Versailles Treaty.

RIGHT-WING CONSPIRATOR

The only government in Europe that was potentially sympathetic to such a cause was the recently formed right-wing regime of Admiral Miklós Horthy in Hungary. Bauer decided to travel to Budapest with Trebitsch to convince Horthy to support a transcontinental revolution. Before they left for Budapest, Trebitsch was sent to Berlin to raise money. Characteristically, he failed to keep a low profile, and within a matter of days he was arrested and thrown into jail. The investigating officers found him in possession of a cache of documents that not only incriminated him, but also Bauer, Ludendorff, and many others, for being involved in activities that the German authorities labeled "high treason." Incredibly, Trebitsch managed to escape from jail and he disappeared from Berlin, much to the dismay of the authorities. The Munich chief of police was informed, and requested that the authorities locate Trebitsch and incarcerate him immediately. But the Munich police chief was a right-wing sympathizer, and rather than arrest Trebitsch he allowed him to leave Munich and escape across the border into Austria. To pay for his travel and other expenses Trebitsch arranged for a correspondent of the Hearst newspaper empire to interview Ludendorff in hiding for a hefty fee, which Ludendorff immediately sent to Trebitsch.

Bauer and Trebitsch made their way to Budapest, arriving there on May 15, 1920. Hungary had been in turmoil since Horthy had launched his violent coup a few months earlier against the Soviet-sympathetic regime of Jewish-born Béla Kun (originally Kohn). Although he was now in complete control of the country, forces loyal to him and other armed militia groups continued to kill suspected Communist sympathizers, and the leading world powers refused to recognize the regime. The only way Horthy could gain international recognition was if he would sign the proposed postwar peace treaty, which meant making humiliating territorial concessions. Within a matter of weeks after Bauer and Trebitsch's arrival in Budapest the treaty was forced on the Hungarians by the Allied powers, a development that was to lead to deep and bitter resentment. (Much later on this was one of the reasons Horthy joined forces with Hitler, with devastating consequences for Hungarian Jewry.)

In the middle of May 1920, with the demands of Versailles looming, and the treaty still unsigned, the new regime was ready to talk to anyone who might help keep the country intact. The timing of the arrival of the two insurrectionists from Germany could, therefore, not have been more fortuitous. Bauer and Trebitsch were given five-star treatment and feted wherever they went. Within a couple of days Horthy met them privately, as a result of which he designated three of his closest reactionary collaborators – all of them squalid ultra-nationalist extremists – to discuss and formulate their proposal. One of them was a brutal paramilitary murderer, Pál Prónay, commander of a violent "white terror" militia group who was also a vicious anti-Semite.

At the first meeting with Bauer and Trebitsch, Prónay agitatedly pulled Bauer aside and, glancing across at Trebitsch, exclaimed in a hoarse whisper, "Colonel, your dark, fat friend is a Jew! I don't feel safe talking in front of him!" Bauer laughed, shook his head, and placed a reassuring arm around Prónay's shoulders, telling him, "I would put my hand in the fire for that man – you can talk in front of him without any fear whatsoever." Prónay was skeptical and remained extremely suspicious of the "dark, fat Jew" throughout their liaisons. Bauer, meanwhile, would soon have cause to regret his confidence in Trebitsch.

For the next few days there were intensive discussions, and a strategy was formulated to combine the forces of all the nationalist, anti-Communist, postwar disillusioned groups of Hungary, Germany, and Russia into one force that would militarily and politically undo the new realities that had been imposed on Europe in Versailles. The plan relied on a cast of characters that included Russian political and military émigrés in Germany, leading German military heroes such as Bauer and Ludendorff, and the new Hungarian government together with its array of reactionary supporters. The funding for the plans was glossed over, but it was assumed that the Hungarian government would take on the initial expenses, and that as the revolution crystallized money would materialize from a number of other sources.

The plan was completed and written up by Trebitsch and signed by Bauer on May 26, 1920. In early June, Hungarian representatives signed the peace treaty at the Trianon Palace in Versailles, leaving Hungary with just twenty-eight percent of the territory it had controlled before the war. Undoubtedly the attitude toward signing had softened with the knowledge that a plan now existed that would potentially render the peace terms irrelevant within a short space of time. Even as the ink was drying on the newly signed treaty the conspiracy was gathering pace in Budapest. Russian czarist generals and Hungarian officials met secretly with Bauer and Trebitsch to finalize the proposed alliance which would lead to "a great Russia, a great Germany, and a great Hungary." There was even the suggestion that Trebitsch should go and meet with the emerging fascist leader in Italy, Benito Mussolini, to secure his support for the revolution, but that meeting never took place.

Then, in the month of July, things began to unravel. Trebitsch became very frustrated that Ludendorff – who commanded enormous respect in Germany and beyond, and whose public support for the plan was crucial – had remained aloof and refused to join him and Bauer in Budapest. The plan also relied heavily on Hungarian government support, but Horthy and his coterie of advisers had begun to lose interest. For all kinds of reasons they had become reluctant to stir up a hornet's nest across Europe, particularly if doing so involved a collection of embittered nationalists with nothing more in common than a desire to turn their resounding defeat into a vindicating victory. Additionally, in the previous month the tide had begun to turn against the anti-Soviet White Army in the Russian civil war, which reduced the importance of the Russian collaborators. Meanwhile the political pendulum in Europe had visibly started to swing to the right, which meant that a violent right-wing pancontinental coup was less urgent. With each passing week Horthy became less inclined to take the lead in what he realized could turn out to be a fiasco.

FAILURE AND BETRAYAL

At around the same time Trebitsch became aware of a plot to kill him. An odious German nationalist involved with the plotters, Franz von Stephani – who was possibly Jewish – wrote to an associate in Budapest asking to have Trebitsch eliminated. Somehow Trebitsch saw the letter and confronted Bauer, who told him he had nothing to fear. But Trebitsch was naturally anxious. He was well aware that many of the people they were dealing with were coldblooded murderers, and he must certainly have known that they were rabid anti-Semites. Stephani's letter abruptly woke him up to the fact that he wasn't involved in some shifty business deal, or a diplomatic row with an ambassador, or a parochial political skirmish. The people he was now involved with were by and large amoral schemers for whom life was cheap and who were ready to kill people without a second thought.

In early September, while on a "mission" to Vienna, Trebitsch suddenly disappeared from sight, taking with him a suitcase full of documents containing all the intricate details of the conspiracy. Bauer was horrified by his disappearance and even more so by the theft of the documents. He desperately tried to locate Trebitsch, but to no avail. He then asked Prónay to find Trebitsch and bring him back to Budapest by any means possible. Prónay dispatched two associates to track Trebitsch down, kidnap him, and bring him back, but although the pair managed to find him they were unable to carry out their orders.

Trebitsch was in hiding, desperately trying to secure his safety and his financial security. He approached both the British and the French embassies in Vienna and tried to sell them the documents, with the claim they contained vital military and political information that would guarantee the future security of Europe. The irony of this dreadful treachery was not that it had been so presciently predicted by Prónay only a couple of months earlier, as much as that it was Trebitsch who had formulated much of the material that he was now offering for sale. The British were understandably wary of Trebitsch. The French were similarly uninterested, and rejected his offer. So Trebitsch offered the documents around and discovered that the Czechoslovakian government was eager to get its hands on them. The newly formed country of Czechoslovakia was made up entirely of territory taken from Hungary and Austria, and its leaders were terrified that Hungary would join forces with reactionary forces within Czechoslovakia and attempt to repossess what it had lost.

Trebitsch journeyed to Prague to negotiate the sale. Once there he managed to secure a substantial price for his document collection.

The Czechoslovak government immediately attempted to use the information in the documents as propaganda by providing the story of the conspiracy to a variety of international newspapers. It also reached out to diplomatic contacts in various countries to inform them of the impending threat. But what was discovered on both fronts was that Trebitsch was considered so unreliable that no one paid much attention to what he had shared with the Czechs, and the British Foreign Office actively dismissed the information as "concoctions."

For Trebitsch this was devastating. For the first time he had actually been in possession of valuable intelligence information, having been at the very heart of a nascent reactionary movement that threatened the stability of the free world, a movement that was the beginning of a trend that would ultimately morph into Fascism and Nazism. But Trebitsch's tarnished reputation militated against anyone of note taking anything he said or conveyed in documents remotely seriously. Even if some believed that he had been involved with Bauer and Ludendorff, Horthy, and the Russians, his very participation in the events he described meant that the plot must be fantasy, and the plotters fantasists. In late December 1920, *The Times* newspaper in London published a three-part summary of Trebitsch's documents in which his name featured frequently. Editorial comment scorned the entire conspiracy, referring to it as the hopeless dreams of a bunch of powerless and delusional ideologues, proven principally by the fact that they had involved Trebitsch.

The one who suffered most from Trebitsch's latest antics was his former mentor and "friend," Colonel Max Bauer. Ridiculed and criticized in equal measure by friend and foe, Bauer went into hiding near Munich, where he wrote a number of confused and confusing accounts of his involvement with his former protégé, which he admitted had been entirely foolish. But his credibility as a political force was shattered.

Trebitsch was also being discredited by the media and the authorities, who claimed variously that he was a fantasist, or a forger, or both. He was compelled to react, particularly to the charges of forgery, as if he was guilty of fabricating the documents this meant the Czechoslovak government would not pay him the remainder of the money. He launched a lawsuit against the Czechs to demand that he be paid what was due to him. This public legal challenge could not be ignored and resulted in his arrest in Vienna in February 1921. He was summarily charged with two contradictory crimes: high treason – a criminal charge punishable by death – and forgery, on the basis of the complaint by the Czechs that the entire cache of documents he had sold them was fabricated for financial gain.

The two-month trial that ensued was a complete debacle. With no one willing to give evidence either for or against Trebitsch, the trial was dominated by Trebitsch, who spoke at great length about his life history, his beliefs, his involvement with the unsuccessful right-wing conspiracy, and his complaints against the Czechoslovak government. The court demanded that the Czechs submit photographs of all the documents they had bought from Trebitsch to establish their authenticity or otherwise, but only a fraction were sent. After a close examination of these photographs, and several other documents confiscated from Trebitsch, the court concluded that they were all undoubtedly genuine. That being the case Trebitsch should have been executed for the crime of high treason, but once again he was in luck. There were certain members of the Austrian coalition government who had also been in touch with right-wing extremists associated with the conspiracy, which meant that if Trebitsch was found guilty it might cause a political crisis. So, in a remarkable twist of fate, he was found not guilty of both charges and released for deportation in late June.

The press was waiting for him as he exited the jail. There had been wild speculation as to what he would do now he was free. It was widely believed, including by Trebitsch himself, that his former associates had assigned assassins to kill him, and with no country eager to give him residency rights there seemed nowhere for him to go. A hushed silence fell as he began a brief statement to the gathered journalists. "My destination," he told them, "is a profound secret. I will disappear as if the earth has swallowed me up, and will reappear in an unexpected place within eight years. Meanwhile, I will have accomplished my task."

ADVENTURES IN CHINA

Over the next few months, Trebitsch was spotted under various aliases in a number of different cities in Europe. In the fall of 1921 he sailed under a false name to the United States. He managed to slip through at the port in New York, but in January 1922 was arrested on immigration charges, then released when he agreed to leave the US via the West Coast. By October he was reported to be in Tokyo. From there he traveled to China, where he soon became involved with a local warlord, General Yang Sen. Soon afterward Trebitsch joined the circle of another warlord, Wu P'ei Fu (who would later deny having ever met Trebitsch). By 1923 he was the adviser to yet another warlord, Wu Hung Chiang, with whom he went to Europe on a quest to find a massive loan, and also to introduce him and his circle to political figures and individuals of influence. One of the first people he visited was Colonel Max Bauer, whose willingness to see Trebitsch can only be wondered at. Bauer took the Chinese delegation to Germany to meet Ludendorff and others, and soon a loan for $25 million was secured from an Austrian industrialist in exchange for mining rights in China. Trebitsch returned to China, but the loan never materialized and before long he was ousted from his advisory position.

In early 1925 Trebitsch once again arrived in New York, where he sold the story of his Chinese exploits to the *New York World* magazine. Fact was heavily laced with fantasy, with Trebitsch claiming to have been at the heart of every major political and military upheaval in China over the previous three years, always one step ahead of the foreign intelligence services and various other foes, real and imagined. But New York had nothing to offer Trebitsch, and he once again went to China where he took to wandering around the country. During that time he decided to explore Buddhism, and within a few months he had moved to Sri Lanka (then Ceylon), where he secluded himself in a Buddhist monastery and began to prepare himself for conversion.

This might have turned out to be just another of Trebitsch's insane flirtations, but a dreadful piece of news from England seems to have pushed him over the edge in a way that nothing had ever done before. Trebitsch's relationship with his family had always been sporadic. Over the years he had seen them from time to time, and his wife and some of his children had even spent time with him in China. One of his sons, Ignatius Jr., was a soldier in the British army. In December 1925, while in a state of complete drunkenness, he and another soldier entered a residential house in an attempt to rob it. In the course of the robbery a resident confronted the pair and Ignatius Jr. drew a pistol and shot him dead. The two soldiers were quickly apprehended and tried, and on January 21, 1926, Ignatius Jr. was sentenced to death.

By the time Trebitsch heard about his son's impending execution, it was already February. Trebitsch immediately boarded a boat to Holland to get to Europe in time to say goodbye, but when he arrived in Amsterdam he was told his son was already dead. The news seems to have jolted Trebitsch into a new realm. From that moment on his flirtation with Buddhism would dominate his life. Through approaches to various official bodies and people of influence he tried to reach Tibet or to meet with the Panshen Lama, who was one of the two holiest figures in Buddhism. But Trebitsch's reputation as a master of intrigue and political agitation dogged him; for the rest of his life he was unable to do even the simplest things without stirring the interest of official bodies and foreign intelligence services.

In 1931 Trebitsch was formally ordained as a Buddhist monk. He was never seen in Western clothes again, and from that time on went only by the name "Chau Kung." His wanderings continued apace, now accompanied by an entourage of Buddhist disciples comprising an eclectic group of European converts, whose lives he ruled with an iron fist. He made several attempts to reinject himself into European life, first by visiting Europe with a plan to open Buddhist monasteries for European converts, and later by trying to insert himself into the diplomatic processes generated by the various flare-ups between the Japanese and Chinese in China. In 1938, five years after the death of the thirteenth Dalai Lama, Trebitsch claimed to have experienced a vision in which he was told he was the new incarnation of the Dalai Lama. His "vision" was well timed. The previous year he had publicly declared his support for the Imperial Japanese after the Japanese army occupied most of Shanghai. It was a politically astute move, as the Japanese would retain control of Shanghai until 1945. In recognition of his vociferous support – most Chinese Buddhists loathed the Japanese – the Japanese government formally recognized him as the Dalai Lama, although in practice this recognition had very little meaning, as the Tibetan-controlled religion rejected the claim outright.

When the Second World War broke out Trebitsch offered to help the Nazis defeat the Allies, claiming to have intelligence information that would benefit their war aims. Perhaps he was motivated by his lifelong obsession with the British, which over the years had vacillated between visceral hatred and a longing to return to England. But nothing came of his flirtation with the Nazis, and as the war progressed he faded into complete obscurity. When Trebitsch died following an operation on his stomach, on October 6, 1943, his death didn't merit a mention in any of the hundreds of newspapers that had reported on him during his lifetime. People who heard about his death speculated that he was poisoned by the Nazis, or by allied sympathizers who despised him for his relationship with the Japanese and the Germans, or by Buddhist extremists who loathed him for his claim to be the Dalai Lama, or by Jews who were disgusted by how he gave them such a bad name; or perhaps he simply died from a stomach ailment, followed by a poorly executed medical operation. We will never know.

Yitzhak Trebitsch, Ignatius Timotheus Trebitsch, Ignatz Timothy Trebitsch-Lincoln, Abbot Chau Kung – and that's just a list of his real names! Over the years this tempestuous chameleon employed dozens of aliases, and adopted the cultures and religions of almost every place he visited. He learned to speak a dozen or more languages fluently and wrote copiously in most of them. He was involved in the politics of countless countries over many decades and his name was recognized by millions across the developed world. He was notorious for his association with agitation, intrigue, espionage, and the shady world of individuals who have no substance and no morals.

And yet, despite his notoriety, he left no lasting imprint, no legacy, and no achievements. His was a life of all wind and no waves. Restless, unhappy, unsuccessful, and ultimately a loser, the Orthodox boy from Hungary who ended his life as a Buddhist monk in Shanghai remains an enigma to all those who have encountered the remarkable story of his peripatetic existence.

Conclusion

"Nonsense is nonsense, but the history of nonsense is scholarship."

PROFESSOR SAUL LIEBERMAN (1898–1983)

Before I draw this book to a close, I feel obliged to write a few lines about my sources and other related topics. While putting this book together, I was in two minds whether or not to include footnotes. After much reflection, and consultation with others, I decided that footnotes would detract from the book rather than add to it, and opted not to include them.

Let me explain. My intention in writing this book was to bring this collection of fascinating Jewish history vignettes to the attention of the widest possible readership. The inclusion of footnotes that many readers would not refer to or be interested in would inevitably have been a distraction, or even deterred people from reading this book. In an academic work aimed at academics, footnotes are a mandatory requirement. But this book is not intended for academics – although they are, of course, welcome to read it.

The subject of every chapter in this book has been amply treated in numerous academic works – by which I mean books, PhD theses, and articles – all of which are fully footnoted, as one would expect them to be. For those reading this book who are curious to learn more about any aspect of this book, a simple Google or JSTOR search will direct them to all the contemporary academic material so that they may enlighten themselves further.

Nevertheless, I do feel I owe the readers at least some information on the source material I relied on when writing the book, particularly as there are chapters that have been written in a style that has much more in common with dramatic fiction than with non-fiction history, including details of private conversations, and descriptive elements that may cause readers to wonder about their accuracy.

For the chapter on Shabbetai Tzvi I relied mainly, although not exclusively, on the superb biography authored by Professor Gershom Scholem (1897–1982), originally published in Hebrew in 1957, later translated into English by Rabbi J. Zwi Werblowsky (1924–2015) and published by Princeton University Press in 1976. This thousand-page book is rich in detail and is principally based on contemporary accounts that recorded the events of the Shabbetai Tzvi episode as they happened. It was the extraordinary level of detail in Scholem's sources, and his own masterful account based on those sources, that enabled me to present the story in a more appealing narrative style.

But even Scholem has his idiosyncratic limitations. Born "Gerhard" Scholem into a highly assimilated, ardently nationalistic German-Jewish family, he rebelled against his parents, initially by zealously opposing the First World War, and then by becoming a devout Zionist. Gerhard turned into Gershom, and thus newly named he announced to family and friends that he was moving to Palestine at the earliest opportunity.

Scholem's parents reacted by doubling up on their loyalty to Germany and its culture, using a variety of passive-aggressive tactics to persuade their son that his German identity was of far greater importance than his Jewish heritage. On one notorious occasion, Scholem's parents ironically presented him with a framed photograph of Theodor Herzl under their Christmas tree, after which he made sure that he was never again home at Christmas time. Eventually, Gershom's father, Arthur Scholem (1863–1925), realizing that his son was thoroughly committed to Zionism and to the study of Judaism, informed him in writing that he was expelled from his parental home and would henceforth be cut off from any financial support.

Gershom was totally undeterred. He befriended the Austrian-born Jewish philosopher Martin Buber (1878–1965), then living in Berlin, and was soon publishing articles about Kabbala in Buber's *Der*

Jude. Arthur reacted with utter contempt, dismissing his son's academic achievements in a scathing letter:

> It's a pity that all this scholarship should have been used so idly, and a double pity that such productive powers and intellectual labor should have been expended so uselessly... three cheers for Hebrew and Jewish studies – but not as a career. Take my word for it, if you don't change course you will experience a bitter shipwreck.

David Biale (b. 1949), Emanuel Ringelblum Professor of Jewish History at the University of California, brilliantly characterizes Gershom Scholem's lifelong obsession with Jewish mysticism, and particularly Sabbatianism, in an excellent article in the second volume of *The Sabbatian Movement and Its Aftermath: Messianism, Sabbatianism and Frankism.* The article is titled "Shabbtai Zvi and the Seductions of Jewish Orientalism" and paints a vivid picture of Scholem's escape from the rigidly ordered world of his Teutonic upbringing into the mystical world of Oriental Kabbala, a journey that included his embrace of Zionism and an uncompromising commitment to Jewish identity, albeit one that was entirely secular.

This bias toward mysticism as the key factor of Sabbatian activism dominates Scholem's analysis of anything connected to Shabbetai Tzvi's Messianism, to the exclusion of any political or other factors. But while Scholem was fascinated by the primeval emotionalism of Jewish mysticism, he was simultaneously repulsed by its raw, magnetic obscurantism. In the end, Scholem was an unreconstructed product of the very background he was struggling to escape.

For all the depth of his understanding of kabbalistic texts, and his appreciation of the kabbalists who authored them, Scholem could never quite put himself in their shoes, nor understand their world as an insider would. His judgment of the wistfulness that marks mystical Judaism is ultimately not too dissimilar to the way his father had judged him. One can almost hear Arthur's scornful voice echo in Gershom's scathing criticism of Vladimir Jabotinsky (1880–1940) and his Revisionist Zionists in the 1930s, and again in later life, when he directed his ire against the Religious Zionist Gush Emunim settler movement, all of whom he disdainfully referred to as "latter-day Sabbatians."

My own judgment of the Shabbetai Tzvi episode in general, and the Sabbatian movement in particular, is rather different, best illustrated in the puzzle of how so many highly intelligent and deeply religious individuals found themselves drawn to Shabbetai Tzvi and his spurious messianic pretensions. Epitomizing this phenomenon is the seemingly incomprehensible transformation of Rabbi Hayim Benveniste (1603–1673) from critic to acolyte, a metamorphosis even Scholem is forced to acknowledge might have been motivated by political considerations.

Rabbi Benveniste was an absolute insider, the author of classic commentaries on earlier halakhic literature that were to become definitive works. When Shabbetai Tzvi returned to Izmir as the "Messiah" in 1666, Rabbi Benveniste was in the midst of a political battle for the top rabbinic spot in the city, and his endorsement of Shabbetai Tzvi resolved the dispute in his favor. Nonetheless, it makes no sense to believe that a rabbi of such distinction could have endorsed this flawed messianic contender purely for personal gain, without having had at least some confidence in Shabbetai Tzvi's credentials as a potential redeemer of the Jews and, crucially, for that potential to be within the framework of normative Judaism.

It also makes no sense for Jewish mysticism to be presented as the sole focus of any group within Judaism, as if Jewish philosophy or Jewish law has no role to play within the group or in how other Jews relate to it. This means that while it might be valid to label Shabbetai Tzvi as the "mystical Messiah" as a way of referencing the fact that he employed Lurianic Kabbala as the engine to drive his movement, to pigeonhole him and Nathan of Gaza, and the movement they launched, as the unadulterated products of Jewish mysticism gone awry is an oversimplification that simply misses the mark.

The Baal Shem of London was a trickier subject to pin down than Shabbetai Tzvi. Details of his life are sketchy, and much of what is known about him is conjecture. Even during his own lifetime he was somewhat of a mystery. The first person to seriously research him was Rabbi Dr. Hermann Adler (1840–1911), chief rabbi of Great Britain and the British Empire from 1891 until his passing in 1911. Adler's research into the Baal Shem took him more than eight years and ultimately resulted in a lecture he gave to the Jewish Historical Society of England, later published in *Transactions of the Jewish Historical Society of England (1902–05).*

Adler's opening words are informative and telling:

> You have heard of the process of whitewashing in so far as it applies to historic criticism. It is a process which has been adopted by several eminent writers in the interests of truth. The great historian, Professor Mommsen, whose recent demise is deplored by the whole world of letters, has essayed to prove that the views commonly entertained about the Roman emperors is not correct, and that Tiberius was by no means a tyrant of so dark a hue as he is ordinarily depicted. Froude endeavors, and not without some measure of success, to clear Henry VIII of the many imputations cast upon him. Marat, the unlovely, has recently been described as the People's Friend. And, indeed, gradually personages who were regarded aforetime as ogres are being transmuted into heroes or saints, so that the present period of historic writing may be described as the age of whitewash. I fear that I shall have to enter upon an opposite course, and cast something of a shadow upon a character that has hitherto loomed before the mind of Anglo-Jewry encircled with a halo of sanctity.

Adler goes on to reveal that the mystique which surrounded the Baal Shem during his lifetime, and which persisted for more than a century after his death, was somewhat overstated and that the truth about him was rather less sensational. And yet, Adler does not comment on the fact that no one seems to have challenged the Baal Shem for being a fraud during his time in London, and that by and large the stories of his supernatural powers were believed and repeated without question long after he had died. In terms of the purposes of this book, perhaps these are the points that are in need of greater reflection.

And then of course there is the amusing mix-up over his portrait, which has further complicated matters and added yet another layer of curiosity to this already strange story.

The Emden-Eybeschutz controversy is a unique historical episode for a whole host of reasons. I grew up being vaguely aware of it, while at the same time I really knew nothing about it. What I did know was that there had been a fierce disagreement between these two great rabbis, and as I grew older I also became aware that the disagreement had something to do with Shabbetai Tzvi.

Anyone who has grown up in a religiously observant Jewish world, as I did, is acutely conscious of the fact that anyone who does anything so radical that it breaks all the accepted rules of Jewish life is identified as a heretic and airbrushed out of history, or alternatively, one only hears about him as a reprobate miscreant. The most striking feature of the Emden-Eybeschutz controversy, considering the magnitude of the storm it generated, is the fact that both Rabbi Yaakov Emden and Rabbi Yonatan Eybeschutz were considered as mainstream as any rabbi could be, and the works of both were studied and utilized with equal reverence, and without comment.

It is totally astonishing that this epic battle had no residual effect on either of the primary protagonists. Bearing in mind how serious the accusations were, and the level of animosity the controversy unleashed, the fact that the reputation of neither party was posthumously affected is nothing short of remarkable. What makes it particularly astounding is the fact that Rabbi Yaakov Emden produced dozens of books and publications condemning his bête noire in vivid detail; indeed, his publications against Rabbi Eybeschutz make up the majority of his literary output by a huge margin. This abundant output was aided considerably by one crucial factor: Rabbi Yaakov Emden owned his own printing press, which meant he was only ever subject to his own censorship, a factor that was clearly non-existent when it came to disparaging Rabbi Yonatan Eybeschutz. These first-hand accounts of the events and of key elements of the controversy by Rabbi Yaakov Emden provide ample details of the raging *maḥloket*, albeit from the rather jaundiced view of his perspective.

Nevertheless, as a result of this body of material, and a lengthy published riposte by Rabbi Yonatan Eybeschutz, we have access to a blow-by-blow narrative of the events, and even much of the dialogue, of the controversy as it unfolded. Other contemporary accounts round off the picture and have allowed historians and scholars to compile comprehensive records of this epic battle. Accordingly, although mainstream Jewish religious literature has tended to ignore the dispute, as if it never happened or at least as if it didn't matter, even if it did happen, in almost every era since the eighteenth century books and articles have appeared that address the broad story, or some detailed aspect of it, allowing us to gain a comprehensive picture of the dispute and its principal characters.

Some of the accounts are biased in favor of Rabbi Yonatan Eybeschutz; others are partial to Rabbi Yaakov Emden. Advocates for the former reject the notion that someone as great as Rabbi Eybeschutz, and as widely accepted by rabbis who would certainly have kept their distance had he been a heretic, could possibly have been a partisan of Sabbatianism, the repulsive theological detritus of Shabbetai Tzvi's failed messianic coup.

Meanwhile, those who argue in favor of Rabbi Yaakov Emden point to the fact that he was not acting alone, citing the active support he received from leading rabbinic colleagues such as Rabbi Yaakov Yehoshua Falk of Frankfurt. Moreover, Rabbi Emden was also revered and respected, widely acknowledged as a sincere and pious man. Why would an eminent man like him have launched a battle against a distinguished fellow rabbi unless he was absolutely certain that the fight was justified? And more pointedly, why does it make more sense to impugn Rabbi Yaakov Emden than it does to offend Rabbi Yonatan Eybeschutz? After all, a great rabbi is a great rabbi, and if we believe that Rabbi Yaakov Emden was a great rabbi too, what justification is there for us to dismiss his claims regarding Rabbi Yonatan Eybeschutz simply because we are not comfortable with them or because Rabbi Eybeschutz denied their validity?

Ultimately, as some less partisan historians have made clear, there is not enough hard evidence to determine Rabbi Eybeschutz's innocence (or guilt) beyond any shadow of doubt, and therefore not enough reason to dismiss Rabbi Emden's single-minded obsessive mission to destroy Rabbi Eybeschutz's reputation as the vile rantings of a lunatic. In hindsight, one can certainly speculate how either side in the dispute might have behaved differently, and consider why it is they behaved the way they did. But whatever the outcome of such alternative scenario considerations, it should not distract us from the fact that we have the data of the story, namely the accusations, their cause, and the consequent reactions and events. Additionally, we have the knowledge that Sabbatianism was far more deep-rooted than many people may have realized at the time, and than we could ever truly understand.

For source material relating to this whole affair I relied on a variety of books and articles, each of which is unique in its own way. The list that follows is not in any particular order, and there may also be other sources from which I gleaned snippets of information that made it into the final narrative. Nevertheless, in terms of the substance of the narrative, and the unusual level of detail that is particularly evident in this chapter of my book, all of it emanates from the sources cited below.

First there are the excellent books about Rabbi Yonatan Eybeschutz, *Beit Yehonatan* (2 volumes; Sighet, 1908) and *HaRav R. Yonatan Eybeschutz* (New York, 1954), by Rabbi Leopold (Yekuthiel Yehuda) Greenwald (1889–1955), the polymath rabbinic scholar who was for over thirty years (1924–55) the rabbi of Congregation Beth Jacob in Columbus, Ohio. Rabbi Greenwald's books and the book by Mortimer J. Cohen, *Jacob Emden – A Man of Controversy* (Philadelphia, 1937), are hostile to Rabbi Yaakov Emden, with Cohen showing particular contempt toward his subject, as the title of his book indicates. Nevertheless, they are thoroughly researched and, if one can look past the inherent bias, they provide the reader with invaluable information.

Another valuable resource was the two-volume *Gedulat Yehonatan* (Warsaw, 1934), a sympathetic biography of Rabbi Yonatan Eybeschutz by David Loeb Zinz (c. 1890–c. 1940). In particular, this work was the source for the dramatic deathbed scene that opens the chapter on the Emden-Eybeschutz controversy. Zinz claims to have heard about this episode at first hand from Rabbi Avraham Shalom Halberstam (1857–1940) of Stropkov, Slovakia, who had in turn heard it from his father, Rabbi Yehezkel Shraga Halberstam (1813–1898), the famous hasidic leader of Sieniawa, in Poland. The latter's father, Rabbi Hayim Halberstam (1793–1876), the preeminent Polish hasidic rabbi of his day, known as the "*Divrei Ḥayim* of Sanz" (Nowy Sacz, Poland), was descended from Rabbi David Ashkenazi (1710–1753), Rabbi Yaakov Emden's younger brother. It appears that the remarkable deathbed incident, which ultimately resulted in Rabbi Yaakov Emden's burial in close proximity to Rabbi Yonatan Eybeschutz, was a well-established family legend.

However, as there is no alternative source for this astonishing version of events, it cannot be treated as irrefutable historical fact. Nevertheless, Rabbi Yaakov Emden's burial so close to the final resting place of Rabbi Yonatan Eybeschutz – the man against whom he waged a bitter battle for over twenty-five years – demands an explanation, and the deathbed story certainly provides us with an account as to how it might have happened. Ultimately I leave it up to you, the reader, to judge whether the story makes any sense or not.

As I have already mentioned, numerous historians and scholars have written about the protagonists in the Emden-Eybeschutz controversy, and I relied on many of their works for details of the events that marked its course. Avraham Hayim Wagenaar's *Toledot Yaavetz* (Amsterdam, 1868), which charts the troubled life of Rabbi Yaakov Emden, was particularly useful, as was the comprehensive account of his life by Rabbi J. J. Schacter in his richly detailed and well-constructed doctoral thesis, "Rabbi Jacob Emden: Life and Major Works" (Harvard University, September 1988). For details of the Nehemiah Hayyun controversy that foreshadowed the Emden-Eybeschutz affair I relied on a number of the Hebrew polemics that were published at the time, as well as Elisheva Carlebach's excellent book, *The Pursuit of Heresy: Rabbi Moses Hagiz and the Sabbatian Controversies* (New York, 1990).

Moshe Aryeh Perlmutter's contentious book, *Rabbi Yehonatan Eybeschutz and His Attitude Toward Sabbatianism* (Tel Aviv, 1947 [Heb.]), is very much in line with the views of his teacher, Professor Gershom Scholem. Perlmutter seizes upon various textual proofs to demonstrate that Rabbi Yonatan Eybeschutz was a Sabbatian believer and concludes that the evidence points distinctly in that direction. Unsurprisingly, Mortimer Cohen vigorously rejected Perlmutter's central thesis in an article entitled "Was Eibeschuetz a Sabbatian?" (*Jewish Quarterly Review*, vol. 39, no. 1).

Cohen's article was merely a proxy attack on his greatest nemesis, the twentieth century's foremost academic expert on the history of Kabbala, Gershom Scholem, who firmly believed that Rabbi Yaakov Emden accurately identified insidiously inserted references to Shabbetai Tzvi in the notorious amulets authored by Rabbi Eybeschutz. In 1937, in his seminal article on Sabbatian antinomianism, "Redemption through Sin," Scholem wrote (translation taken from G. Scholem, *The Messianic Idea in Judaism* [New York, 1971]):

> I cannot conceal the fact ... that after thoroughly examining both Eybeschütz' own kabbalistic writings and all the polemical works that they engendered, I have been forced to conclude that he was indeed a Sabbatian, as both Jacob Emden and, in a later age, Heinrich Graetz insisted.

Although this confident assertion was the result of years of research, and of having previously expressed this view verbally to other scholars of Jewish history, its publication produced a storm of protest from Torah-observant scholars of Jewish studies, for whom the idea that an acclaimed rabbinic luminary of the yesteryear was a closet heretic was an attack on traditional Judaism they could never allow.

Soon enough, Rabbi Reuven Margolies (1889–1971), a prolific author and polymath who bridged the world of traditional rabbinic scholarship and modern academia, took Scholem to task in an article titled "The Reason for Rabbi Yaakov Emden's Opposition to Rabbi Yehonatan Eybeschutz" (Tel Aviv, 1941 [Heb.]). In it he expressed the view that Scholem had missed the point completely, and that the Emden-Eybeschutz controversy had its roots in a particular if rather obscure episode. According to Margolies, the genesis of Rabbi Yaakov Emden's animosity toward Rabbi Eybeschutz was a public position he had taken against Hakham Tzvi Ashkenazi (1656–1718), Rabbi Yaakov Emden's father, regarding a halakhic case involving a chicken found not to have a heart. As a result, said Margolies, Rabbi Emden bore bitter personal animosity toward Rabbi Eybeschutz, whom he considered an insolent upstart with no right to challenge the erudite scholarship of his revered father, and he was consequently willing to destroy Rabbi Eybeschutz's reputation on the basis of the flimsy amulet-based evidence of Sabbatianism.

Scholem responded to Margolies's article in an article titled "*Leket Margalyiot*" (Tel Aviv, 1941), in which he vigorously defended his position and rejected Margolies's theory as baseless conjecture. In the years that followed, the Margolies thesis was dismissed piece by piece and, as recently as 2015, Rabbi Edward Reichman M.D. presented incontrovertible evidence that there was no connection between Rabbi Yonatan Eybeschutz's stance on the chicken without a heart and Rabbi Yaakov

Emden's antipathy toward his adversary (see E. Reichman, "A Letter from a Torah Sage of the 18th Century to the Medical Faculty of the University of Halle [January, 1763]: The Selective Deference of Rabbi Yonatan Eybeschutz to Medical Expertise as a Lesson in the Complex Relationship Between Medicine and Halakhah," *Verapo Yerapei: Journal of Torah and Medicine of the Albert Einstein College of Medicine Synagogue* 6 [2015]: 89–112). It is worth noting, however, that disproving Margolies does not mean Scholem was correct in his certainty.

The richest sources of information about the dispute are without any doubt the numerous books and pamphlets authored by Rabbi Yaakov Emden, both during and after the controversy. His candid recollections of the events as they unfolded, coupled with salacious accusations against his opponent and his supporters, all clearly garnered from third-party sources, make surprising reading bearing in mind the author – a respected senior rabbi and the author of highly acclaimed works of serious scholarship.

Rabbi Yaakov Emden's extreme language, and his utter disdain for Rabbi Yonatan Eybeschutz, jumps out of the pages of his various publications. Plainly, they record just one side of the dispute, and no similar narrative emerged from the pen of his nemesis, whose one publication was restricted to a spirited defense of the controversial amulets. Nevertheless, if one sidesteps the extreme rhetoric in Rabbi Emden's publications, focusing instead on the narrative sections that record the actual evolution of the controversy, and the events that unfolded as the affair intensified, Rabbi Emden's writings are an invaluable resource.

Of particular interest and importance is Rabbi Yaakov Emden's autobiography, *Megillat Sefer*. Discovered and published over a century after his death, the autobiography has long been the subject of fascination. Until it was published, it had been assumed that Rabbi Emden's caustic rhetoric – copiously evident in his various Emden-Eybeschutz controversy-related polemics – was solely reserved for Rabbi Yonatan Eybeschutz and those he suspected of even the slightest sympathy or support for his foe. The autobiography laid that myth to rest. His candor is disconcerting, to say the least. No one is spared his acerbic criticisms, including senior rabbinic personalities with whom he maintained good relations. Surprisingly, Rabbi Emden even critiques himself, writing candidly about his innermost struggles and most intimate secrets without any attempt to gloss them over or to censor uncomfortable truths for self-serving purposes.

The autobiography has been published several times, but the editions cited most often are the Kahana edition and the Bick edition. The first was published in 1897 by the Odessa-based Jewish history scholar David Kahana (1838–1915), while the second was published in 1979 by a curious misfit called Avraham Bick (1914–1990). Bick, who claimed descent from Rabbi Yaakov Emden, was an Orthodox rabbi in New York, the grandson of Rabbi Yitzhak Bick (1864–1932), onetime member of the Russian Duma, and later the distinguished rabbi of Providence, Rhode Island.

Bick was notorious as a prominent Communist sympathizer and advocate, an activity that was unusual for an Orthodox rabbi, to say the least. He published a number of pamphlets in Yiddish advocating Communism to American Jews and in 1956 was summoned to appear before Senator Joseph McCarthy's House Committee on Un-American Activities, where he pled the Fifth Amendment seventy-three times. Eventually he moved to Israel, where he worked as an editor for the Mossad Harav Kook publishing house. He died in 1990, childless and in complete obscurity.

Both editions of Rabbi Yaakov Emden's *Megillat Sefer* are ostensibly based on an original manuscript at the Bodleian Library in Oxford. Kahana's edition is undoubtedly the more reliable of the two, despite a number of problematic editing issues that are beyond the scope of this concluding chapter. Bick's edition, however, despite his insistent claims of superiority vis-à-vis the Kahana edition, is so flawed and faulty that Rabbi J. J. Schacter, who has been working on a critical edition of *Megillat Sefer* for many years, summarily dismissed it in his masterful dissertation as "uncritical, incomplete and simply sloppy. It is barely more useful than an earlier historical novel in Yiddish about Emden by the same author.... In general, all of Bick's work is shoddy and irresponsible, and cannot be taken seriously."

In 2008, Rabbi Dr. Meir Wise published a translation of *Megillat Sefer*, which he claimed was based directly on the Oxford manuscript. Although I agreed to be one of the sponsors of the project, after reading the published book it became clear to me that Wise had used Bick's thoroughly flawed "transcription" as the basis for his translation, and had never seen the original manuscript, never mind read it.

Consequently, I wrote a critical review for the highly respected rabbinic publishing and bibliography website *Seforim Blog* to set the record straight (http://seforim.blogspot.com/2012/03/megillat-sefer-translation-review-by.html). Among other things, I pointed out that:

> [Any] claim that the original Bodleian manuscript was used is too ridiculous to refute, as it is patently untrue. Clearly the source for this translation is the Bick edition. This decision to rely on the Bick edition of *Megillat Sefer*, on the basis of Bick's introduction to his version, is so puzzling as to put into question the depth, if any, of Rabbi Wise's ... knowledge of contemporary academic research and opinion regarding Rabbi Emden, and in particular his autobiography.

Meanwhile, in 2014, Rabbi Avraham Shmuel Yehuda Gestetner, presiding rabbi of the controversial Shar Hamishpot rabbinical court in Monsey, New York, published a perplexing book titled *Megillat Plaster*, in which he made the startling claim that *Megillat Sefer* was actually a forgery, authored by an agenda-driven proto-Reform Jew in the nineteenth century. This preposterous proposition was accompanied by *ad hominem* attacks on anyone who had questioned this thesis, following the publication of an earlier, truncated version of the book in 2009. What was most remarkable about Gestetner's intemperate dismissal of his critics, and indeed ironic, was that a central plank of his argument against the authenticity of *Megillat Sefer* was that it was inconceivable that a rabbi of Rabbi Yaakov Emden's stature and credentials would be so critical of his rabbinic colleagues in a work intended for publication.

In summary, the foregoing survey of the sources I utilized in the compilation of the Emden-Eybeschutz chapter demonstrates the vast and varied range of literature the affair generated. The publication frenzy commenced even as the *maḥloket* raged across Europe in the 1750s and has continued unabated ever since. Each era has had its own literary relationship with the controversy, and disagreements over the causes of the dispute and the motivations of those involved have meant that the actual story was lost in the background, as agenda-driven debates drew attention away from what actually occurred. And as I have shown, these debates continue to act as a distraction even today.

My intention in writing the chapter on the Emden-Eybeschutz controversy was to open up the actual story of what happened to a broad audience. Consequently, I deliberately reduced the confusing analysis and agenda-driven critiques that overshadow so much of the literature and focused instead on the narrative sequence of events, using the pertinent information scattered across the sources as my guide. To the extent that it is possible to remain neutral, I have tried to do so, and hopefully readers will be able to evaluate for themselves how the controversy unfolded and why it caused so much turmoil to the various communities and individuals who were involved.

The *Get* of Cleves controversy was a landmark legal dispute that escalated into a full-scale polemic involving dozens of rabbis and communities in the late eighteenth century, and although it did not have quite the same devastating consequences as the earlier Emden-Eybeschutz dispute, it nonetheless left its mark on the halakhic system and continues to reverberate to this day.

About fifteen years ago I was asked to get involved in a tragic situation on behalf of an estranged wife who was unable to obtain a *get* (Jewish divorce document) from her recalcitrant husband. He had apparently been very abusive toward her during their time together, and the marriage had irretrievably broken down. The husband had initially refused to grant her a *get* under any circumstances, a situation that would have meant she could never remarry according to Jewish law – a bitter life sentence for an Orthodox Jewish woman. Eventually, however, the husband "conceded" and told his wife's family he would give the *get* in exchange for an exorbitant sum of money.

It was a straightforward case of extortion, and sadly the wife's family were simply not able to come up with the extravagant sum the husband was demanding. It was at that point that they approached me to see if I would be able to get the husband to drop or at least reduce his demands in exchange for the *get*.

I was utterly outraged. Even if the family were able to come up with the money, I felt it would be a disgrace to give in to this man's sick demands. After consulting with the distinguished *dayanim* (rabbinic judges) of the London Beth Din, I informed the husband and his family that I would be conducting a public campaign against him and anyone associated with him – namely, his family, his business associates, his supporters – until he gave his wife her *get*, with no strings attached. I told them we would organize demonstrations outside homes and businesses, publish adverts in the newspapers, and write to every synagogue and institution he was associated with to explain how he was a *mesarev ledin*, the Jewish legal term for a person who has been formally declared in contempt of court.

I was quite confident that this strategy would be effective, as I was aware that the husband's family was terrified of negative publicity and would be loathe for such a situation to erupt. Then, out of the blue, I got a phone call from a close friend of the husband's family. The man informed me that a few years earlier the husband had been diagnosed with a chronic mental condition, and that if I went through with my threatened action the family would use his history of mental illness as proof that he was legally incompetent, which would mean he could not give the *get*.

After the call ended I sat for a while in contemplation, not sure what to do. Before receiving the call everything had seemed so simple. I had been convinced that the matter would be resolved quickly. Now it appeared that I had been outsmarted by this ploy. I decided to call one of my uncles, whose knowledge in Talmud and halakhic precedent is unsurpassed, and whose devoted attention to my Torah studies as my personal rebbe had been the springboard for my own enthusiasm for Torah knowledge – and, in fact, all knowledge. I called him, explained what had happened, and asked for his opinion. Was it time for me to give up?

After hearing me out, and chastising me for my initial over-confidence and for being so adversarial, he asked if I had ever heard of the *Get* of Cleves.

"No," I admitted, "although I have heard of Anne of Cleves." Anne of Cleves was the fourth of Henry VIII's unfortunate wives. "Did Henry VIII give Anne a *get* when they divorced?" I asked my uncle.

I remembered that Henry VIII had been interested in obtaining the Talmud tractate on divorce when he tried to end his first marriage to Catherine of Aragon in the face of vehement opposition by the Catholic

Church, at that time headed by Pope Clement VII. Perhaps the plan that failed for Catherine had succeeded for Anne?

My uncle chuckled at my informed ignorance. "No, no, not Anne of Cleves – I'm talking about the *Get* of Cleves. Just look into the story of the *Get* of Cleves and you will see why any threat to thwart a *get* by claiming that the husband is insane and legally incompetent is totally empty. The man who called you has no idea what he is talking about, and clearly has no concept of the halakhot surrounding insanity and incompetence when it comes to giving a *get*. After the *Get* of Cleves, being insane enough so that you can't give a *get* is more or less impossible."

The first stop on my quest to find out about the *Get* of Cleves was an excellent article by the indefatigable Rabbi Aaron Rakeffet (Rothkoff) titled "The Divorce in Cleves" (*Gesher*, vol. 4, no. 1 [New York, 1969]). Rabbi Rakeffet began with the following astonishing quote from a responsum of Rabbi Moshe Feinstein (1895–1986) regarding a man with messianic delusions whose wife wanted to divorce him in Rabbi Feinstein's then community of Lyuban, in 1929 (*Iggerot Moshe, Even HaEzer* 1:120):

> Because of this belief [that he was the Messiah] he acted foolishly and constantly strove to read the Torah and to serve as the cantor at public services. Even when the congregation did not permit him to do so, he still fought for these privileges. He traveled from city to city in order to correct the world. At times, he took the property of others and did not return the items until the owners contributed to charity. He climbed trees in order to preach to passersby. He even appeared publicly in the nude, as he claimed he was like Adam before the sin. All this came about because of his belief that he was the Messiah. *Otherwise he was completely normal.*

I was so taken aback by the last sentence of this quote, that I decided I had to check it out for myself in the original. After all, things can get misconstrued in translation, and perhaps Rakeffet was erring on the side of amplification and hyperbole. I flicked through the pages of *Iggerot Moshe*, and there it was:

Uveshe'arei devarim haya pike'aḥ gamur behavanat hadavar, vezo-kher veyode'a hakol, umedaber vesho'el ka'inyan.

In every other area he was totally normal in his under-standing of the matter at hand, and he remembered and knew everything, and he was focused when he conversed or asked a question.

In other words, the man's aberrant behavior and delusional self-image only affected actions that involved his mission to be recognized as the Messiah. With regard to everything else, whether it was discussions on any other subject or life decisions he needed to make, these were seemingly unaffected by his messianic madness. Consequently, and after much deliberation, Rabbi Feinstein concluded that the messianic pretender was capable of giving his wife a *get*. To support this decision, he offered a lengthy explanation based on sources spanning centuries of Jewish legal opinion, demonstrating why the man was halakhically sane and sufficiently competent to understand what it meant to divorce his wife and to execute a *get*.

At no point in his extensive responsum did Rabbi Feinstein men-tion the *Get* of Cleves, although much of the material he applied to his own deliberations had been similarly utilized by those who addressed the vexed situation 150 years earlier, and the two cases were eerily con-gruent. The principal difference between the two, as I would discover, was that the *get* executed at Cleves in 1766 was challenged by one of the most formidable rabbinic courts of Europe, while Rabbi Moshe Feinstein's Lyuban *get* never drew so much as a critical comment, nei-ther when it occurred, nor when he published the responsum some forty years later.

Evidently the broad principles of halakhic sanity with regard to giving a *get* had been settled in the furor of the Cleves controversy and, at least for the purposes of this sensitive issue, Rabbi Feinstein – several of whose more original responsa had been subjected to fierce critical objection – could comfortably associate himself with the halakhic con-sensus generated by the eighteenth-century debate.

Aside from the article by Rakeffet, I was soon introduced to the original works published by the protagonists of the story: *Or Yisrael*

(Cleves, 1770) by Rabbi Yisrael Lipschuetz (d. 1782), in two variant editions, and *Or HaYashar* (Amsterdam, 1769) by Rabbi Aharon Shimon Copenhagen (d. 1786). Both works offer an account of the story from the perspective of those who arranged and advocated for the *Get* of Cleves and include a bounty of associated literature, all of it supportive.

The book by Rabbi Lipschuetz is full of barbed references to his interlocutors and critics, and in particular Rabbi Nathan Maas (1720–1793) of the Frankfurt rabbinate, who is compared in one reference to "Nathan of Gaza," Shabbetai Tzvi's notorious co-conspirator. This is a particularly grave insult in the immediate wake of the Emden-Eybeschutz affair, as Rabbi Maas was a devoted student of Rabbi Yaakov Yehoshua Falk (1680–1756), the venerated author of *Pnei Yehoshua* on the Talmud, who had lost his job as chief rabbi of Frankfurt as a direct result of his strident stance against Rabbi Yonatan Eybeschutz in the amulet controversy.

Over a century after the publication of these two books, the rabbi of Frankfurt, Rabbi Marcus Horovitz (1844-1910), published a four-volume work in German on the history of the Frankfurt rabbinate, titled *Frankfurter Rabbinen* (Frankfurt, 1882–1885). This monumental publication – later translated into Hebrew (*Rabbanei Frankfurt* [Jerusalem, 1972]) – contained a detailed account of the *Get* of Cleves controversy, although this time with a pro-Frankfurt rabbinate slant, along with a slew of details that had never previously emerged.

The Horovitz version of the story was immediately censured by contemporary rabbinic colleagues who questioned the accuracy, and even the existence, of Horovitz's primary source material. Horovitz never responded to his critics, and the truthfulness of certain aspects of his account remains an unresolved mystery. In any event, the world of Jewish law came down firmly on the side of the *Get* of Cleves, as evidenced in the responsum by Rabbi Feinstein and numerous other examples, not least of which was the story that had introduced me to this whole episode in the first place.

After a couple of weeks of research, I got back in touch with the recalcitrant husband's friend and told him he was welcome to reveal the husband's mental health problems, if that is what the family wanted to do. Moreover, I added, if he wanted any help to get this information out to a wider audience, I would do everything I could to assist him.

Meanwhile, we were planning to proceed with the demonstrations and public shaming as originally scheduled. The man was quite taken aback by this response and told me that he needed to consult with the husband and his parents and would then get back to me. Unsurprisingly, I never heard from him again, but a few days later the *get* was given and the nightmare was over.

Let me turn now to the curious event that introduced me to the eccentric British aristocrat who converted to Orthodox Judaism in the late eighteenth century, Lord George Gordon. In 2006, as part of my summer vacation reading, I selected the recently published biography of William Pitt the Younger (1759–1806), prime minister of Great Britain for some twenty years during the latter part of the eighteenth century and the early part of the nineteenth century. The book, *William Pitt the Younger: A Biography* (London, 2004), which is excellent, was written by William Hague (b. 1961), now Lord Hague, former leader of the UK's Conservative Party and Parliamentary Opposition, who later served as Britain's foreign secretary and as leader of the House of Commons. In describing the background to Pitt's remarkable ascent to the position of prime minister at the tender age of twenty-four in 1883, Hague mentioned the notorious Gordon Riots of 1780, the worst outbreak of civil unrest in modern British history.

The riots were named for a man called Lord George Gordon, a young, devoutly Protestant, anti-Catholic agitator who, as a member of the British Parliament, was energetically trying to reverse the recent repeal of the anti-Catholic laws. His role as the actual instigator of the riots was debatable, but the effect of a week of widespread uncontrolled violence was extremely significant at the time, whoever was ultimately to blame. I recalled having previously heard about Lord George Gordon in some kind of Jewish context, but could not quite remember the details. In those pre-WiFi, pre-smartphone days I was unable to instantly turn to Google to research it further, so I made a mental note to look into Gordon when I returned to London after our vacation in Israel.

That was August. For one reason or another I never got around to Googling him, and before I knew it several months had passed. Eventually, during an unusually quiet day in November, I began my research, and I soon discovered why Gordon's name was so familiar. It turns out that Lord George Gordon, the Protestant firebrand of the eponymous

Gordon Riots, had later abandoned Christianity and converted to Judaism, becoming a full-fledged, mitzva-observant Jew, even adopting the beard and clothing of the Polish Jews of his day. More remarkably, he died in jail relatively young, after being incarcerated for five years for the preposterous "crime" of insulting the French queen, Marie Antoinette.

I was so intrigued by this story that I began to look for any books that could better inform me about Gordon and his background. Charles Dickens (1812–1870) wrote a fictionalized account of the Gordon Riots in his book *Barnaby Rudge*, and a number of political-history books included descriptions of Gordon during that period. Nevertheless, his conversion to Judaism, which is what really interested me about Gordon, always seemed to be a footnote.

There was, however, one book that caught my eye, as it was mentioned in every referenced article about Gordon. Written by his faithful secretary, Robert Watson (1746–1838), it was published just two years after Gordon's death, in 1795, but was never subsequently republished. I scoured book dealers' websites to see if I could get my hands on a copy and eventually found one at a rural secondhand bookstore for £125. I called the owner to ascertain the condition of the book, and we agreed on a slightly lower price, although I told him I still needed to think about it and would call him back to confirm the transaction, or to cancel it.

Just to be sure I wasn't being overcharged for this obscure eighteenth-century biography, I telephoned a dear friend of mine, a hasidic book dealer from Stamford Hill in North London. Having dealt in antiquarian books for over fifty years, my friend was familiar with every aspect of this murky trade, and I fully trusted his judgment and integrity. I just wanted his confirmation before I made the purchase. I asked him if he had ever heard of Lord George Gordon. There was a long pause at the other end of the line.

"Yes," he replied, "but why do you want to know?"

I explained how Gordon had cropped up in a book I had recently read, and that I now wanted to buy this book about him and was just calling him to check that the price made sense.

"But why today?" he asked me. "Why specifically today?"

"You're totally right," I responded, not detecting the wonder in his voice, "I should have done this in August when Gordon's name first came up, but you know how it is – between one thing and another, it has taken me until today to finally get to this. That's why it's today."

This time the pause was a little longer.

"That's really very strange," my friend said, finally, "because today is Lord George Gordon's *yahrtzeit* (death date anniversary), and this morning I was part of the group that went out to the site of his burial in Central London to say *Tehillim* (psalms) and Kaddish."

I was totally speechless. After a while my friend spoke again.

"Buy the book," he said, "it's a good price. And say some *Tehillim* for his *neshama* (soul). His Hebrew name was *Yisrael ben Avraham Avinu*."

Watson's book turned out to be a great resource. Moreover, I discovered that Watson had himself led an extremely eventful life. In the 1776 revolutionary war he served with George Washington and emerged from that adventure with the rank of colonel. An inveterate revolutionary, when he moved back to Britain he was immediately drawn to Gordon, and soon became his personal secretary. He remained utterly devoted to his employer through the Gordon Riots, the legal battles, Gordon's disappearance and then his reappearance as a Jew, his imprisonment, and even after his death. The book was an uncritical tribute to Gordon, whom Watson had clearly adored and idolized.

In 1796, Watson was arrested in London for revolutionary activities, and imprisoned at Newgate. He somehow managed to escape, whereupon he fled to Paris, where he became Napoleon Bonaparte's personal English-language tutor. After serving as the head of the Scottish College in Paris for several years, he moved to Rome, where he inadvertently discovered and purchased an unknown cache of the controversial "Stuart Papers" that had belonged to the royal revolutionary, "King" James III (1688–1766), youngest legitimate son of Great Britain's King James II (1633–1701), who abortively attempted to replace George I (1660–1727) and George II (1683-1760) as the reigning monarch of Great Britain.

When the Papal authorities realized what Watson had obtained, they seized the papers from him and handed them over to the British government, which nonetheless compensated Watson for his loss.

In old age, the once notorious Watson disappeared from the limelight and ultimately descended into penury. Then, in 1838, his notoriety was morbidly rekindled when he committed suicide at a nondescript tavern in London. He was ninety-two years old, making him the oldest known person to commit suicide since records began.

Another useful resource was *The Strange History of Lord George Gordon* (London, 1937) by Percy Colson (1873-1952), although the parts of the book that deal with Gordon's conversion to Judaism were written by the renowned scholar of Anglo-Jewish history, Cecil Roth (1899-1970), who later become editor-in-chief of the magnificent sixteen-volume *Encyclopedia Judaica* (Jerusalem, 1971–72). An abridged account of Gordon's conversion based on the Colson book was published under Roth's name in *Essays and Portraits in Anglo-Jewish History* (London, 1953). The comprehensive article, "Lord George Gordon's Conversion to Judaism" by Israel Solomons (d. 1923), in *Transactions of the Jewish Historical Society of England* (vol. 7 [1911–1914]: 222–271), was invaluable, as was *King Mob: The Story of Lord George Gordon and the Riots of 1780* (London, 1958) by the "most widely read popular historian of our time," Christopher Hibbert (1924–2008).

One particularly interesting account of Gordon's life is a book called *Lord George Gordon* (Lakewood, 1992) by Yirmeyahu Bindman, an "author and researcher living in Jerusalem, specializing in Jewish historical biography and the Noahide Laws." Presented as a "dramatic biography of a notorious British aristocrat who became a *ger tzedek*, a righteous convert, during the turbulent era of the American Revolution," the reason it is interesting is because it was written exclusively for the strictly Orthodox community. As is typical of such books, the narrative is conveyed in a gushing hagiographic style, presenting Gordon as a selfless social-activist hero who ultimately embraced the one true faith, Judaism, a choice that was personally very challenging for him and added further difficulty to an already complicated life.

After reading the book, I was interested to know whether Bindman had come across any references to Gordon in rabbinic literature, or in contemporary Jewish correspondence of the eighteenth century, or whether he had relied on the non-Orthodox sources that chart Gordon's turbulent life. I finally got around to contacting him while writing this conclusion, and he responded that he didn't know of any strictly Orthodox sources contemporary to Gordon which mentioned him. He then added the following:

> The community in England was so small, and [Gordon's] relationship with them so fraught, that nothing of that kind was set to paper that could be traced. The Anglo-Jewish records were destroyed in the London Blitz. He was certainly a fine Jew, one of the most important religious figures that Britain has ever produced, but like many prominent [converts to Judaism] of the ghetto period, the consensus was that he would have to leave his country of origin. It became impossible to refuse his conversion, simply because he was an important politician and so nothing could be gained by pushing him back to the British system. There are only the fragmentary accounts of his jail period, where many people were impressed both with his *simḥa* (joy) in adversity and with the Torah which inspired him.

A number of things about Bindman's missive struck me as odd, not least the assertion that Gordon was "one of the most important religious figures that Britain has ever produced." After all, Britain is the country that produced Sir Thomas More (1478–1535), Lord high chancellor of England during the reign of Henry VIII, whose opposition to the Protestant Reformation resulted in his execution for treason and subsequent canonization by the Catholic Church. And in Gordon's day there was John Wesley (1703–1791), the charismatic founder of the Methodist Church. On what scale Bindman supposed that Gordon was more important than either of these two, among many others, escaped me.

Perhaps Bindman meant "one of the most important *Jewish* religious figures," although even if that was the case Gordon was up against some strong competition, such as Rabbi Yitzhak Isaac Halevi Herzog (1888–1959), an extraordinary scholar and activist who would become the first chief rabbi of the State of Israel. Herzog was born in Lomza, Lithuania, but he spent his formative years in Leeds, where his father was a rabbi.

I wrote back to Bindman, expressing surprise that no private third-party Jewish correspondence had ever emerged discussing Gordon's conversion. He lived in an energetically active literary period, and rabbinic correspondence at the time was notably frank on every kind of topic imaginable. I also added the general observation that while Gordon was certainly sincere, he was clearly quite eccentric.

Bindman's second response was even more curious than his first. He dismissed the idea that Gordon was eccentric, suggesting that "he was possessed of the roots of a very great spiritual [soul], and this made him seem intense and not focused on the common concerns of non-Jewish society." Bindman even proposed that Gordon's conversion to Judaism had mitigated his intensity, "since his striving for truth had been gratified." So far, so startling, but Bindman then went on to make one of the most extraordinary assertions I have ever seen. As proof that Gordon was not an eccentric, Bindman reminded me that Gordon "had a good sense of humor, something not generally found in eccentric individuals."

I actually laughed out loud when I read that sentence, although I'm pretty sure it was not intended as evidence of Bindman's sense of humor. We do know that Gordon used comedy in his social and professional interactions, but the claim this meant he could not possibly have been eccentric is simply absurd. Rather, it would appear Bindman was adhering to the strictly observed unwritten law of Orthodox hagiographies that insists a Jewish hero can never be nuanced, or be compromised in any way by character or personality anomalies.

The reality, as we know, is quite different. Sincerity and piety may very well be coupled with eccentricity, or anxiety, or a host of other challenging personality traits, and this does not diminish a hero's accomplishments in any way. If anything, it demonstrates that no such handicap is a barrier to achieving great spiritual heights. Surely this is a far more positive message.

After some reflection, I chose not to engage in any further correspondence with Bindman, and to leave it at that.

Hagiography, however misguided, is a benign form of literary fraud. Literary forgery, on the other hand, is fraud of an entirely different magnitude. The subject of the chapter on the Maharal's Haggada, Rabbi Yehuda Yudel Rosenberg (1859–1935), was a serial literary forger whose various publications on the history of the *Golem* of Prague became the widely accepted version of a historical episode of dubious origin, and which may never have happened at all. Curiously, his literary forgery was not only limited to the relatively harmless genre of narrative story-telling, as the Haggada attests.

The Scottish poet and novelist Andrew Lang (1844–1912), in *Books and Bookmen* (New York, 1886), his self-declared "swan-song of a book-hunter," includes a sardonic yet insightful chapter on literary forgers. "The literary forger," he says, "is usually a clever man, and it is necessary for him to be at least on a level with the literary knowledge and critical science of his time." As to the motives behind literary forgery, Lang offers a variety of ideas:

> The motives of the literary forger are curiously mixed; but they may, perhaps, be analyzed roughly into piety, greed, "push," and love of fun. Many literary forgeries have been pious frauds, perpetrated in the interests of a church, a priesthood, or a dogma. Then we have frauds of greed, as if, for example, a forger should offer his wares for a million of money to the British Museum.... Next we come to playful frauds, or frauds in their origin playful.... Occasionally it has happened that forgeries, begun for the mere sake of exerting the imitative faculty, and of raising a laugh against the learned, have been persevered with in earnest.... Then there are forgeries by "pushing" men, who hope to get a reading for poems which, if put forth as new, would be neglected. There remain forgeries of which the motives are so complex as to remain forever obscure. We may generally ascribe them to love of notoriety in the forger.... More difficult still to understand are the forgeries which real scholars have committed or connived at for the purpose of supporting some opinion which they held with earnestness. There is a vein of madness and self-deceit in the character of the man who half-persuades himself that his own false facts are true.

I wonder what Lang would have made of Rosenberg, a unique example of a literary forger who managed to check almost every one of Lang's boxes. Rosenberg was both devoutly religious and a notable rabbinic scholar, and he evidently had an interest in influencing Jewish religious practice with books such as the Haggada.

Indeed, I have another of Rosenberg's pamphlets, which is bibliographically unknown. Titled *Seder Hakafot* (Piotrkow, 1909), it purports to be a record of customs for the seven-circuit dance with the Torah scrolls on the festival of Simhat Torah as practiced by Rabbi Pinhas Shapiro of Korecz (1726–1790), one of the earliest pioneers of the hasidic movement. The bulk of Rabbi Shapiro's manuscripts were lost after his passing, resulting in a paucity of published works.

On the title page of *Seder Hakafot*, Rosenberg claims to have purchased the manuscript on which he based the work from a man he called "Bertche Katz" who, according to Rosenberg, was a descendant of Rabbi Shapiro. Without the existence of any independent verification of Bertche Katz's existence, and with incontrovertible proof that Rosenberg was an incorrigible literary forger, one must assume that *Seder Hakafot* was just another of Rosenberg's forgeries. This one, however, if taken seriously, might well have resulted in the introduction of baseless customs into an ancient annual festival ceremony.

Did Rosenberg compose *Seder Hakafot* and the Maharal Haggada as "pious frauds"? Or was he driven to use his forgery skills by greed, desperate for the money their sales would generate? Perhaps he was a "playful fraud," motivated by an inventive spirit that needed an outlet, or by a twisted sense of humor that secretly took pleasure when his forgeries were taken seriously. Or maybe he simply wanted to bask in limelight that would otherwise have evaded him. I guess we will never really know, although one can detect all of the above in the range of forgeries Rosenberg was responsible for.

What is essential for us to understand is how elements of Rosenberg's literary activities were insidious to the point of being highly immoral, and that there seems to have been no rule he was not willing to break in order to serve some purpose he deemed important. Rabbi Professor Shnayer Leiman wrote an excellent survey article on Rosenberg's numerous forgeries and proclivity for literary dishonesty, "The Adventure of The Maharal of Prague in London: Rabbi Yudl Rosenberg and the Golem of Prague," in *Tradition* 36:1 (New York, 2002). In it he reveals how Rosenberg even faked a discovery of material he claimed was written by a follower of Rabbi Yaakov Emden, which he published to correct an earlier literary slip-up in which he had cited Rabbi Emden's view that the Zohar was a post-talmudic work, implying that it was inauthentic:

> R. Yudl's translation of the Zohar into Hebrew was nothing less than a messianic act on his part. As he explains in the introduction to his translation, the Zohar itself claims that the spread of its teaching will culminate in the Messianic Age. But, asks R. Yudl, how could its teaching spread among Jews who, for the most part, do not understand Aramaic, the language of the Zohar? Hence the necessity of translating the Zohar into Hebrew.
>
> In the introduction to his translation of the Zohar on Leviticus, published in 1925, R. Yudl discusses the controversy surrounding the authenticity and antiquity of the Zohar. In passing, he notes that R. Jacob Emden (d. 1776), the distinguished rabbi and polemicist, was among the Zohar's severest critics. Indeed, added R. Yudl, Emden concluded that the Zohar was post-talmudic in origin.
>
> Apparently, R. Yudl regretted publicizing the fact that a distinguished rabbi considered the Zohar a post-talmudic work (i.e., a work falsely ascribed to R. Shimon bar Yohai and, therefore, inauthentic). Emden's view, in effect, undermined the very purpose of R. Yudl's translation. So later in 1925, in a supplement to his translation of the Zohar, R. Yudl stated that while in Lodz he chanced upon a worn copy of a book entitled *Tzur Devash*. The title page was torn and lacked the portion with the name of the author. But a careful reading of the volume enabled R. Yudl to establish that its author was a disciple of R. Jacob Emden.
>
> According to R. Yudl, the volume contained some brief legal responsa, as well as a series of letters, written by Emden. R. Yudl cites a passage from one of Emden's letters which supports the antiquity and authenticity of the Zohar. The passage explains away the earlier position of Emden which offered a scathing critique of the antiquity and authenticity of the Zohar.

It does so by indicating that the earlier position was intended only as a means of pulling the rug out from under the feet of Sabbatian teaching and, therefore, was not to be taken seriously by normative Jews.

While the alleged Emden passage cited by R. Yudl may well be an accurate reflection of Emden's sentiments, the book from which it is drawn does not exist. Apparently, neither the title nor the passage, neither the legal responsa nor the letters, have been cited (or: sighted) by anyone other than R. Yudl.

Aside from literary projects in general, and literary fraud in particular, Rosenberg led a fairly typical life for a rabbi of his era, initially in Eastern Europe, where, like many other rabbis, he struggled to make a living. In middle age he moved to Canada, spending just over twenty years there, first in Toronto and later in Montreal, where he was involved in endless *maḥlokot* with the senior rabbi of the city, Rabbi Tzvi Hirsch Cohen (1865–1950), the beloved "Maggid of Montreal." Rosenberg's volatile rabbinic career in Canada has been treated in great detail by Ira Robinson, in his book *Rabbis and Their Community: Studies in the Immigrant Orthodox Rabbinate in Montreal, 1896–1930* (Calgary, 2007).

Of particular interest is the book by Rosenberg's daughter, Leah (Lily) Rosenberg (1906?–1997), *The Errand Runner: Reflections of a Rabbi's Daughter* (New York, 1981), a deeply personal account of her life and the life of her immediate family. Leah had drifted away from Torah-observant Orthodox Judaism and is best known for her unflattering portrayal in fiction works by her son, the famous Canadian satirical novelist Mordecai Richler (1931–2001), author of *The Apprenticeship of Duddy Kravitz* (Ontario, 1959).

Relations between Richler and his mother were terrible. In 1976, after years of festering rage marked by endlessly bitter interactions, he wrote to her for the last time: "If your old age tastes of ashes, if you are wretched, lonely, worried about your health, money, I am sorry. But now that you are seventy, can't you at last grasp that you have brought most of this on yourself." The source of the friction was an extramarital affair between Leah and a German-Jewish boarder at their home in

1944 that resulted in the divorce of Leah and Richler's father, Moses. Leah and Moses' marriage had been a disaster from the start, arranged by their parents for all the wrong reasons – the outgoing daughter of an illustrious old-world rabbi marrying the introverted son of a successful, worldly junkyard dealer.

Leah's book might never have been published had it not been for her son's semi-autobiographical novel *Joshua Then and Now* (Toronto, 1980), in which the main character's mother is depicted as a burlesque dancer, possibly a barbed reference to Leah's stint working at Montreal's notorious Esquire Show Bar. Whether or not it was this that prompted *Errand Runner*'s publication, so that Leah could set the record straight, the book is a rich source of information about Rabbi Yudel Rosenberg's transition from struggling Polish rabbi to distinguished Canadian rabbinic luminary, and how the unpredictable life of Orthodox rabbis at that time affected the lives of their children.

Let me now turn to Ignatz (Ignatius) Timothy (Timotheus) Trebitsch-Lincoln (1879–1943), the subject of the book's final and most compelling chapter. He was perhaps best summed up by the eminent literary critic John Gross (1935–2011) in his *New York Times* review of Professor Bernard Wasserstein's exhaustive biography, *The Secret Lives of Trebitsch Lincoln* (New Haven/London, 1988):

> Few Hungarian Jews can have been ordained as both Anglican clergymen and Buddhist monks. Few Presbyterian missionaries can have gone on to promote dubious oil companies in the Balkans and serve as advisers to Chinese warlords. It is unusual, to say the least, for a former British Member of Parliament to escape from jail in Brooklyn, face a possible charge of high treason in Austria, and help organize a right-wing Putsch in Berlin. Yet these are only some of the parts played by a single man – originally called Ignacz Trebitsch, though he was to use many other names as well – in the course of his improbable career.

Gross pertinently points out that Trebitsch's adventurous life was "remarkable for variety rather than quality," a feature that struck me forcefully as I went through the manuscript for the final edit. On more than one occasion I found myself laughing out loud at the sheer insanity of this man's life. He tumbled from one crisis to another, always at the center of some chaotic scenario, his shrill voice and exaggerated prose the soundtrack to yet another misadventure. So much energy, such incredible skills, so bright – and yet, in the final analysis he had nothing to show for it, unless you count an unrivaled rollercoaster yarn that no fiction writer would have ever dared to dream up.

Aside from Wasserstein's magnificent book, on which my own account is based, I obtained a copy of Trebitsch's *Revelations of an International Spy* (New York, 1916) after finding it online in all its first-edition glory for under ten dollars. Written during his time in a Brooklyn jail cell, it makes for a remarkable read, full of the self-assured confidence of a conman whose detailed version of pseudo-reality is so comprehensive that he knows it will be impossible for the less informed to detect that it is nothing more than a confluence of fact and fantasy deliberately woven to dazzle its audience into submission.

Interestingly, Wasserstein sees Trebitsch as a false Messiah – a twentieth-century Shabbetai Tzvi who never emerged from the chrysalis of self-deluded importance, perhaps because he never found a Nathan of Gaza to propel him into the stratospheric notoriety he so craved. He certainly had all the hallmarks of someone with acute *folie-de-grandeur*, convinced of his own superiority and greatness, destined to lead and trail blaze, and leave his indelible mark on humanity.

The last word goes to Wasserstein, recorded in a *New York Times* article (May 8, 1988) that coincided with the publication of his book. Wasserstein reflects on his quest to find the true Trebitsch during the many years of research that ultimately resulted in the published biography:

> Trebitsch-Lincoln died in Shanghai in October 1943. Yet, even in death, he retains a capacity to astound, and I suppose it is possible he may yet rise from his grave in the Shanghai Municipal Cemetery, in the form of a posthumous cache of papers, to contradict everything I have found out about him. Notwithstanding that faint possibility, I felt, by the end of my researches, that my archival burrowings and merciless badgering of witnesses, along

with some outstanding strokes of good fortune, had yielded the closest accessible approach to the true history of a false Messiah.

This is a fitting reminder that all historical narrative is, in the end, incomplete. If it is true to say that one can never truly know someone in life, it is doubly true of that person in death, and exponentially more so when the narrative encompasses numerous people, places, times, and conditions, as well as extraordinary circumstances outside the realms of ordinary existence. Despite this handicap, it is the historian's duty to provide as accurate a picture as possible, based on the details that are available, and the broader background knowledge that years of scholarship have furnished, so that those who are interested in discovering the rich patchwork that is world history can at the very least know what there is to know, and use that as their base.

This book, drawn from all of the many sources recorded above, is my humble contribution to that patchwork base.

Index

The fonts used in this book are from the Arno family